NATIONAL IDENTITY

Professor Anthony D. Smith took his first degree in Classics and Philosophy at Wadham College, Oxford, and his master's degree and doctorate in Sociology at the London School of Economics. He also holds a doctorate in History of Art from the University of London. He is currently Professor of Ethnicity and Nationalism at the University of London in the London School of Economics.

His publications include *Theories of Nationalism* (1971, second edition 1983), *The Concept of Social Change* (1973), *Nationalism in the Twentieth Century* (1979), *The Ethnic Revival* (1981), *State and Nation in the Third World* (1983), *The Ethnic Origins of Nations* (1986), *Nations and Nationalism in the Global Era* (1995) and *Nationalism and Modernism* (1998). He is currently working on a book on nationalism and religion.

NATIONAL IDENTITY

ANTHONY D. SMITH

PENGUIN BOOKS

PENGUIN BOOKS

Published by the Penguin Group
Penguin Books Ltd, 27 Wrights Lane, London W8 5TZ, England
Penguin Books USA Inc., 375 Hudson Street, New York, New York 10014, USA
Penguin Books Australia Ltd, Ringwood, Victoria, Australia
Penguin Books Canada Ltd, 10 Alcorn Avenue, Toronto, Ontario, Canada M4V 3B2
Penguin Books (NZ) Ltd, 182–190 Wairau Road, Auckland 10, New Zealand

Penguin Books Ltd, Registered Offices: Harmondsworth, Middlesex, England

First published 1991
6

Copyright © Anthony D. Smith, 1991
All rights reserved

The moral right of the author has been asserted

Printed in England by Clays Ltd, St Ives plc
Set in 10/12 pt Monophoto Bembo

TABLE OF CONTENTS

Introduction

This book aims to provide a straightforward introduction to the nature, causes and consequences of national identity as a collective phenomenon. With the present resurgence of the tide of nationalism in many parts of the world, notably the Soviet Union and Eastern Europe, a synoptic account of the field of national phenomena is timely. As yet, there are only a few general accounts of the field that go beyond historical surveys of nationalism. At the same time the ethnic revival in the West has turned the attention of both the public and the academic community to the issues posed by ethnic nationalism and has led to important debates, intellectual as well as political, in this area. The allied study of ethnicity in North America has also stimulated interest in the problems of polyethnic states around the globe.

The present book is an attempt to provide an historical sociology of national identity and applies the concepts developed in my *Ethnic Origins of Nations* (1986) for the mainly *pre*-modern period to the modern world of nations and nationalism. Its underlying assumption is that we cannot understand nations and nationalism simply as an ideology or form of politics but must treat them as cultural phenomena as well. That is to say, national*ism*, the ideology and movement, must be closely related to *national identity*, a multidimensional concept, and extended to include a specific language, sentiments and symbolism.

While for analytical purposes it is necessary to distinguish the ideological movement of national*ism* from the wider phenomenon of *national identity*, we cannot begin to understand the power and appeal of nationalism as a political force without grounding our analysis in a wider perspective whose focus is national identity treated as a collective cultural phenomenon.

Such an approach requires in turn an historical sociology of the bases and formation of national identities. This means that we must first grasp the pre-modern antecedents of modern nations and relate national identity and nationalism to questions of ethnic identity and community.

Having treated some of these issues elsewhere, I have chosen instead to present my own view of the problem of continuity between pre-modern *ethnie* and modern nations and of the means by which the latter were formed and created. There is an extensive literature on rival approaches to ethnicity, which I have only touched on here (see especially the essays in Taylor and Yapp (1979) and in Stack (1986) as well as McKay (1982) and A. D. Smith (1988a)).

In this book I have focused on four main issues. The first is the characteristics of national as opposed to other kinds of collective cultural identification. The second is the role of different ethnic bases in the formation of modern nations and the ways in which they emerged in early modern Europe. The third is the nature of different kinds of nationalist ideology and symbolism and their impact on the formation of territorial and ethnic political identities. My final concern is the political consequences of different kinds of national identity, their potential for the proliferation of ethnic conflicts and the chances of superseding the identities and ideologies that give rise to such endemic instability.

Nationalism provides perhaps the most compelling identity myth in the modern world, but it comes in various forms. Myths of national identity typically refer to territory or ancestry (or both) as the basis of political community, and these differences furnish important, if often neglected, sources of instability and conflict in many parts of the world. It is no accident that many of the most bitter and protracted 'inter-national' conflicts derive from competing claims and conceptions of national identity. An understanding of these ideas and claims is vital if we are ever to ameliorate, let alone resolve, some of these conflicts and create a genuine international community (on which see the excellent treatment in Mayall (1990)).

These are the concerns that have shaped the argument and plan of this book. I start with a cursory examination of different kinds of collective cultural identity in order to highlight the special features of *national* identity. Chapter 2 looks at the ethnic bases of modern nations and identifies their features, dynamics and survival potential. Chapter 3 traces the two main ways in which nations were formed and asks why the first modern national states developed in the West. The contrast between the processes of bureaucratic incorporation of lower strata and outlying ethnic groups by strong states formed by aristocratic ethnic communities, and the mobilization of the 'people' by intellectuals and professionals in popular ethnic communities, is one first found in early-modern Europe. However, it appears soon afterwards in other continents, and it forms a constant motif in the culture and politics of the modern world.

Chapter 4 introduces the concept of nationalism as an ideology, language and sentiment, emphasizing the symbols, ceremonies and customs of national identity, and distinguishing territorial from ethnic varieties of nationalism. As an ideology and language, nationalism emerged in eighteenth-century Europe, and it is therefore necessary to explore briefly the cultural matrix and role of the intellectuals in its emergence.

Chapter 5 and 6 examine in turn the ways in which territorial and ethnic kinds of national identity are formed, and their impact on the politics of different parts of the world. Chapter 5 looks at the creation of territorial political communities out of former empires and colonies, and the way in which intelligentsias help to create 'civic nations' by design. Chapter 6 traces the recurrent waves of popular 'ethno-nationalism' in nineteenth-century Eastern Europe and the Middle East, in twentieth-century Africa and Asia, and in Europe and the Soviet Union since the 1960s. In each case, a similar process of 'vernacular mobilization', mobilization of the people in and through their indigenous culture and history, challenged the existing system of states and prompted powerful movements of ethnic secession and irredentism, though the forms and timing have varied.

The final chapter looks at the possibilities of a new 'post-national' world, a world without nationalism and perhaps without nations. Given the current limitations imposed on multinational corporations, the erosion of power-blocs and the nationalization of global communications networks, the chances of imminent supersession of nationalism look bleak. Nevertheless, signs of regional associations under the cultural auspices of 'pan' nationalisms may herald a new stage in collective identifications, at least in some parts of the globe.

This will probably be a slow and uncertain process. All that we can say with some degree of certainty is that national identity and nationalism are likely to remain powerful and proliferating forces in the foreseeable future. Hence the urgent need to increase our understanding of so global a condition and so explosive a force.

Anthony D. Smith,
London School of Economics
21 March 1990

CHAPTER 1

National and Other Identities

The year 429 BC marked a turning-point for Athens. In that year Pericles, after thirty years as the Athenian leader, succumbed to the plague that ravaged Athens. From that moment Athens' power visibly declined.

In the same year Sophocles staged what many consider to be his greatest tragedy, *Oedipus Tyrannos* (Oedipus the King). It is sometimes seen as the playwright's warning to his countrymen about the perils of pride and power, but its central theme is the problem of identity.

The play opens with a plague. But this one ravages Thebes, not Athens. We soon learn that it has been sent by the gods because of an unsolved murder long ago, that of the Theban king, Laius. Shortly after that murder on the road to Delphi Oedipus arrived in Thebes and freed the city from the terror of the Sphinx by correctly answering her riddles. Oedipus became king, married the widowed queen, Jocasta, and had with her four children, two boys and two girls.

At the beginning of the play Oedipus promises that he will discover the unclean presence that has brought the plague and must be banished. He sends for the blind seer, Teiresias; but Teiresias only answers darkly that he, Oedipus, is the unclean presence who must be sent into exile. Oedipus suspects that Teiresias has been put up to such an accusation by Jocasta's scheming brother Creon. But Jocasta heals their quarrel and reveals that her former husband, Laius, was murdered by robbers at a place 'where three roads meet'. This stirs Oedipus' memory of a moment when he killed some strangers. One man, however, survived, and on his return to Thebes begged to be sent away to the pastures. Oedipus sends for him. He must find out what happened to Laius.

A messenger arrives from Corinth and brings the news that Polybus, the king of that city and Oedipus' father, has died. This prompts Oedipus to reveal why he left Corinth long ago, never to return. It was because of an oracle from Delphi, which said that he would kill his father and marry his mother. Even now he cannot return to Corinth for fear of marrying his mother, Merope.

But the Corinthian messenger has a surprise for Oedipus. He is not, after all, the son of the king and queen of Corinth. He was a foundling given to the royal couple because they were childless, and he was given to them by none other than the messenger himself long ago when he was a shepherd on Mount Cithaeron. If the messenger had not received him from his counterpart, the Theban shepherd, Oedipus would have died of exposure, his little feet swollen from the thongs that pierced them: hence his name, Oedipus (Swollen-foot). Who is this Theban shepherd, and where did he get the child with the pierced feet? Jocasta has realized the terrible truth and begs Oedipus to desist. He refuses. He must find out 'who he is'. Jocasta rushes out and hangs herself. Oedipus exults:

> Let all come out, however vile! However base it be,
> I must unlock the secret of my birth. The woman,
> With more than woman's pride, is shamed by my low origin.
> I am the child of Fortune, the giver of good,
> And I shall not be shamed. She is my mother;
> My sisters are the Seasons; my rising and my falling
> March with theirs. Born thus, I ask to be no other man
> Than that I am, and will know who I am.[1]

The Theban shepherd is now brought in. He turns out to be the same man who fled when Laius was murdered, and the very man who gave the baby to the Corinthian messenger on Mount Cithaeron long ago, rather than let it die of exposure. Reluctantly at first, in mounting terror later, the Theban shepherd reveals the truth: he was the trusted servant of Laius and Jocasta; they gave him the baby to expose on Mount Cithaeron; it was because of an oracle; the baby was the child of Laius and Jocasta . . .

Oedipus rushes out, finds Jocasta hanging from the ceiling and blinds himself. The rest of his life becomes one long quest, first in Thebes, then in exile with Antigone, for the meaning of his strange destiny; until, in the grove of the Eumenides in Colonus outside Athens, the earth itself swallows him up, and by that act he hallows

Athens for ever. That was the poet's last thought, in 406 BC, at the end of his long life.[2]

MULTIPLE IDENTITIES

There are many motifs, and more than one level, in Sophocles' play. But the question of identity, collective as well as individual, broods over the action. 'I will know who I am': the discovery of self is the play's motor and the action's inner meaning. But each 'self' that Oedipus uncovers is also a social self, a category and a role, even when it proves to be erroneous for Oedipus. Only after the shattering revelation of 'who he is' does he begin to glimpse the meaning of his destiny. He is not a successful ruler, a normal husband and father, or saviour of his city. In turn, he becomes a defiling presence, a murderer, a low-born slave, a foreigner, a child of Fortune. Only at the end does he see what, though sighted, he was unable to 'see' and what only Teiresias, the blind seer, could see. He will become another Teiresias, another blind seer, with the power to heal and save through his suffering and his unique fate.[3]

In Sophocles' drama Oedipus traverses a series of categories and roles. These roles and categories are at the same time so many collective identities, well known to fifth century Greeks. Even if they had no experience of kingship or murder, ancient Greeks were well acquainted with the symbolic and mythical significance of such subjects. The very strangeness of Oedipus' ultimate fate made the false roles he consecutively 'put on' seem familiar and easily intelligible.

Oedipus, like the other heroes whose exploits were dramatized by the Athenian tragedians, represented the normal person placed in unusual circumstances and set apart by a unique fate. He is normal in so far as the roles he occupied before the revelation of his origins represent so many collective identities and 'locations'. Like others, Oedipus has a series of such role-identities – father, husband, king, even hero. His individual identity is, in large part, made up of these social roles and cultural categories – or so it would appear until the moment of truth. Then his world is turned upside down, and his former identities are shown to be hollow.

The tale of Oedipus throws into sharp relief the problem of

identity. It reveals the way in which the self is composed of multiple identities and roles – familial, territorial, class, religious, ethnic and gender. It also reveals how each of these identities is based on social classifications that may be modified or even abolished. The revelation of Oedipus' birth teaches us that another, unseen world touches our material world, turns its social categories upside down and destroys all familiar identities.

What are these categories and roles of which each individual self is normally composed?

Most obviously and fundamentally, the category of gender. If not immutable, gender classifications are universal and pervasive. They also stand at the origin of other differences and subordinations. We are in many subtle as well as overt ways defined by our gender, as are many of our opportunities and rewards in life. At the same time the very universality and all-encompassing nature of gender differentiation makes it a less cohesive and potent base for collective identification and mobilization. Despite the rise of feminism in specific countries, gender identity, which spans the globe, is inevitably more attenuated and taken for granted than other kinds of collective identity in the modern world. Geographically separated, divided by class and ethnically fragmented, gender cleavages must ally themselves to other, more cohesive identities if they are to inspire collective consciousness and action.[4]

Second, the category of space or territory. Local and regional identity is equally widespread, particularly in pre-modern eras. Localism and regionalism also appear to possess the cohesive quality that gender differentiation generally lacks. But the appearance often proves to be deceptive. Regions easily fragment into localities, and localities may easily disintegrate into separate settlements. Only rarely do we meet a powerful and cohesive regional movement, as in the Vendée during the French Revolution; but, as in this case, its unity is likely to derive as much from ideology as from ecology. In most other cases 'regionalism' is unable to sustain the mobilization of its populations with their separate grievances and unique problems. Besides, regions are geographically difficult to define; their centres are often multiple and their boundaries ragged.[5]

A third type of collective identity is socio-economic, the category of social class. Oedipus' fear that he prove to be 'slave-born' mirrors

the ancient Greek fears of slavery and poverty – fears that have
often provided the motors of political action, even when slavery
was replaced by serfdom. In Marx's sociology class is the supreme,
indeed the only relevant, collective identity and the sole motor of
history. Certain kinds of social class – aristocracies of various
kinds, bourgeoisies, proletariats – have sometimes provided bases
for decisive political and military action. Sometimes: not always,
not even frequently. United action by an 'aristocracy' is less
common than factional conflicts within aristocracies. Conflicts of
sectors and fractions of a national bourgeoisie are not uncommon,
starting with the French Revolution itself, let alone conflict between the bourgeoisies of different nations. As for the working
class, while the myth of the international brotherhood of the pro-
letariat is widely accepted, that of the unity of workers within a
given nation is equally prevalent and important, as workers divide
into industrial sectors and along skill levels. Workers' revolutions
are almost as rare as peasant ones; in both cases, sporadic, localized
revolts have been the norm.[6]

The difficulty with treating social class as a basis for an enduring
collective identity is its limited emotional appeal and lack of cultural
depth. Whether we define 'class', with Marx, as a relationship to the
means of production or, with Weber, as an aggregate of those with
identical life-chances in the market, there are clear limits to any
attempt to use class as a basis for a sense of identity and community.
Classes, like gender divisions, are often territorially dispersed. They
are also largely categories of economic interest, and are hence likely
to subdivide according to differences in income and skill levels.
Besides, economic factors are subject to rapid fluctuations over
time; hence the chances of retaining different economic groups
within a class-based community are likely to be slim. Economic
self-interest is not usually the stuff of stable collective identities.

There is a further aspect of class identity that both favours and
militates against the formation of a stable community. 'Class' signifies a social relationship. There are always two or more classes in a
given social formation in conflict, which helps to sharpen class
differences, and hence identities, as studies of working-class culture
in Britain have revealed. At the same time, by definition, only part
of a given territorially bounded population will be included in such

5

class identities. If a more inclusive collective identity covering the whole population in that territory were to emerge, it would necessarily be of quite a different kind from an identity based on class and economic interests. Such wider collective identities might even challenge more restricted class identities, and perhaps undermine or divide them through an appeal to quite different criteria of categorization.

This is just what has often happened. Both religious and ethnic identities have striven to include more than one class within the communities created on their bases. Religious communities, where they aspire to be Churches, have appealed to all sectors of a given population or even across ethnic boundaries. Their message is either national or universal. It is never addressed to a particular class as such, even when in practice the religion is reserved for, or primarily aimed at, a particular class. Fifth-century Mazdakism in Sassanid Persia was undoubtedly a movement of social justice for the lower classes, but its message was, in principle, universal. Similarly, Anglicanism in eighteenth-century England was largely an upper-class and middle-class preserve, although in principle open to any Englishman. The many different forms of 'class religion' noted by Weber suggest the close links between class and religious identities and the frequent 'sliding' from one to the other.[7]

Nevertheless, 'religious identity' is based on quite different criteria from those of 'social class' and emerges from quite different spheres of human need and action. Whereas class identities emerge from the sphere of production and exchange, religious identities derive from the spheres of communication and socialization. They are based on alignments of culture and its elements – values, symbols, myths and traditions, often codified in custom and ritual. They have therefore tended to join in a single community of the faithful all those who feel they share certain symbolic codes, value systems and traditions of belief and ritual, including references to a supra-empirical reality, however impersonal, and imprints of specialized organizations, however tenuous.[8]

Religious communities are often closely related to ethnic identities. While the 'world religions' sought to overstep, and abolish, ethnic boundaries, most religious communities coincided with ethnic groups. The Armenians, Jews and Monophysite Amhara offer classic instances of this coincidence, as did the Copts before the Arab conquest of Egypt. The relationship can be even closer. What began as a purely religious community may end up as an exclusive ethnic community. The Druse, a schismatic Muslim sect founded in Egypt but persecuted there, removed to the fastnesses of Mount Lebanon, where they welcomed Persians and Kurds as well as Arabs into their ranks for about ten years in the early eleventh century. But, with the death of their last great teacher, Baha'al Din (d. AD 1031), proselytization ceased. Membership of the community became fixed, largely because of fear of religious foes outside. Entry to, and exit from, the community of the faithful was no longer permitted. Soon the Druse became as much a community of descent and territory. To be a Druse today, therefore, is to belong to an 'ethno-religious' community.[9]

Even now many ethnic minorities retain strong religious bonds and emblems. Catholics and Protestants in Northern Ireland, Poles, Serbs and Croats, Maronites, Sikhs, Sinhalese, Karen and Shi'i Persians are among the many ethnic communities whose identity is based on religious criteria of differentiation. Here, too, as John Armstrong demonstrates, it is easy to 'slide' from one type of identity to another, and overlap is frequent. For the greater part of human history the twin circles of religious and ethnic identity have been very close, if not identical. Each people in antiquity possessed its own gods, sacred texts, rituals, priesthoods and temples, even where minority or peasant groups might also share in the dominant religious culture of their rulers. Even in early medieval Europe and the Middle East the world religions of Islam and Christianity sometimes subdivided into ethnically demarcated Churches or sects, as with the Armenians and Copts and, later, the Persian Shi'ites. Though one cannot argue conclusively for ethnic causation, there are enough circumstantial cases to suggest strong links between forms of religious identity, even within world religions, and ethnic cleavages and communities.[10]

Nevertheless, analytically the two kinds of cultural collective identity must be clearly distinguished. Religious community may, after all, divide an ethno-linguistic population, as happened among the Swiss or Germans and in Egypt. For a long time religious cleavages prevented the emergence of a strong and enduring ethnic consciousness among these populations – until the era of nationalism succeeded in uniting the community on a new, political basis. Similarly, though world religions like Buddhism and Christianity may be adapted to pre-existing ethnic communities that they in turn reinforce, as in Sri Lanka and Burma, they may, equally, help to erode ethnic differences, as happened to several barbarian peoples when they converted to Christianity and merged with neighbouring peoples, as was the case with Angles, Saxons and Jutes in England.[11]

In the next chapter I shall explore the particular features of ethnic identity that mark it off from other, including religious, identities. For the moment the similarities between religious and ethnic identity need to be stressed. Both stem from similar cultural criteria of classification. They frequently overlap and reinforce one another. And singly or together, they can mobilize and sustain strong communities.

THE ELEMENTS OF 'NATIONAL' IDENTITY

One kind of collective identity, so important and widespread today, is barely mentioned in Sophocles' Theban plays. Though they sometimes hinge on conflict between cities, they never raise the question of 'national' identity. Oedipus' identities are multiple, but being 'foreign' (i.e. non-Greek) is never one of them. Collective conflicts are, at most, wars between Greek city-states and their rulers. Did this not, in fact, mirror the state of ancient Greece in the fifth century BC?

It was Friedrich Meinecke who in 1908 distinguished the *Kulturnation*, the largely passive cultural community, from the *Staatsnation*, the active, self-determining political nation. We may dissent from his use of these terms, indeed from the terms themselves; but the distinction itself is valid and relevant. Politically, there was no 'nation' in ancient Greece, only a collection of city-states, each jealous of its sovereignty. Culturally, however, there existed an ancient Greek community, Hellas, that could be invoked, for example by Pericles, in the political realm – usually for Athenian purposes. In other words we can speak of a Greek cultural and ethnic community but not of an ancient Greek 'nation'.[12]

This suggests that, whatever else it may be, what we mean by 'national' identity involves some sense of political community, however tenuous. A political community in turn implies at least some common institutions and a single code of rights and duties for all the members of the community. It also suggests a definite social space, a fairly well demarcated and bounded territory, with which the members identify and to which they feel they belong. This was very much what the *philosophes* had in mind when they defined a nation as a community of people obeying the same laws and institutions within a given territory.[13]

This is, of course, a peculiarly Western conception of the nation. But then the Western experience has exerted a powerful, indeed the leading, influence on our conception of the unit we call the 'nation'. A new kind of policy – the rational state – and a new kind of community – the territorial nation – first emerged in the West, in close conjunction with each other. They left their imprint on subsequent non-Western conceptions, even when the latter diverged from their norms.

It is worth spelling out this Western or 'civic' model of the nation in more detail. It is, in the first place, a predominantly spatial or territorial conception. According to this view, nations must possess compact, well-defined territories. People and territory must, as it were, belong to each other, in the way that the early Dutch, for example, saw themselves as formed by the high seas and as forging (literally) the earth they possessed and made their own. But the earth in question cannot be just anywhere; it is not any stretch of land. It is, and must be, the 'historic' land, the 'homeland', the 'cradle' of our people, even where, as with the Turks, it is not the land of ultimate origin. A 'historic land' is one where terrain and people have exerted mutual, and beneficial, influence over several generations. The homeland becomes a repository of historic memories and associations, the place where 'our' sages, saints and heroes lived, worked, prayed and fought. All this makes the homeland unique. Its rivers, coasts, lakes, mountains and cities become 'sacred' – places of veneration and exaltation whose inner meanings can be fathomed only by the initiated, that is, the self-aware members of the nation. The land's resources also become exclusive to the people; they are not for 'alien' use and exploitation. The national territory must become self-sufficient. Autarchy is as much a defence of sacred homelands as of economic interests.[14]

A second element is the idea of a *patria*, a community of laws and institutions with a single political will. This entails as least some common regulating institutions that will give expression to common political sentiments and purposes. Sometimes, indeed, the *patria* is expressed through highly centralized and unitary institutions and laws, as in post-Revolutionary France, though even there the various regions retained their local identities into the early twentieth century. At the other extreme we find unions of separate colonies, provinces and city-states, whose federal institutions and laws are designed as much to protect local or provincial liberties as to express a common will and common political sentiments. Both the United States of America and the United Provinces of the Netherlands offer well-documented cases of such national unions. In many ways the primary purpose of the Union of Utrecht in 1579 and of the Netherlands' States General was to protect the ancient liberties and privileges of the constituent provinces, which had been so rudely assailed by Habsburg policies of centralization under Charles V and Philip II. Nevertheless, the ferocity and duration of the war against Spain soon bred a sense of common purpose and identity (quite apart from Calvinist influence) that expressed a growing Dutch national political community, albeit incomplete.[15]

Concurrent with the growth of a sense of legal and political community we may trace a sense of legal equality among the members of that community. Its full expression is the various kinds of 'citizenship' that sociologists have enumerated, including civil and legal rights, political rights and duties, and socio-economic rights. Here it is legal and political rights that the Western conception considers integral to its model of a nation. That implies a minimum of reciprocal rights and obligations among members and the correlative exclusion of outsiders from those rights and duties. It also implies a common code of laws over and above local laws, together with agencies for their enforcement, courts of final appeal and the like. As important is the acceptance that, in principle, all members of the nation are legally equal and that the rich and powerful are bound by the laws of the *patria*.

Finally, the legal equality of members of a political community in its demarcated homeland was felt to presuppose a measure of common values and traditions among the population, or at any rate its 'core' community. In other words, nations must have a measure of common culture and a civic ideology, a set of common understandings and aspirations, sentiments and ideas, that bind the population together in their homeland. The task of ensuring a common public, mass culture has been handed over to the agencies of popular socialization, notably the public system of education and the mass media. In the Western model of national identity nations were seen as culture communities, whose members were united, if not made homogeneous, by common historical memories, myths, symbols and traditions. Even where new, immigrant communities equipped with their own historic cultures have been admitted by the state, it has taken several generations before their descendants have been admitted (in so far as they have been) into the circle of the 'nation' and its historic culture through the national agencies of mass socialization.[16]

Historic territory, legal–political community, legal–political equality of members, and common civic culture and ideology; these are the components of the standard, Western model of the nation. Given the influence of the West in the modern world, they have remained vital elements, albeit in somewhat altered form, in most non-Western conceptions of national identity. At the same time a rather different model of the nation sprang up outside the West, notably in Eastern Europe and Asia. Historically, it challenged the dominance of the Western model and added significant new elements, more attuned to the very different circumstances and trajectories of non-Western communities.

We can term this non-Western model an 'ethnic' conception of the nation. Its distinguishing feature is its emphasis on a community of birth and native culture. Whereas the Western concept laid down that an individual had to belong to some nation but could choose to which he or she belonged, the non-Western or ethnic concept allowed no such latitude. Whether you stayed in your community or emigrated to another, you remained ineluctably, organically, a member of the community of your birth and were for ever stamped by it. A nation, in other words, was first and foremost a community of common descent.

This ethnic model also has a number of facets. First, obviously, is the stress on descent – or rather, presumed descent – rather than territory. The nation is seen as a fictive 'super-family', and it boasts pedigrees and genealogies to back up its claims, often tracked down by native intellectuals, particularly in East European and Middle Eastern countries. The point here is that, in this conception, the nation can trace its roots to an imputed common ancestry and that therefore its members are brothers and sisters, or at least cousins, differentiated by family ties from outsiders.

This emphasis on presumed family ties helps to explain the strong popular or demotic element in the ethnic conception of the nation. Of course, the 'people' figure in the Western model too. But there they are seen as a political community subject to common laws and institutions. In the ethnic model the people, even where they are not actually mobilized for political action, nevertheless provide the object of nationalist aspirations and the final rhetorical court of appeal. Leaders can justify their actions and unite disparate classes and groups only through an appeal to the 'will of the people', and this makes the ethnic concept more obviously 'inter-class' and 'populist' in tone, even when the intelligentsia has little intention of summoning the masses into the political arena. Popular mobilization therefore plays an important moral and rhetorical, if not an actual, role in the ethnic conception.[17]

Similarly, the place of law in the Western civic model is taken by vernacular culture, usually languages and customs in the ethnic model. That is why lexicographers, philologists and folklorists have played a central role in the early nationalisms of Eastern Europe and Asia. Their linguistic and ethnographic research into the past and present culture of the 'folk' provided the materials for a blueprint of the 'nation-to-be', even where specific linguistic revivals failed. By creating a widespread awareness of the myths, history and linguistic traditions of the community, they succeeded in substantiating and crystallizing the idea of an ethnic nation in the minds of most members, even when, as in Ireland and Norway, the ancient languages declined.[18]

Genealogy and presumed descent ties, popular mobilization, vernacular languages, customs and traditions: these are the elements of an alternative, ethnic conception of the nation, one that mirrored the very different route of 'nation-formation' travelled by many communities in Eastern Europe and Asia and one that constituted a dynamic political challenge. It is, as we shall see, a challenge that is repeated to this day in many parts of the world, and it reflects the profound dualism at the heart of every nationalism. In fact every nationalism contains civic and ethnic elements in varying degrees and different forms. Sometimes civic and territorial elements predominate; at other times it is the ethnic and vernacular components that are emphasized. Under the Jacobins, for example, French nationalism was essentially civic and territorial; it preached the unity of the republican *patrie* and the fraternity of its citizens in a political–legal community. At the same time a linguistic nationalism emerged, reflecting pride in the purity and civilizing mission of a hegemonic French culture preached by Barère and the Abbé Gregoire. In the early nineteenth century French cultural nationalism began to reflect more ethnic conceptions of the nation, whether Frankish or Gallic; later these became validating charters for radically different ideals of France. The clerical–monarchist Right was particularly wedded to genealogical and vernacular conceptions of an 'organic' nation, which it opposed to the republican territorial and civic model, notably during the Dreyfus Affair.[19]

Nevertheless, even during the most severe conflicts mirroring opposed models of the nation certain fundamental assumptions tied the warring parties together through a common nationalist discourse. In the French example just cited both republicans and monarchists accepted the idea of France's 'natural' and historic territory (including Alsace). Similarly, there was no real dispute about the need to inculcate national ideals and history through a mass, public education system, only about some of its content (notably the Catholic dimension). Devotion to the French language was also universal. Similarly, nobody questioned the individuality of France and the French as such; differences arose only over the historical content of that uniqueness and hence the lessons to be drawn from that experience.

This suggests that behind the rival models of the nation stand certain common beliefs about what constitutes a nation as opposed to any other kind of collective, cultural identity. They include the idea that nations are territorially bounded units of population and that they must have their own homelands; that their members share a common mass culture and common historical myths and memories; that members have reciprocal legal rights and duties under a common legal system; and that nations possess a common division of labour and system of production with mobility across the territory for members. These are assumptions, and demands, common to all nationalists and widely accepted even by their critics, who may then go on to deplore the ensuing global divisions and conflicts created by the existence of such nations.

The existence of these common assumptions allows us to list the fundamental features of national identity as follows:

1. an historic territory, or homeland
2. common myths and historical memories
3. a common, mass public culture
4. common legal rights and duties for all members
5. a common economy with territorial mobility for members.

A nation can therefore be defined as *a named human population sharing an historic territory, common myths and historical memories, a mass, public culture, a common economy and common legal rights and duties for all members.*[20]

Such a provisional working definition reveals the complex and abstract nature of national identity. The nation, in fact, draws on elements of other kinds of collective identity, which accounts not only for the way in which national identity can be combined with these other types of identity – class, religious or ethnic – but also for the chameleon-like permutations of national*ism*, the ideology, with other ideologies like liberalism, fascism and communism. A national identity is fundamentally multi-dimensional; it can never be reduced to a single element, even by particular factions of nationalists, nor can it be easily or swiftly induced in a population by artificial means.

Such a definition of national identity also sets it clearly apart from any conception of the state. The latter refers exclusively to public institutions, differentiated from, and autonomous of, other social institutions and exercising a monopoly of coercion and extraction within a given territory. The nation, on the other hand, signifies a cultural and political bond, uniting in a single political community all who share an historic culture and homeland. This is not to deny some overlap between the two concepts, given their common reference to an historic territory and (in democratic states) their appeal to the sovereignty of the people. But, while modern states must legitimate themselves in national and popular terms as the states of particular nations, their content and focus are quite different.[21]

This lack of congruence between the state and the nation is exemplified in the many 'plural' states today. Indeed, Walker Connor's estimate in the early 1970s showed that only about 10 per cent of states could claim to be true 'nation-states', in the sense that the state's boundaries coincide with the nation's and that the total population of the state share a single ethnic culture. While most states aspire to become nation-states in this sense, they tend to limit their claims to legitimacy to an aspiration for political unity and popular sovereignty that, even in old-established Western states, risks being challenged by ethnic communities within their borders. These cases, and there are many of them, illustrate the profound gulf between the concepts of the state and the nation, a gulf that the historical material to be discussed shortly underlines.[22]

SOME FUNCTIONS AND PROBLEMS OF NATIONAL IDENTITY

Let me recapitulate. National identity and the nation are complex constructs composed of a number of interrelated components – ethnic, cultural, territorial, economic and legal–political. They signify bonds of solidarity among members of communities united by shared memories, myths and traditions that may or may not find expression in states of their own but are entirely different from the purely legal and bureaucratic ties of the state. Conceptually, the nation has come to blend two sets of dimensions, the one civic and territorial, the other ethnic and genealogical, in varying proportions in particular cases. It is this very multidimensionality that has made national identity such a flexible and persistent force in modern life and politics, and allowed it to combine effectively with other powerful ideologies and movements, without losing its character.

We can illustrate this multifaceted power of national identity by looking at some of the functions it fulfils for groups and individuals.

In line with the dimensions listed above, we can conveniently divide these functions into 'external' and 'internal' objective consequences.

The external functions are territorial, economic and political. Nations, first, define a definite social space within which members must live and work, and demarcate an historic territory that locates a community in time and space. They also provide individuals with 'sacred centres', objects of spiritual and historical pilgrimage, that reveal the uniqueness of their nation's 'moral geography'.

Economically, nations underwrite the quest for control over territorial resources, including manpower. They also elaborate a single division of labour, and encourage mobility of goods and labour, as well as the allocation of resources between members within the homeland. By defining the membership, the boundaries and the resources, national identity provides the rationale for ideals of national autarchy.[23]

Politically, too, national identity underpins the state and its organs, or their pre-political equivalents in nations that lack their own states. The selection of political personnel, the regulation of political conduct and the election of governments are grounded in criteria of national interest, which is presumed to reflect the national will and national identity of the inclusive population.

But perhaps the most salient political function of national identity is its legitimation of common legal rights and duties of legal institutions, which define the peculiar values and character of the nation and reflect the age-old customs and mores of the people. The appeal to national identity has become the main legitimation for social order and solidarity today.

National identities also fulfil more intimate, internal functions for individuals in communities. The most obvious is the socialization of the members as 'nationals and 'citizens'. Today this is achieved through compulsory, standardized, public mass education systems, through which state authorities hope to inculcate national devotion and a distinctive, homogeneous culture, an activity that most regimes pursue with considerable energy under the influence of nationalist ideals of cultural authenticity and unity.[24]

The nation is also called upon to provide a social bond between individuals and classes by providing repertoires of shared values, symbols and traditions. By the use of symbols — flags, coinage, anthems, uniforms, monuments and ceremonies – members are reminded of their common heritage and cultural kinship and feel strengthened and exalted by their sense of common identity and belonging. The nation becomes a 'faith-achievement' group, able to surmount obstacles and hardships.[25]

Finally, a sense of national identity provides a powerful means of defining and locating individual selves in the world, through the prism of the collective personality and its distinctive culture. It is through a shared, unique culture that we are enabled to know 'who we are' in the contemporary world. By rediscovering that culture we 'rediscover' ourselves, the 'authentic self', or so it has appeared to many divided and disoriented individuals who have had to contend with the vast changes and uncertainties of the modern world.

This process of self-definition and location is in many ways the key to national identity, but it is also the element that has attracted most doubt and scepticism. Given the wide range of human attitudes and perceptions, it is hardly surprising if nationalists, their critics and the rest of us have been unable to agree on the criteria for national self-definition and location. The quest for the national self and the individual's relationship to it remains the most baffling element in the nationalist project.

These doubts are both philosophical and political. Because of the many kinds of national self that present themselves in practice (a natural result of the multifaceted nature of the nation), nationalist doctrine has been attacked as logically contradictory or incoherent. The indeterminacy of national criteria and their vague, shifting, often arbitrary character in the writings of nationalists have undermined the ideology's credibility, even where respect has been accorded to individual nationalist propositions such as the idea of cultural diversity. At best the idea of the nation has appeared sketchy and elusive, at worst absurd and contradictory.[26]

Intellectual scepticism is paralleled by moral condemnation. In the name of 'national identity' people have allegedly been willing to surrender their own liberties and curtail those of others. They have been prepared to trample on the civil and religious rights of ethnic, racial and religious minorities whom the nation could not absorb. International, or more accurately inter-state, relations have similarly suffered. The ideal of the nation, transplanted across the globe from its Western heartlands, has brought with it confusion, instability, strife and terror, particularly in areas of mixed ethnic and religious character. Nationalism, the doctrine that makes the nation the object of every political endeavour and national identity the measure of every human value, has since the French Revolution challenged the whole idea of a single humanity, of a world community and its moral unity. Instead nationalism offers a narrow, conflict-laden legitimation for political community, which inevitably pits culture-communities against each other and, given the sheer number and variety of cultural differences, can only drag humanity into a political Charybdis.[27]

This is a familiar indictment, and its scope and intensity proclaim the emotional and political power of the ideal that it so utterly condemns. But an ideal and an identity that can fulfil so many functions, collective and individual, are bound to have the most varied social and political consequences, given the variety of circumstances in which nationalists must operate. We could, equally, catalogue the benign effects of nationalism: its defence of minority cultures; its rescue of 'lost' histories and literatures; its inspiration for cultural renascences; its resolution of 'identity crisis'; its legitimation of community and social solidarity; its inspiration to resist tyranny; its ideal of popular sovereignty and collective mobilization; even the motivation of self-sustaining economic growth. Each of these effects could, with as much plausibility, be attributed to nationalist ideologies as the baneful consequences listed by critics. No more striking, or revealing, testimony could be offered to the ambiguous power of national identity and nationalism or to their profound relevance, for good or ill, to most people in most areas of the world today.

Why this should be so, and what the deeper roots of the power exerted today by national identities are, we must now explore.

CHAPTER 2

The Ethnic Basis of National Identity

The origins of what we have termed national identity are as complex as its nature. I am not saying simply that the origins of each nation are in many ways unique and that there is great variation in the starting-points, trajectories, rates and timings of modern nations. The very question 'what are the origins of nations?' needs to be broken down into several further questions, such as: who is the nation? Why and how is the nation? When and where is the nation?

In fact we can conveniently use these questions to seek a general explanation of the origins and development of modern nations in three parts.

1. *Who* is the nation? What are the ethnic bases and models of modern nations? Why did these particular nations emerge?
2. *Why* and *how* does the nation emerge? That is, what are the general causes and mechanisms that set in motion the processes of nation-formation from varying ethnic ties and memories?
3. *When* and *where* did the nation arise? What were the specific ideas, groups and locations that predisposed the formation of individual nations at particular times and places?

Through answers to these questions, albeit of a general and necessarily incomplete nature, we may hope to shed some light on the vexed problem of national origins and development.

ETHNIE AND ETHNO-GENESIS

If myths like that of Oedipus can be seen as widely believed tales told in dramatic form, referring to past events but serving present purposes and/or future goals, then the nation stands at the centre of one of the most popular and ubiquitous myths of modern times: that of nationalism. Central to this myth is the idea that nations exist from time immemorial, and that nationalists must reawaken them from a long slumber to take their place in a world of nations. The hold of the nation lies, as we shall see, partly in the promise of the nationalist salvation drama itself. But this power is often immeasurably increased by the living presence of traditions embodying memories, symbols, myths and values from much earlier epochs in the life of a population, community or area. So it is these pre-modern ethnic identities and traditions that we must first explore.[1]

The concept of 'ethnicity' has received a good deal of attention in recent years. For some it has a 'primordial' quality. It exists in nature, outside time. It is one of the 'givens' of human existence (this is a view that has received some backing recently from sociobiology, where it is regarded as an extension of processes of genetic selection and inclusive fitness). At the other extreme ethnicity is seen as 'situational'. Belonging to an ethnic group is a matter of attitudes, perceptions and sentiments that are necessarily fleeting and mutable, varying with the particular situation of the subject. As the individual's situation changes, so will the group identification; or at least, the many identities and discourses to which the individual adheres will vary in importance for that individual in successive periods and different situations. This makes it possible for ethnicity to be used 'instrumentally' to further individual or collective interests, particularly of competing élites who need to mobilize large followings to support their goals in the struggle for power. In this struggle ethnicity becomes a useful tool.[2]

Between these two extremes lie those approaches that stress the historical and symbolic–cultural attributes of ethnic identity. This is the perspective adopted here. An ethnic group is a type of cultural collectivity, one that emphasizes the role of myths of descent and historical memories, and that is recognized by one or more cultural differences like religion, customs, language or institutions. Such collectivities are doubly 'historical' in the sense that not only are historical memories essential to their continuance but each such ethnic group is the product of specific historical forces and is therefore subject to historical change and dissolution.

At this point it is useful to distinguish between *ethnic categories* and *ethnic communities*. The former are human populations whom at least some outsiders consider to constitute a separate cultural and historical grouping. But the populations so designated may at the time have little self-awareness, only a dim consciousness that they form a separate collectivity. Thus Turks in Anatolia before 1900 were largely unaware of a separate 'Turkish' identity – separate, that is, from the dominant Ottoman or the overarching Islamic identities – and besides, local identities of kin, village or region were often more important. The same can be said for the Slovak inhabitants of the Carpathian valleys before 1850, despite their common dialects and religion. In both cases a myth of common origins, shared historical memories, a sense of solidarity or an association with a designated homeland were largely absent.[3]

An ethnic community, on the other hand, can be distinguished by just these attributes, even if they are firmly held and clearly enunciated by only small segments of the designated population and even if some of these attributes are more intense and salient than others at a given period. We may list six main attributes of ethnic community (or *ethnie*, to use the French term):

1. a collective proper name
2. a myth of common ancestry
3. shared historical memories
4. one or more differentiating elements of common culture
5. an association with a specific 'homeland'
6. a sense of solidarity for significant sectors of the population.[4]

The more a given population possesses or shares these attributes (and the more of these attributes that it possesses or shares), the more closely does it approximate the ideal type of an ethnic community or *ethnie*. Where this syndrome of elements is present we are clearly in the presence of a community of historical culture with a sense of common identity. Such a community must be sharply differentiated from a *race* in the sense of a social group that is held to possess unique hereditary biological traits that allegedly determine the mental attributes of the group.[5] In practice, *ethnies* are often confused with races, not only in this social sense but even in the physical, anthropological sense of subspecies of *Homo sapiens* such as Mongoloid, Negroid, Australoid, Caucasian and the like. Such a confusion is the product of the widespread influence of racist ideologies and discourses, with their purportedly 'scientific' notions of racial struggle, social organisms and eugenics. In the hundred years from 1850 to 1945 such notions were applied to the purely cultural and historical differences of *ethnies*, both inside Europe and in colonial Africa and Asia, with results that are all too well known.[6]

But a glance at the above list of ethnic attributes reveals not only their largely cultural and historical content, but also (with the exception of number 4) their strongly subjective components. Most important, it is myths of common ancestry, not any fact of ancestry (which is usually difficult to ascertain), that are crucial. It is fictive descent and putative ancestry that matters for the sense of ethnic identification. Indeed, Horowitz has likened ethnic groups to 'super-families' of fictive descent because members view their *ethnie* as composed of interrelated families, forming one huge 'family' linked by mythical ties of filiation and ancestry. Such a linkage between family and nation reappears in nationalist mythologies and testifies to the continuing centrality of this attribute of ethnicity. Without such descent myths it is difficult to see *ethnies* surviving for any length of time. The sense of 'whence we came' is central to the definition of 'who we are'.[7]

What I have termed 'shared historical memories' may also take the form of myth. Indeed, for many pre-modern peoples the line between myth and history was often blurred or even non-existent. Even today that line is not as clear-cut as some would like it to be; the controversy over the historicity of Homer and the Trojan War is a case in point. So are the tales of Stauffacher and the Oath of the Rütli, and of William Tell and Gessler, which have entered the 'historical consciousness' of every Swiss. It is not only that widely believed dramatic tales of the past serving present or future purposes grow up readily around kernels of well-attested events: in addition, myths of political foundation, liberation, migration and election take some historical event as their starting-point for subsequent interpretation and elaboration. The conversion of Vladimir of Kiev to Christianity (in AD 988) or the founding of Rome (in 753 BC?) may be treated as historical events, but their significance resides in the legends of foundation with which they are associated. It is these associations that confer on them a social purpose as sources of political cohesion.[8]

Similarly, attachments to specific stretches of territory, and to certain places within them, have a mythical and subjective quality. It is the attachments and associations, rather than residence in or possession of the land that matters for ethnic identification. It is where we belong. It is also often a sacred land, the land of our forefathers, our lawgivers, our kings and sages, poets and priests, which makes this our homeland. We belong to it, as much as it belongs to us. Besides, the sacred centres of the homeland draw the members of the *ethnie* to it, or inspire them from afar, even when their exile is prolonged. Hence, an *ethnie* may persist, even when long divorced from its homeland, through an intense nostalgia and spiritual attachment. This is very much the fate of diaspora communities like the Jews and Armenians.[9]

It is only when we come to the varying elements of a common culture that differentiate one population from another that more objective attributes enter the picture. Language, religion, customs and pigmentation are often taken to describe objective 'cultural markers' or differentiae that persist independently of the will of individuals, and even appear to constrain them. Yet it is the significance with which colour or religion is endowed by large numbers of individuals (and organizations) that matters more for ethnic identification even than their durability and independent existence, as the growing political significance of language and colour over the last two or three centuries demonstrates. It is only when such markers are endowed with diacritical significance that these cultural attributes come to be seen as objective, at least as far as ethnic boundaries are concerned.[10]

All of this suggests that the *ethnie* is anything but primordial, despite the claims and rhetoric of nationalist ideologies and discourses. As the subjective significance of each of these attributes waxes and wanes for the members of a community, so does the cohesion and self-awareness of that community's membership. As these several attributes come together and become more intense and salient, so does the sense of ethnic identity and, with it, of ethnic community. Conversely, as each of these attributes is attenuated and declines, so does the overall sense of ethnicity, and hence the *ethnie* itself would dissolve or be absorbed.[11]

How does an *ethnie* form? We can give only some very tentative answers. Where such processes are visible in the historical record they suggest certain patterns of ethnic formation. Empirically, these are of two main kinds: coalescence and division. On the one hand, we can trace ethnic formation through the coming together of separate units, and this in turn can be broken down into processes of amalgamation of separate units, such as city-states, and of absorption of one unit by another, as in the assimilation or regions or 'tribes'. On the other hand, *ethnies* may be subdivided through fission, as with sectarian schism, or through what Horowitz calls 'proliferation', when a part of the ethnic community leaves it to form a new group, as in the case of Bangladesh.[12]

The frequency of such processes suggests the shifting nature of ethnic boundaries and the malleability, within certain limits, of their members' cultural identity. It also reveals the 'concentric' nature of ethnic, and more generally collective cultural, affiliations. That is to say, individuals may feel loyalty not only to their families, villages, castes, cities, regions and religious communities, as well as to class and gender identifications; they may also feel allegiances to different ethnic communities at different levels of identification simultaneously. An example of this in the ancient world would be the sentiment of ancient Greeks as members of a *polis*, or the 'sub-*ethnie*' (Dorians, Ionians, Aeolians, Boeotians, etc. – really ethnic identities in their own right) and of the Hellenic cultural *ethnie*.[13] In the modern world the various clans, languages and ancestral 'sub-*ethnies*' of the Malays or Yoruba furnish examples of the concentric circles of ethnic identity and allegiance. Of course, at any one time one or other of these concentric circles of allegiance may be to the fore for political, economic or demographic reasons; but this serves only to reinforce 'instrumentalist' arguments against the primordial nature of ethnic communities and to highlight the importance of boundary changes.[14]

At the same time this is the only part of the story. We must not overstate the mutability of ethnic boundaries or the fluidity of their cultural contents. To do so would deprive us of the means of accounting for the recurrence of ethnic ties and communities (let alone their original crystallizations) and their demonstrable durability over and above boundary and cultural changes in particular instances. It would dissolve the possibility of constituting identities that were more than successive fleeting moments in the perceptions, attitudes and sentiments of identifying individuals. Worse, we would be unable to account for any collectivity, any group formation, from the myriad moments of individual sentiment, perception and memory. But the fact remains that, as with other social phenomena of collective identity like class, gender and territory, ethnicity exhibits both constancy and flux side by side, depending on the purposes and distance of the observer from the collective phenomenon in question. The durability of some *ethnies*, despite changes in their demographic composition and some of their cultural distinctiveness and social boundaries, must be set against the more instrumentalist or phenomenological accounts that fail to consider the importance of antecedent cultural affinities that set periodic limits to the redefinitions of ethnic identities.[15]

Any realistic account of ethnic identity and ethno-genesis must, therefore, eschew the polar extremes of the primordialist–instrumentalist debate and its concerns with, on the one hand, fixity of cultural patterns in nature and, on the other, 'strategic' manipulability of ethnic sentiments and continuous cultural malleability. Instead we need to reconstitute the notion of collective cultural identity itself in historical, subjective and symbolic terms. Collective cultural identity refers not to a uniformity of elements over generations but to a sense of continuity on the part of successive generations of a given cultural unit of population, to shared memories of earlier events and periods in the history of that unit and to notions entertained by each generation about the collective destiny of that unit and its culture. Changes in cultural identities therefore refer to the degree to which traumatic developments disturb the basic patterning of the cultural elements that make up the sense of continuity, shared memories and notions of collective destiny of given cultural units of population. The question is how far such developments disrupt or alter the fundamental patterns of myth, symbol, memory and value that bind successive generations of members together while demarcating them from 'outsiders' and around which congeal the lines of cultural differentiation that serve as 'cultural markers' of boundary regulation.[16]

We may illustrate these points by considering briefly some cases of disruptive culture change that nevertheless renewed, rather than destroyed, the sense of common ethnicity and its identity as we defined it above. Typical events that generate profound changes in the cultural contents of such identity include war and conquest, exile and enslavement, the influx of immigrants and religious conversion. The Persians, at least from the Sassanid period, were subjected to conquest by Arabs, Turks and others, were gradually converted to Islam and experienced more than one influx of immigrants. Yet, despite all the changes of collective cultural identity consequent on these processes, a Persian sense of distinctive ethnic identity persisted, and at times received a new lease of life, notably in the renaissance of the New Persian linguistic and literary revival of the tenth and eleventh centuries.[17] The Armenians too experienced traumatic events that had profound consequences for the cultural contents of their ethnic identity. They were the first constituted kingdom and people to convert to Christianity, were fought over by Sassanids and Byzantines, were defeated, excluded and partly exiled, received considerable influxes of immigrants and were finally subjected to mass deportation and genocide in part of their homeland. Yet, despite changes in location, economic activities, social organization and parts of their culture over the centuries, a sense of common Armenian identity has remained throughout their diaspora, and the forms of their antecedent culture, notably in the sphere of religion and language/script, have ensured a subjective attachment to their cultural identity and separation from their surroundings.[18]

These examples suggest the further observation that a combination of often adverse external factors and a rich inner or 'ethno'-history may help to crystallize and perpetuate ethnic identities. If the origins of cultural differentiation itself are lost in the last states of prehistory, we may at least attempt to isolate those recurrent forces that appear to coalesce the sense of ethnic identification and ensure its persistence over long periods.

Of these, state-making, military mobilization and organized religion appear to be crucial. Long ago Weber commented on the importance of political action for ethnic formation and persistence, arguing 'It is primarily the political community, no matter how artificially organized, that inspires the belief in common ethnicity.'[19] It is possible to exaggerate the role of state-making in ethnic crystallization (one thinks of the failure of Burgundy, and the qualified success of Prussia); yet, clearly, the foundation of a unified polity, as in ancient Egypt, Israel, Rome, Sassanid Persia, Japan and China, not to mention France, Spain and England, played a major role in the development of a sense of ethnic community and, ultimately, of cohesive nations.[20]

Warfare is, if anything, even more important. Not only does 'war make the state (and the state makes war)', as Tilly declared; it fashions ethnic communities not only from the contestants but even from third parties across whose territories such wars are often conducted. The case of ancient Israel is only the most striking, caught as it was between the great powers of the ancient Near East, Assyria and Egypt. Armenians, Swiss, Czechs, Kurds and Sikhs afford other instances of strategically located communities whose sense of common ethnicity, even when it did not originate from these events, was crystallized time and again by the impact of protracted warfare between foreign powers in which they were caught up. As for the contestants themselves, we need note only the frequency with which *ethnies* are antagonistically paired: French and English, Greeks and Persians, Byzantines and Sassanids, Egyptians and Assyrians, Khmers and Vietnamese, Arabs and Israelis . . . While it would be an exaggeration to deduce the sense of common ethnicity from the fear of the 'outsider' and paired antagonisms, there is no denying the central role of warfare, not, as Simmel suggested, as a crucible of ethnic cohesion (war may fracture that cohesion, as it did in the Great War in some European countries) but as a mobilizer of ethnic sentiments and national consciousness, a centralizing force in the life of the community and a provider of myths and memories for future generations. It is perhaps this last function that enters most deeply into the constitution of ethnic identity.[21]

As for organized religion, its role is both spiritual and social. The myth of common ethnic origins is often intertwined with creation myths – such as that of Deucalion and Pyrrha in Hesiod's *Theogony* and that of Noah in the Bible – or at least presupposes them. Very often the heroes of the ethnic community are also those of religious lore and tradition, albeit treated as 'servants of God' rather than ethnic founders or leaders, as was the case with Moses, Zoroaster, Muhammad, St Gregory, St Patrick and many others. The liturgy and rites of the Church or community of the faithful supply the texts, prayers, chants, feasts, ceremonies and customs, sometimes even the scripts, of distinctive ethnic communities, setting them apart from neighbours. And over all this heritage of cultural difference stand the 'guardians of the tradition', the priests, scribes and bards who record, preserve and transmit the fund of ethnic myths, memories, symbols and values encased in sacred traditions commanding the veneration of the populace through temple and church, monastery and school, into every town and village within the realm of the culture–community.[22]

State-making, protracted warfare and organized religion, though they figure prominently in the historical record of ethnic crystallization and persistence, may also operate to break up, or cut across, ethnic identifications. This happened when empires like those of Assyria and Achaemenid Persia created the conditions for a sustained intermingling of ethnic categories and communities in an Aramaic-speaking and syncretistic civilization, and when prolonged wars and rivalries put an end to ethnic states and communities like the Carthaginians and Normans (in Normandy). Ethnic identity also developed when religious movements burst across ethnic frontiers and founded great supra-territorial organizations, Buddhist, Catholic or Orthodox, or conversely, through schism, divided the members of ethnic communities such as the Swiss or Irish. Yet, for all these cases, we may find many more that confirm the close links between ethnic crystallization and the antecedent role of states, warfare and organized religion.

ETHNIC CHANGE, DISSOLUTION AND SURVIVAL

The importance of these and other factors can also be seen when we turn to the closely related questions of how *ethnies* change in character, dissolve or survive.

Let me start with ethnic change and with a well-known example, that of the Greeks. Modern Greeks are taught that they are the heirs and descendants not merely of Greek Byzantium, but also of the ancient Greeks and their classical Hellenic civilization. In both cases (and there have in fact been two, rival, myths of descent at work since the early nineteenth century), 'descent' was seen in largely demographic terms; or rather, cultural affinity with Byzantium and ancient Greece (notably Athens) was predicated on demographic continuity. Unfortunately for the classicist Hellenic myth, the demographic evidence is at best tenuous, at worst non-existent. As Jacob Fallmereyer demonstrated long ago, Greek demographic continuity was brutally interrupted in the late sixth to eighth centuries AD by massive influxes of Avar, Slav and, later, Albanian immigrants. The evidence from the period suggests that the immigrants succeeded in occupying most of central Greece and the Peloponnese (Morea), pushing the original Greek-speaking and Hellenic inhabitants (themselves already intermingled with earlier Macedonian, Roman and other migrants) to the coastal areas and the islands of the Aegean. This shifted the centre of a truly Hellenic civilization to the east, to the Aegean, the Ionian littoral of Asia Minor and to Constantinople. It also meant that modern Greeks could hardly count as being of ancient Greek descent, even if this could never be ruled out.[23]

There is a sense in which the preceding discussion is both relevant to a sense of Greek identity, now and earlier, and irrelevant. It is relevant in so far as Greeks, now and earlier, *felt* that their 'Greekness' was a product of their descent from the ancient Greeks (or Byzantine Greeks), and that such filiation made them *feel* themselves to be members of one great 'super-family' of Greeks, shared sentiments of continuity and membership being essential to a lively sense of identity. It is irrelevant in that *ethnies* are constituted, not by lines of physical descent, but by the sense of continuity, shared memory and collective destiny, i.e. by lines of cultural affinity embodied in distinctive myths, memories, symbols and values retained by a given cultural unit of population. In that sense much has been retained, and revived, from the extant heritage of ancient Greece. For, even at the time of Slavic migrations, in Ionia and especially in Constantinople, there was a growing emphasis on the Greek language, on Greek philosophy and literature, and on classical models of thought and scholarship. Such a 'Greek revival' was to surface again in the tenth and fourteenth centuries, as well as subsequently, providing a powerful impetus to the sense of cultural affinity with ancient Greece and its classical heritage.[24]

This is not to deny for one moment either the enormous cultural changes undergone by the Greeks despite a surviving sense of common ethnicity or the cultural influence of surrounding peoples and civilizations over two thousand years. At the same time in terms of script and language, certain values, a particular environment and its nostalgia, continuous social interactions, and a sense of religious and cultural difference, even exclusion, a sense of Greek identity and common sentiments of ethnicity can be said to have persisted beneath the many social and political changes of the last two thousand years.[25]

I shall return in a moment to the role of ethnic exclusion in ensuring ethnic persistence. For the present I want to look at the other side of the coin: ethnic dissolution. We say how *ethnies* can be dissolved through fission or proliferation. But in a sense the ethnic community remains in *some* form in such cases – smaller, perhaps, or reduplicated, but none the less still 'in the field'. Can we then speak of ethnic extinction – the disappearance of an *ethnie*, not just in the form it possessed until that point but in any form?

I think we can if we hold to the historical, cultural and symbolic criteria of ethnic identity I have been employing. There are two main kinds of ethnic extinction in the full sense: genocide and ethnocide, which is sometimes – at times misleadingly – called 'cultural genocide'. In one sense genocide is a rare and probably modern phenomenon. It includes those cases where we know that mass death of a cultural group was premeditated and the basis of that targeting was exclusively the existence and membership of that cultural group. Nazi policies towards the Jews and a part of the Gypsies were of this kind; so perhaps were European actions towards the Tasmanian Aborigines, and the Turkish actions in Turkish Armenia.[26] Other policies and actions were genocidal in their consequences rather than their intentions; such ethnic destruction occurred when the American Whites encountered the American Indians, and when the Spanish conquistadors encountered the Aztec and other Indian populations of Mexico (though here disease played a larger part). In these cases ethnic extinction was not deliberately aimed at, yet no attempt was made to mitigate those policies whose side-effect was genocidal. These genocidal actions need to be distinguished again from large-scale massacres like those by the Mongols in the thirteenth century or in modern times by the Soviets and Nazis of selected populations (for example, the Katyn massacre or the reprisals of Lidice and Oradour), which are designed to break a spirit of resistance by terrifying the civilian population or rendering it leaderless.[27]

The interesting point about genocide and genocidal actions, at least in modern times, is how rarely they achieve their stated goals or unintended consequences. They rarely extinguish *ethnies* or ethnic categories. In fact they may do the opposite, reviving ethnic cohesion and consciousness, or helping to crystallize it, as they did with the Aborigines' movement or Romany Gypsy nationalism. Perhaps there are deep-rooted facets of modernity that both encourage and preclude successful genocide (where success is measured by total extinction), and this may have much to do with the conditions and diffusion of nationalism. It may have been easier to destroy an *ethnie* in pre-modern times. At any rate, when at last the Romans decided to destroy Carthage once and for all they erased the city and massacred three quarters of its population, selling off the rest into slavery. Though vestiges of Punic culture persisted till the time of St Augustine, the Carthaginians as a western Phoenician *ethnie* and ethnic state were extinguished.[28]

The same fate awaited several peoples of the ancient world, including the Hittites, Philistines, Phoenicians (of Lebanon) and Elamites. In each case loss of political power and independence presaged ethnic extinction, but usually through cultural absorption and ethnic intermingling. These are cases of ethnocide rather than genocide, despite the drama of the political events that precipitated them. When he destroyed Susa and eliminated the Elamite state from politics in 636 BC Asshur-bani-pal, king of Assyria, did not set about exterminating every Elamite (the Assyrians in fact usually deported the élites of the peoples they conquered). Yet so massive was the act of destruction that Elam never recovered, new peoples settled within its borders, and, though its language persisted into the Achaemenid Persian period, no Elamite community or state re-emerged to sustain the myths, memories, values and symbols of Elamite religion and culture.[29]

The fate of Assyria itself was even more swift and dramatic. Nineveh fell in 612 BC to a combined onslaught of Cyaxares' Medes and Nabopolassar's Babylonians, and her last prince, Asshur-uballit, was defeated at Harran three years later. Thereafter, we hear little of 'Assyria'. Its gods were received by Cyrus back into the pantheon at

Babylon, but there is no further mention of state or people, and when Xenophon's army marched through the province of Assyria he found all her cities in ruins with the exception of Erbil. Was this a case of genocidal actions or even genocide? [30]

It is unlikely. The goal of Assyria's enemies was destruction of her hated rule. That meant destroying her major cities so that there was no chance of a revival of her political fortunes. True, Nabopolassar talked about 'turning the hostile land into heaps and ruins', but this did not mean exterminating every Assyrian, even if this had been feasible. Perhaps the Assyrian élites were evicted; but, in any case, in terms of religion and culture they were less and less differentiated from the Babylonian civilization they sought to emulate. Besides, the latter days of the vast Assyrian empire witnessed severe social divisions both in the army and the countryside, and considerable ethnic intermingling in the empire's heartlands, and use of an Aramaic lingua franca for commercial and administrative purposes following a large influx of Arameans. Hence the ethnic distinctiveness of the Assyrians was severely compromised well before the downfall of the empire, and cultural syncretism and ethnic intermingling helped to ensure the attenuation and absorption of the Assyrian ethnic community and its culture by the surrounding peoples and cultures. [31]

As with the Phoenicians, Elamites and others, the relatively swift disappearance of an Assyrian culture and community must be seen as an example of ethnocide. In the ancient world at least, destruction of a community's or state's gods and temples was seen as the means of destroying the community itself; that seems to have been the aim of the Persians when they destroyed the Babylonian temples in 482 BC, and perhaps of the Romans when they destroyed the Temple in Jerusalem in AD 70. [32] The aim in all such cases was the eradication of the group's culture, rather than the group itself, and it differs in its intended effects from the much slower, unplanned processes of cultural absorption which have undermined many small ethnic categories and communities.

History is replete with instances of unintended cultural absorption and ethnic dissolution. Engels, surveying the ethnic map of Europe in 1859, referred to these dying ethnic cultures and communities as so many 'ethnographic monuments', which he hoped would soon disappear to make way for the large capitalist nation–state. He has, in fact, been largely disappointed. At the same time the diminution of many former *ethnies*, and the attenuation of their sentiments, as in the cases of the Occitanie, Sorbs, Wends and many others, demonstrates these widespread processes of gradual absorption through incorporation and fragmentation.

But, equally, they suggest the other side of the coin – the durability of ethnic ties, the longevity of their cultures and the persistence of collective identities and even communities over several centuries. If ethnic boundaries and cultural contents undergo periodic change, how shall we account for ethnic survival potential, sometimes across millennia?

Again, it is useful to consider a well-known example. Jews trace their ancestry to Abraham, their liberation to the Exodus, their founding charter to Mount Sinai, and their golden age to (variously) the Davidic and Solomonic kingdom or the era of the sages in the late Second Temple period and after. These are all myths in the sense outlined above, and they retain their religious potency today. But their potency is not only religious. They remain, even for secular Jews, charters of their ethnic identity. Here, too, as with the Greeks and Armenians, the Irish and Ethiopians, there is a *felt* filiation, as well as a cultural affinity, with a remote past in which a community was formed, a community that despite all the changes it has undergone, is still in some sense recognized as the 'same' community. To what is this sense of continuity, of shared memory and of collective destiny owed?

The simple answer, that peoples survive in some form because they are rooted in their homelands and enjoy a large measure of independent statehood, will clearly not do in the Jewish case. The Jews have been exiled from both for nearly two thousand years. Not that either is unimportant to the Jewish sense of identity; but both figure more as symbol than as living memory. Certainly this is true of statehood, the Hasmonean being the last truly independent Jewish state – unless we include the kingdom of the Khazars. The land of Israel was at times more than a symbol of messianic restoration; groups of Jews made their way there from time to time and founded synagogues. Yet here too the yearning for Zion was often more spiritual than actual, a vision of perfection in a restored land and city.[33]

Another common view, which this time is directed specifically to diaspora peoples, is that their survival depends on their ability to find a distinct economic niche in host societies, usually as middlemen or artisans, between military and agrarian élites and the peasant masses. That Jews, Greeks and Armenians, like Lebanese and Chinese traders, found such niches in medieval European and early modern societies is not in question and neither is the role of such occupational niches in reinforcing residential patterns and cultural segregation where these already exist. What is at issue is the method by which the category 'occupational niche' is separated from the nexus of conditions that make up typical diasporas and assigned a prior casual weight in ensuring ethnic survival and status. Rather, as Armstrong has argued, archetypal diasporas that stem from religious and cultural differences must be seen as a totality of interrelated aspects and dimensions in which occupational segregation and middleman status serves to reinforce and articulate, but not necessarily to ensure, ethnic difference and survival. Certainly, in Moorish Spain Jews held every kind of occupational position, but their ethnic survival was bound up with more fundamental religious and cultural distinctions from their neighbours.[34]

A more basic consideration stems from the earlier emphasis on organized religion. In the case of diaspora communities, as of sects-turned-*ethnies* like the Druse, Samaritans, Maronites and Sikhs, religious rituals, liturgy and hierarchies have played a powerful conserving role, ensuring a high degree of formal continuity between generations and from community to community. Add to this the separating power of sacred languages and scripts, texts and calendars, and the apparent mystery of millennial diaspora survival appears soluble.

But there are difficulties here, too. For one thing this says nothing about the shape, size or location of the surviving community. The Samaritans, for example, were till quite recently heading for ethnic extinction, because after centuries of decimation endogamy could no longer replenish their numbers. In the case of the Beta Israel (or Falasha) of northern Ethiopia the attrition of their numbers in war, and the isolation of their craftsman community, might have spelt absorption had it not been for a wider Jewish ethnic self-renewal and the rise of Zionism and the state of Israel.[35]

This thesis also says nothing about the vitality of the community.

Religion may become petrified and antiquarian, as did the Assyrian state religion; in that case, as we saw, it contributed nothing to the chances of ethnic survival. The same inner decay can be found in later Roman religion, as in the Pharaonic religion of Ptolemaic Egypt. In neither case could we hang an argument for ethnic survival, let alone ethnic vitality, on any movement within the traditional religion.[36]

Religion, then, may preserve a sense of common ethnicity as if in a chrysalis, at least for a period, as was the case with Greek Orthodoxy for the self-governing Greek Orthodox *millet* under Ottoman rule. But unless new movements and currents stir the spirit within the religious framework, its very conservatism may deaden the *ethnie* or it may become a shell for an attenuated identity.[37] Clearly, organized religion by itself is not enough. What then are the characteristic mechanisms of ethnic self-renewal? I would single out four such mechanisms:

1. *Religious reform* Having accepted the importance of organized religion for ethnic survival potential, we need to consider the role of movements of religious reform in stimulating ethnic self-renewal. In the case of the Jews there are a number of instances. These range from the Prophetic and Deuteronomic movements in eighth-century and seventh-century BC Judah to Ezra's reforms in the mid-fifth century BC, the rise of Pharisaism and Mishnaic rabbinism in the second century AD, right up to the Chassidic and neo-Orthodox movements of the eighteenth and nineteenth centuries. In each case religious reform was intertwined with ethnic self-renewal; the community's mode of renewal was religiously inspired.[38]

Conversely, failure of religious reform or petrified conservatism may turn the modes of ethnic self-renewal elsewhere. This occurred among the Greeks at the beginning of the nineteenth century. The Greek Orthodox hierarchy in Constantinople became increasingly remote from middle-class and popular aspirations, including those of the lower clergy who supplied the revolt in the Morea with some of its leaders. Here Greek aspirations found increasingly secular ideological discourses for their goals.[39]

2. *Cultural borrowing* In the wider field of culture ethnic survival finds sustenance not from isolation but from selective borrowing

and controlled culture contact. Here again we can find an example from Jewish history. The stimulus of Hellenistic culture, from the time of Alexander on, provoked a lively encounter between Greek and Jewish thought that, though it had fierce political repercussions, strengthened through enrichment the whole field of Jewish culture and identity.[40] There are many other examples of the ways in which external cultural stimuli and contacts have renewed the sense of ethnic identity through selective cultural appropriation; nineteenth-century Japan, Russia and Egypt afford well-known cases.

3. *Popular participation* Socially, too, we can discern modes of ethnic self-renewal in the movements of social strata and classes. Of these, the most relevant are popular movements for greater participation in the cultural or political hierarchy. The great socio-religious popular movement of the Mazdakites in fifth-century Sassanid Persia renewed the severely damaged fabric of Sassanid Persian and Zoroastrian community at the same time as it undermined the foundations of the Sassanid state. This in turn provoked a repressive, but also ethnically regenerative, movement under Chosroes I in the sixth century, which included the codification of the basis of the *Book of Kings*, a return to Iranian mythology and ritual, and a national revival in literature, protocol, learning and the arts.[41] The popular movements in Judaism, from the Mosaic era to the Chassidim just mentioned, also served to renew a demotic *ethnie* through enthusiastic popular participation and missionary zeal. The same is true of various popular movements in Islam, including its foundation and the movements of Sunni or Shi'ite purification and messianism to this day, such as Wahhabism, Mahdism and the Shi'ite revolution in Iran.[42]

4. *Myths of ethnic election* In many ways myths of ethnic chosenness go to the heart of the modes of ethnic self-renewal and hence survival. What we notice, first of all, is that *ethnies* that, for all their ethnocentrism towards others, lacked such myths (or failed to instil them in the general population) tended to be absorbed by other communities after losing their independence. This may of course be an argument from silence. Generally speaking, it is *ethnies* with religious myths of ethnic election that possess the specialist classes whose position and outlook are so heavily bound up with the success and influence of election myths – and it is they who are often our

only literary witnesses. Nevertheless, when we consider the fate of many *ethnies* that possessed such classes but boasted no such myth of *ethnic* election (as opposed to royal election), then, as the cases of Assyria, Phoenicia and the Philistines reveal, it is clear that their chances of ethnic survival were considerably diminished.

This, of course, merely puts the onus of explanation back on to the conditions which foster and sustain myths of ethnic election. Yet such a method short-circuits the process of ethnic survival through exclusive election. For what the myth of election promises is a conditional salvation. This is vital for grasping its role in survival potential. Its *locus classicus* is found in the book of Exodus: 'Now therefore, if ye will obey my voice indeed, and keep my covenant, then shall ye be a peculiar treasure unto me from all the peoples; for all the earth is mine; and ye shall be unto me a kingdom of priests, and an holy nation.' [43] To see oneself as potentially 'an holy nation' is to link chosenness indissolubly with collective sanctification. Salvation is accessible only through redemption, which in turn requires a return to former ways and beliefs, which are the means of sanctification. Hence the recurrent note of 'return' in many ethno-religious traditions that inspire movements of both religious reform and cultural restoration. Given the ineluctable subjectivity of ethnic identification, this moral summons to re-sanctify the potential elect provides a powerful mechanism for ethnic self-renewal and hence long-term survival. This is certainly one key to the problem of Jewish survival in the face of adversity, but we can also trace its revitalizing effects among other peoples – Amharic Ethiopians, Armenians, Greeks converted to Orthodoxy, Orthodox Russians, Druse, Sikhs, as well as various European *ethnies* like the Poles, Germans, French, English, Castilians, Irish, Scots and Welsh, to name a few. So widespread a phenomenon clearly bears more thorough-going investigation.[44]

'ETHNIC CORES' AND THE FORMATION OF NATIONS

Religious reform, cultural borrowing, popular participation and myths of ethnic election: these are some of the mechanisms that, along with location, autonomy, polyglot and trading skills and organized religion, help to ensure the survival of certain ethnic communities across the centuries despite many changes in their social composition and cultural contents. These cases again bring us up sharply against the central paradox of ethnicity: the coexistence of flux and durability, of an ever-changing individual and cultural expression within distinct social and cultural parameters. The latter take the form of a heritage and traditions received from one generation to another, but in slightly or considerably changed form, which set limits to the community's outlook and cultural contents. A certain tradition of images, cults, customs, rites and artefacts, as well as certain events, heroes, landscapes and values, come to form a distinctive repository of ethnic culture, to be drawn upon selectively by successive generations of the community.

How do such traditions influence subsequent generations? In premodern communities it is the priests, scribes and bards, often organized into guilds and castes, who recount, re-enact and codify traditions. Often as the only literate strata, and being necessary for intercession with divine forces, priests, scribes and bards achieve considerable influence and prestige in many communities. Organized in their brotherhoods and temples and churches, they form a network of socialization in the major towns and much of the surrounding countryside – depending upon their degree of organization and mental monopoly in the community's territory. Indeed, in many ancient and medieval empires priesthoods and their temple and scribal infrastructure formed indispensable partners in government and/or rival centres of power to the Court and bureaucracy, especially in ancient Egypt and Sassanid Persia.[45]

Even in diaspora communities we find the priests, rabbis and doctors of law, organized along more or less centralized lines, forming an encompassing network of tribunals and counsel, and endowing far-flung enclaves with religious, legal and cultural unity in the face of an often hostile environment. Especially among Jews and Armenians, as Armstrong has demonstrated, this highly evolved network of religious officials and institutions was able to ensure the subjective unity and survival of the community and its historical and religious traditions.[46]

It is through such unifying and embracing mechanisms that what we may term 'ethnic cores' are gradually built up. These are fairly cohesive and self-consciously distinctive *ethnies* which form the kernel and basis of states and kingdoms such as the barbarian *regna* of the early medieval era. Among the kingdoms of the Franks, Lombards, Saxons, Scots and Visigoths the sense of a community of customs and common descent played a vital role, despite the fact that many of their inhabitants did not belong to the dominant ethnic community. Nevertheless, in popular perception, such *regna* were seen as increasingly communal and possessed of a unifying cultural basis.[47] By the later medieval period these subjectively unified communities of culture formed the core around which large and powerful states erected their administrative, judicial, fiscal and military apparatus, and proceeded to annex adjacent territories and their culturally different populations. Under Edward I, for example, the English (Anglo-Norman) state expanded into Wales, destroying the Welsh kingdoms and bringing most Welshmen into the realm as a peripheral cultural community under the domination of the English state. Something similar happened in France under Louis VIII to the *pays d'oc*, notably the County of Toulouse, at the time of the Albigensian Crusade.[48]

Locating such ethnic cores tells us a good deal about the subsequent shape and character of nations – if (and when) such nations emerge. It helps us to answer in large part the question: *who* is the nation? and to some extent: *where* is the nation? That is to say, a state's ethnic core often shapes the character and boundaries of the nation; for it is very often on the basis of such a core that states coalesce to form nations. Though most latter-day nations are, in fact, polyethnic, or rather most nation-states are polyethnic, many have been formed in the first place around a dominant *ethnie*, which annexed or attracted other *ethnies* or ethnic fragments into the state to which it gave a name and a cultural charter. For, since *ethnies* are by definition associated with a given territory, not infrequently a chosen people with a particular sacred land, the presumed boundaries of the nation are largely determined by the myths and memories of the dominant *ethnie*, which include the foundation charter, the myth of the golden age and the associated territorial claims, or ethnic title-deeds. Hence the many conflicts, even today, for sundered parts of the ethnic homeland, – in Armenia, in Kosovo, in Israel and Palestine, in the Ogaden, and elsewhere.

Both the close relationship and the differences between the

concepts of *ethnie* and nation and their historical referents may also be seen by recalling our definition of the nation. A nation, it was argued, is *a named human population sharing an historic territory, common myths and historical memories, a mass, public culture, a common economy and common legal rights and duties for all members*. By definition the nation is a community of common myths and memories, as is an *ethnie*. It is also a territorial community. But whereas in the case of *ethnies* the link with a territory may be only historical and symbolic, in the case of the nation it is physical and actual: nations possess territories. In other words nations always require ethnic 'elements'. These may, of course, be reworked; they often are. But nations are inconceivable without some common myths and memories of a territorial home.

This suggests a certain circularity in the argument that nations are formed on the basis of ethnic cores. There is, indeed, considerable historical and conceptual overlap between *ethnies* and nations. Nevertheless, we are dealing with different concepts and historical formations. Ethnic communities do not have several of the attributes of the nation. They need not be resident in 'their' territorial homeland. Their culture may not be public or common to all the members. They need not, and often do not, exhibit a common division of labour or economic unity. Nor need they have common legal codes with common rights and duties for all. As we shall see, these attributes of nations are products of particular social and historical conditions working upon antecedent ethnic cores and ethnic minorities.

On the other side of the picture we should note the possibility of forming nations without immediate antecedent *ethnie*. In several states nations are being formed through an attempt to coalesce the cultures of successive waves of (mainly European) immigrants – in America, Argentina and Australia. In other cases states were formed out of the provinces of empires which had imposed a common language and religion, notably in Latin America. Here, too, creole élites began a process of nation-formation in the absence of a distinctive *ethnie*. In fact, as nation-formation proceeded it was found necessary to fashion a distinctively Mexican, Chilean, Bolivian, etc. culture, and to emphasize the specific characteristics – in terms of separate symbols, values, memories, etc. – of each would-be nation.[49]

The dilemma is even sharper in sub-Saharan Africa, whose states were created, if not deliberately across *ethnies*, at least with little reference to them. Here the colonial states had to foster a purely territorial patriotism, a sense of political loyalty to the newly created states and their embryonic political communities. In the independent states born of these territorial communities several *ethnies*, ethnic fragments and ethnic categories were drawn together by political regulation and social boundaries that had come to include previously unrelated groups in the post-colonial political system, and had brought them, even against their will, into a new struggle for scarce resources and political power. In these circumstances the ruling élites, who may often have been recruited from a dominant *ethnie* or coalition of ethnic groupings, were tempted to fashion a new political mythology and symbolic order not only to legitimate their often authoritarian regimes, but also to head off threats of endemic ethnic conflict and even movements of secession. In these cases the state is utilized to fashion the 'civil religion' whose myths, memories, symbols and the like will provide the functional equivalent of a missing or defective dominant *ethnie*. So the project of nation-formation in sub-Saharan Africa suggests the creation of the components of a new ethnic identity and consciousness that will sub-sume, by drawing together, some of the loyalties and cultures of the existing *ethnies*. At least that has been the national 'project' of many African and Asian élites.[50]

This means that the relationship of modern nations to any ethnic core is problematic and uncertain. Why then should we seek the origins of the nation in pre-modern ethnic ties when not every modern nation can point back to an ethnic base? There are, I think, three reasons why we should do so.

The first is that, historically, the first nations were, as we shall see, formed on the basis of pre-modern ethnic cores; and, being powerful and culturally influential, they provided models for subsequent cases of the formation of nations in many parts of the globe.

The second reason is that the ethnic model of the nation became increasingly popular and widespread not only for the foregoing reason, but also because it sat so easily on the pre-modern 'demotic' kind of community that had survived into the modern era in so many parts of the world. In other words the ethnic model was sociologically fertile.

And third, even where a nation-to-be could boast no ethnic antecedents of importance and where any ethnic ties were shadowy or fabricated, the need to forge out of whatever cultural components were available a coherent mythology and symbolism of a community of history and culture became everywhere paramount as a condition of national survival and unity. Without some ethnic lineage the nation-to-be could fall apart. These three factors in the formation of nations provide the point of departure for our analysis in the next two chapters.

CHAPTER 3

The Rise of Nations

If the presence and reconstruction of ethnic ties and pasts tends to determine which units of population are eligible and likely to become nations, it tells us little about why and how this transformation comes about. To answer the question: what are the general causes and mechanisms of the formation of nations on the basis of variable ethnic ties and memories? we need to examine the main patterns in the formation of identities, and the broad changes that promoted their development.

In this context the term 'formation of nations' is significant. It reminds us that though for convenience we delimit and define a specific concept of the nation, we are in fact dealing with a complex set of processes over time rather than with fixed 'essences'. In chapter 1 the complex and abstract nature of the concept of 'national identity' was highlighted. As a *named human population sharing an historic territory, common myths and historical memories, a mass, public culture, a common economy and common legal rights and duties for all members*, the nation is a multidimensional concept, an ideal type that provides a standard or touchstone which concrete examples imitate in varying degrees. We must expect individual examples to show considerable variation in the degree to which different processes, along the several dimensions, have developed and combined to produce an approximation to the ideal type of the nation. It is necessary to bear this in mind when we explore the causes and mechanisms of the emergence of nations.

NATIONS BEFORE NATIONALISM?

I mentioned, at the beginning of chapter 2, the nationalist belief that nations have existed from time immemorial, though often in prolonged slumber. To the nationalist, as to an earlier generation of scholars, there was therefore no special problem about the origins and causes of nations, no need to explore the processes of their formation.

Nations were perennial; only their degree of self-awareness and activism varied.[1]

Against this familiar older view a modern generation of scholars has demonstrated the contingency of nations and nationalism in history, and their relative modernity. For most scholars, nationalism, the movement and ideology, can be dated to the late eighteenth century. Before the period leading up to the French Revolution we have only fleeting expressions of a national sentiment, and vague intimations of the central ideas of nationalism, with its emphasis on the autonomy of culturally distinctive nations. Even the nation is a purely modern construct, though here there is considerable disagreement among 'modernists' as to the period of its emergence in Europe, with some favouring the eighteenth century or earlier and others preferring the late nineteenth and early twentieth century, when the masses were finally 'nationalized' and women enfranchised. Clearly, among the modernists – those who claim the nation is wholly 'modern' – different ideas of the nation are at work.[2]

Nevertheless, if the modernists are right there can be neither nations nor nationalism in pre-modern eras. The conditions that have brought the nation into being were absent in antiquity and the middle ages, and the differences between pre-modern and modern collective cultural identities are too great to be subsumed under a single concept of the nation. Mass 'citizen-nations' can only emerge in the era of industrialism and democracy.[3]

There is much truth in this view, but it needs to be qualified in important ways. It presumes that a single criterion, the inclusion of the masses and women, is decisive for determining the emergence and presence of the nation. This is unduly restrictive, if not misleading. Besides, by this criterion units of population which mobilized the masses for military and political activity would constitute nations – shall we then call the early Sumerian city-states or the early Swiss cantons nations? Shall we deny the appellation of nation to the ancient Egyptians and Assyrians, simply because the masses were excluded from political activity or representation? Is this not to impose a very Western concept of the nation on to quite different areas and periods?[4]

But can we escape doing just this, at least in some form and to some degree? I think not. Even if we employ a more multidimensional concept of the nation, like the one I have urged, in practice we shall still be measuring differences between collective cultural identities in pre-modern and modern periods through a number of processes and dimensions. Let me try to illustrate what I mean.

We can start by asking whether there were nations and nationalism in antiquity. Ancient Egypt is an obvious choice. The river Nile and the surrounding deserts have endowed it with a fairly fixed and compact territory, except to the south perhaps. Once unification of Upper and Lower Egypt had been achieved the long history of dynastic rule there gave contemporaries every impression of a strong, unified bureaucratic state with the inhabitants subject to a single Pharaonic code of laws, and with the river affording the basis for a unified economic system. In terms of culture too, the monopoly position of Pharaonic religion and customs lent Egyptians of all classes a distinctive cultural profile at least till the final decline of the state.[5]

Here we seem to have a named population with a historic territory, myths, memories and mass culture, and even a common economy and legal code. Did not ancient Egypt approximate in every sense to an ideal–typical nation, as much, if not more than, Assyria, Safavid Persia or Tokugawa Japan?

There is no doubt that the ancient Egyptians, like the Assyrians, Persians of the Safavid period and Japanese of the Tokugawa era, constituted what I have termed an *ethnie*, with a corresponding ethnocentrism. But they were in several important respects some way from approximating the ideal type of the nation. Economically, despite the trading unity promoted by the Nile, Egypt was divided into regions and districts, with an economy based largely on village subsistence farming. Legally, too, while all Egyptians were subject to Pharaonic regulation there was not the least hint of shared rights and duties, let alone any idea of citizenship such as one finds in ancient Greece. Indeed, as in all these states, there were different laws for different classes and strata, the priesthoods constituting a category all to themselves. Education, too, was class divided, the sons of the Egyptian nobility receiving quite separate training from that provided by the scribal schools of the temples. Thus, while there were common myths and memories as well as a common pantheon and rituals that served to differentiate Egyptians from other peoples, the public culture of the Pharaonic state operated largely through the religious institutions, which were themselves subject to divisions and were unable to compensate for the regionalism that so often undermined the unity of the Egyptian state. In later periods the growing division between the élites and the peasantry and artisans led to disaffection with the old Pharaonic temple religion and lower class resort to the new mystery cults and ultimately Christianity.[6]

We may perhaps characterize ancient Egypt more fruitfully as an ethnic state than as a nation, as we have defined it. The ancient Egyptian state signally failed to break free of its aristocratic and priestly bases, unlike the French and British states. Like the other ethnic states of Assyria, Persia and Japan, it failed to inculcate a public culture in the middle and lower classes and made little attempt to unify the population either through a single occupation system throughout the territory or by prescribing common rights and duties for all members of the kingdom. The ethnic state remained the pre-modern equivalent of the modern nation, and it would need a revolution to break the mould.

Can we speak, then, of an ancient Egyptian nationalism without falling into a retrospective determinism? We know that Egyptian monarchs, including Akhnaton, had a clear idea of Egypt as a kingdom and (later) an empire, and Akhnaton's hymn to the sun attributes value even to other peoples ('The Nile in heaven, it is for the foreign peoples'). But such sentiments seem to have been confined to the élites and to have been invoked to resist foreigners and guard the old order. As the Theban prince, Kamose, who drove out the Hyksos kings in c. 1580 BC put it:

> I will grapple with them, and cut open their belly!
> I will save Egypt and overthrow the Asiatics![7]

If nationalism signified merely resistance to cultural and political outsiders, then Kamose and his successors were nationalists, and nationalism can be found in every era and continent. But if by nationalism we wish to designate ideologies and movements that presuppose a world of nations, each with its own character, and a primary allegiance to the nation as the sole source of political power and the basis of world order, then we shall be hard put to find movements inspired by such ideals in the ancient, or medieval, worlds, let alone in ancient Egypt.

Ancient Egypt, then, presents us with a clear example of an ethnic state where there is a close fit between the dynastic state and a population with a relatively homogeneous historical culture. Only Japan could boast a similar degree of ethnic homogeneity, despite the presence of Ainu and Korean minorities. Other ethnic states – Assyria, Elam, Urartu, Persia, China – soon annexed outlying areas with culturally different peoples or invited (or deported) outsiders into their homelands and allowed them to intermarry with the dominant ethnic community.

In assessing the degree to which nations or nationalisms are present in the ancient world, we are greatly hampered by lack of evidence, even from the small ruling strata. Perhaps this is one reason why, in the two cases where we have more evidence, we are more prepared to admit the possibility of nations and nationalisms.

I refer, of course, to ancient Greece and Israel. Here, if anywhere, we might expect to confront a strong sense of *national* identity and an equally vivid nationalism. Yet even here the evidence is at best ambiguous.

We have already seen how such unity as there was among ancient Greeks was strictly cultural rather than political. In fact, the cultural picture is even more complex, because the ethnic divisions *within* the wider Hellenic ethnic community, the cleavages between Ionians, Aeolians, Boeotians and Dorians, also played a role in social and even political life. The distinction between Dorian 'fortitude' and Ionian 'refinement' could be invoked (usually negatively as 'uncouth strength' and 'effeminacy') by the parties to the Peloponnesian War in the quest for allies and justifications. This diversity also played an important role in social and religious life; tribal divisions, religious rituals, calendars and artistic forms varied with each ethnic category. Yet even these divisions did not constitute effective communities, since each was subdivided into *poleis*, the city-states that commanded a Greek's primary allegiance and that, despite the later amphictyonies, never ceased to do so.[8]

This is also the main reason for the failure of ancient Greeks to evince more than a semblance of nationalism. Once again, as in ancient Egypt, we are dealing with the typical ethnocentrism displayed by most cultural communities in antiquity, an ethnocentrism that in moments of crisis could impel the constituent parts of the Hellenic cultural community (in fact by no means all of them) to come together to resist the common enemy. Successful resistance to Persia did in fact inspire panhellenic cultural sentiments and fuel the sense of Greek superiority to 'enslaved' barbarians – but it singularly failed to unite them, despite the efforts of Kimon and Pericles, in the crusade against Persia. Persian gold remained more potent than pan-Greek sentiment.[9]

There was perhaps greater unity and more nationalism among the Jews of Judea. This was a relatively late development. Ancient Israel had undoubtedly drawn on common myths of origin, shared memories and traditions, and a common religious culture. But its unity had been fractured by tribal divisions and the simmering conflict between the northern and southern tribal regions. Repeated wars with Canaanites and Philistines engendered some political unity, but it was really the Jerusalem priesthood and the prophetic movement that stemmed the tide of cultural assimilation after the fall of the northern kingdom of Israel in 722 BC. Similarly, it was the reforms of Ezra and the political measures of Nehemiah that preserved the Judean commonwealth in the Achaemenid empire and under their successors, the Ptolemies. In the great crisis of Hellenization that ensued, and that the measures of the Seleucid Antiochus Epiphanes exacerbated, these religious currents once again turned the tide of cultural assimilation under the Maccabees, the Pharisees and Zealots and finally the Rabbis and Sages.[10]

But, even here, can we speak of a Jewish nation and Jewish nationalism? Are we to view the Maccabees and Zealots as early examples of latterday nationalist guerrillas and freedom fighters?

The difficulty in arriving at a clear answer lies in the near-identity in Jewish thought and practice of what we consider to be separate, namely the religious community and the nation with religious messianism and nationalism. For the Zealots, in particular, the land of Israel belonged to God and was therefore inalienable. It was the duty of every Jew to recover it from the Romans as a prelude to the end of days. Such eschatological hopes were focused on the realization of the Covenant between Israel and the Lord. The messianic promise of God's kingdom on earth would be fulfilled in a Jewish theocracy in the land of Israel. In this conception no distinction was possible between a Jewish nation and the religious community of Israel, or between Jewish messianism and the aspirations of the Jewish people.[11]

Though, as we shall see, nationalism is a fundamentally secular ideology, there is nothing unusual about a religious nationalism. Not only have nationalists often found it necessary to appeal to the religious sentiments of the masses, but they have also found it relatively easy to identify the nation with the religious community wherever the latter defines the circle of the ethnic community, as in Sri Lanka, Armenia, Poland and Ireland. But in these latter cases the invocation of the ethno-religious community occurs self-consciously in the age of nationalism, whereas in the ancient Jewish case there was no European or worldwide tradition of nationalist ideas to draw on, and hence no ideology of the nation *per se*. From what we know of the period it is unlikely that the Zealots of first-century AD Judea (or any other Jew) entertained the possibility of a secular concept of the nation separate from Judaism. But arguments from silence must be treated with caution.[12]

Can we speak, perhaps, of a Jewish nation in the period of the Second Temple? There was certainly a vivid sense of common ethnicity embodied in a common name and myths of descent, shared historical memories, a fervent attachment to the land, and shared languages (Hebrew and Aramaic) and common religious culture. In other respects, however, the evidence is less clear. Though the extent of the Land of Israel was set down by tradition ('from Dan to Beersheba'), actual territorial extent and unity varied, with Galilee and the coastal plain (and the southern Negev) standing somewhat apart from the Judean centre. This entailed corresponding economic divergences, despite the unifying role of the Temple as entrepôt of merchandise. Galilee, in particular, was the largely self-sufficient home of prosperous farmers (olive oil and vineyards were favoured), especially in the later Mishnaic period. How far Jews in the Hasmonean commonwealth were united by common civic rights and duties is also unclear, but religious ordinances and duties applied equally to all adult males, who, in theory at least, received the same religious education. With the rise of the synagogue and the Pharisees, local religious education became a reality for everyone, though it was perhaps only in the subsequent Mishnaic period that the common man (*Am Ha-Aretz*) came into his own in terms of legal rights and duties. By then, of course, any remaining hopes of political autonomy had been extinguished.[13]

This suggests a closer approximation to the ideal type of the nation among the Jews of the late Second Temple period than perhaps anywhere else in the ancient world, and it must make us wary of pronouncing too readily against the possibility of the nation, and even a form of religious nationalism, before the onset of modernity. The profound consequences of the concept of a chosen people, the passionate attachment to sacred lands and centres, and the abiding imprint of sacred languages and scriptures proved to be an enduring legacy for many peoples from late antiquity to modern times, sustaining their sense of uniqueness and nurturing their hopes of regeneration.[14]

Can we then expect to find similar approximations in the medieval period? In fact several medieval kingdoms and peoples came to see themselves as latterday 'children of Israel', chosen by God to perform heroic feats through divinely inspired rulers – as communities of common customs and descent, possessed of sacred lands and centres.

In the West some of the barbarian *regna* that arose on the ruins of the Roman empire claimed the prestige of lineal Trojan and/or Biblical descent. Popular beliefs soon came to identify their communities of common beliefs and descent with the illustrious pedigrees of their princely houses. Among the Visigoths, Saxons, Franks and Normans there emerged a myth of ethnic election, which held their rulers to be the successors of David and their communities the heirs of ancient Israel. However the reality fell far short of the model, both in terms of an ideology of the national cause and the processes necessary for the formation of nations, whether cultural, educational, legal, territorial or economic. It is only in the later medieval era that such processes began to develop in a manner that laid the basis for national formation and consciousness. I shall return to these processes shortly.[15]

At the other end of Europe, in Poland and Russia, similar *regna* were established in the tenth to twelfth centuries, only to suffer dismemberment and, in the Russian case, the 'Mongol captivity'. Despite Slav predominance in both kingdoms, ethnic homogeneity was never as great as in ancient Egypt or Judea, nor was there as much economic or legal unification, let alone a public education system. Only their linguistic and religious cultures, the one Catholic, the other Orthodox, succeeded in crystallizing a sense of common and distinctive ethnicity, abetted by the memories of their early statehood under the Piasts and Rurikids (of Kievan Rus'). These memories were to play an important role in the later formation and definition of the Polish and Russian nations from the fifteenth century on.[16]

If we are dealing with ethnic states rather than nations in Europe before about AD 1300, can we speak of nationalism before the late medieval era? Hardly, if we are referring to an *ideological movement aiming to attain or maintain autonomy, unity and identity for a social group which is deemed to constitute a nation*. There are plenty of expressions of ethnocentric sentiments in the early and high middle ages, even if our records come mainly from clerical and bureaucratic strata. But the ideas and activities we associate with nationalism are generally lacking before the Anglo-French Wars and the breakup of Western Christendom through the rival claims of powerful dynastic states. Ideas and doctrines such as the cultural determination of politics, auto-emancipation, the primacy of the nation and popular sovereignty, had to wait until the seventeenth and eighteenth centuries for more than fleeting expression, as did their translation into nationalist activities and movements.[17] Only with such oft-cited expressions and movements as the Scots Declaration of Arbroath in 1320, or the Swiss Oath of the Rütli in 1291, renewed in 1307, does a more activist note appear – a desire for autonomy based on cultural difference and distinctive laws and customs of the people, which echoes the religious sense of ethnic election (with Bruce cast as 'another Maccabeus or Joshua') of the Maccabees and Zealots. But though they inspired resistance such ideals did not, in the long run, help to build a Scots or Swiss nation as part of a world of nations.[18]

TYPES OF ETHNIC COMMUNITY

It is clear that, whatever might be said of individual instances, collective cultural communities in antiquity and the early middle ages do not, on the whole, approximate to the ideal type of the nation, nor do their ideals and sentiments typically express the ideas and beliefs that we associate with nationalism in more recent periods. How far this reflects our working definitions, and how far it mirrors an important historical and sociological difference, must remain a matter of interpretation. That such a difference is present in the historical record seems clear enough; but its relative significance is a matter of judgement. The very fact that inspection of that record reveals considerable doubt suggests a greater continuity between pre-modern *ethnies* and ethnocentrism and more modern nations and nationalism than modernists of all kinds have been prepared to concede.

This means that attempts to explain how and why nations emerged must start from the ethnic ties and identities that have commonly formed their cultural basis and that, as I hope to show, have played an important part in the formation of the first and subsequent nations.

My point of departure is a distinction that needs to be drawn between two kinds of ethnic community, the 'lateral' and the 'vertical'.

Among the barbarian principalities of Western Europe, the Norman duchy of Normandy, founded by Rollo in AD 913, maintained a vivid sense of community based on customs and myths of descent, which united the Norse settlers and French-speaking inhabitants of the area, until its conquest by France in AD 1204. For nearly three centuries they maintained their élite status as a warrior community, even when they sent expeditions as far afield as Ireland and Sicily. Yet it was really only the upper strata that composed the Norman *ethnie*. This was not necessarily because they scorned the native inhabitants, with whom, after all, they intermarried, and whose language and many of whose customs they adopted. The point is that their sense of community, their myths of descent and their historical memories all clustered round the ruling house. It was the genealogies and exploits of the Norman dukes that Dudo of St

Quentin and Orderic Vitalis celebrated. The ruling house stood for the whole class of warrior–aristocrats who had founded and settled the duchy; other classes were simply subsumed under the common myths and customs attached to the glories of the ruling house.[19]

The Norman community of Normandy, as elsewhere wherever Norman arms prevailed, reveals a type of ethnic community that can conveniently be termed 'lateral'. This type of *ethnie* was usually composed of aristocrats and higher clergy, though it might from time to time include bureaucrats, high military officials and the richer merchants. It is termed lateral because it was at once socially confined to the upper strata while being geographically spread out to form often close links with the upper echelons of neighbouring lateral *ethnies*. As a result, its borders were typically 'ragged', but it lacked social depth, and its often marked sense of common ethnicity was bound up with its *esprit de corps* as a high status stratum and ruling class.

In contrast, the 'vertical' type of *ethnie* was more compact and popular. Its ethnic culture tended to be diffused to other social strata and classes. Social divisions were not underpinned by cultural differences: rather, a distinctive historical culture helped to unite different classes around a common heritage and traditions, especially when the latter were under threat from outside. As a result the ethnic bond was often more intense and exclusive, and barriers to admission were higher. In contrast to the surrounding aristocratic *ethnies* like the Canaanites and Philistines, the Israelite tribal confederacy and kingdoms evinced a more exclusive ethnocentric zeal and active mobilization of all strata for protracted wars. Other examples of more demotic, vertical *ethnies* included the Druse, Sikhs, Irish and Basques. In all of these communities there were marked differences between strata, and even class conflict, but ethnic culture was not the preserve of one stratum to the exclusion of the others – rather, it was the property of all members of the community, to a greater or lesser degree.[20]

Obviously, the distinction between lateral and vertical ethnic communities is an ideal–typical one, and it conceals differences within each category, while suggesting too sharp a division between the types. Aristocratic, lateral communities might be of the conquest variety, like the noble Hittite charioteers or the Hungarian knights.

Or they might be indigenous, like the Sassanid Persian monarchs, nobles and Zoroastrian clergy who revived Persian glory (notably under Chosroes I, AD 531–76) among the upper strata, while failing to incorporate the rural masses and the urban minorities, Manichean, Christian and Jewish, as the Mazdakite movement demonstrated.[21] Similarly, the demotic, vertical communities included urban city-state confederacies, sects and diaspora enclaves, as well as the more rurally based tribal confederations (Arabs, Mongols, Irish) and the 'frontier' warrior *ethnies* like the Catalans or Swiss. But, as these examples reveal, we are in fact dealing more with historical and social processes than fixed types. Given historical communities may undergo transformation from one polar type to another, or even mix elements from both. Arabs, who began their political career as a loose tribal confederation united into a community of the faithful by the Prophet, soon became 'aristocratized' in the main centres of their settlement and rule, either as a lateral, conquest *ethnie* or more indigenously through Islamization and intermarriage, but with only ragged boundaries between sultanates.[22] Armenian feudal nobles, no longer able to rule an independent state, became more 'de-motized', or rather, the shared Armenian religio-ethnic culture was diffused down the social scale, until in the diaspora a more popular vertical community (or series of enclave communities) emerged in place of the earlier more aristocratic and lateral *ethnie*.[23]

Now the importance of the distinction between the two kinds of ethnic community resides not only in highlighting a persistent source of ethnic conflict and ethnic survival in pre-modern eras, but also in offering different types of ethnic core around which nations could be constructed, and furnishing the two main routes by which nations could be formed. It is these trajectories that we must now explore.

LATERAL *ETHINES* AND BUREAUCRATIC INCORPORATION

Let me start with the lateral route. Aristocratic ethnic communities have the capacity for self-perpetuation to the extent that they can incorporate other strata of the population within their cultural orbit. Quite often they made little attempt to diffuse their culture down the social scale. Hittites, Philistines, even Assyrians, were content to rule over culturally alien annexed populations, and managed to ensure the survival of their own élite culture for several centuries or more. But, ultimately, their polities were destroyed and their cultures absorbed by alien immigrants. In a few other cases – the Persians and Egyptians spring to mind – lateral *ethnies* survived by 'changing their character', that is, by adopting new religions and/or customs, even new languages, while preserving their name, myths of common descent, high historical memories and their homeland.[24]

A few aristocratic *ethnies* managed to retain their identity for many centuries, even millennia, partly through strict adherence to distinctive forms of religion, but also through the inclusion within their political boundaries of other ethnic groups, and by a limited diffusion of their religious culture down the social scale. The efforts of the Amhara kings of the medieval 'Solomonic' dynasty to incorporate outlying regions and lower strata into their Monophysite ethnic culture met with only partial success, but it was enough to ensure their own survival in the face of Muslim onslaughts and subsequent European encroachments, at least in their heartlands.[25]

The efforts of some of the Western European ethnic states were more successful. In England, France, Spain, Sweden and to some extent in Poland and Russia, the dominant lateral *ethnie*, which formed the state's ethnic core, was gradually able to incorporate middle strata and outlying regions into the dominant ethnic culture. The primary agency of such incorporation was the new bureaucratic state. Through its military, administrative, fiscal and judicial apparatus it was able to regulate and disseminate the fund of values, symbols, myths, traditions and memories that formed the cultural heritage of the dominant aristocratic ethnic core. In this way the aristocratic ethnic state was able to define a new and broader cultural identity for the population, even though in practice this often entailed some degree of accommodation between the dominant and peripheral ethnic cultures within the parameters set by the power of the dominant core.[26]

Accommodation was the hallmark of developments in England after the Norman Conquest. There was during the twelfth and thirteenth centuries considerable linguistic borrowing, intermarriage and élite mobility between conquering Normans and subordinate upper-stratum Saxons, all within a common framework of growing, if interrupted, state centralization and an English Catholic ecclesiastical organization. This meant that the bureaucratic incorporation of subordinate ethnic populations entailed considerable social intercourse and cultural fusion between Anglo-Saxon, Danish and Norman elements. By the fourteenth century linguistic fusion had crystallized into Chaucerian English, and a common myth of 'British descent', propounded in the twelfth century by Geoffrey of Monmouth, had received wide social and political recognition.[27]

This is not to claim that by the fourteenth century an English nation had come into existence, only that some of the processes that help to form nations had become discernible. The ethnic elements of the nation were already well developed. Not only was there a common name and myth of ethnic descent, but also a variety of historical memories and traditions, fed by prolonged wars with neighbours in Scotland, Wales and France. There was also a growing sense of common culture revealed in the English language but based as much on an influential English Church organization. This was greatly aided by a growing attachment to an island homeland, which was especially fervent during the long wars in France although visible much earlier. At the same time unity was slow to appear in other respects. We cannot really speak of a common public educational system in the medieval period, despite the pervasive influence of the Church. In its full secular form this would indeed have to wait for several centuries, but an élite educational system was established by the later sixteenth century. Economic unification, too, was minimal, despite growing fiscal and administrative intervention by the state from Henry II onwards. Regionalism persisted for a long time, as did the subsistence economy in those areas unaffected by the wool trade. Even the boundaries of the kingdom were in dispute, with the annexations in Wales and the continual border wars with Scotland, not to mention the Plantagenet possessions across the Channel. As for common legal rights and duties, despite Magna Carta and the growth of the common law these applied only to a highly restricted upper stratum of society. It was only much later that these rights were generalized to wider sections of society, and then often through struggle with encroaching monarchs and landlords.[28]

Nevertheless, the centralizing Norman state and English Church did succeed in laying the foundations of a national culture and national identity quite early on, even if their full expression had to await the Tudor renaissance and Reformation. Interestingly, it was at this point that the older, British myth of descent began to give way to an Anglo-Saxon myth, which traced English origins back to the Germanic tribes and their ancient liberties and 'free' institutions. It was also the moment when a new national religion came to define the peculiar identity of Englishmen, in opposition to the universal claims of Rome and its imperial Spanish ally. While the nation clearly did not include the artisans and peasantry, by the sixteenth century if not earlier, the former aristocratic Anglo-Norman lateral ethnic community had bequeathed a state tradition and administration strong enough to incorporate the upper middle classes, albeit often through conflicts, as well as outlying regions in the north, west and Welsh borders. Here, then, is an example of the way in which the nation emerges through state action (abetted by the Church), which in turn was built around a relatively homo-geneous, albeit upper-stratum, ethnic core.[29]

Similar processes of ethnic bureaucratic incorporation can be dis-cerned in French history, though here developments were slower and more piecemeal. Some amalgamation of upper-stratum Frankish with Romano-Gallic ethnic culture occurred under the Christianized Merovingians, but the French *regnum* really only emerged in the late twelfth century in the central Ile de France area. Of course the Capetian kings were able to utilize the identity myths and glory of the old Frankish kingdom and the Carolingian empire for their own ends, largely because the kingdom of the eastern Franks came, after the division of Charlemagne's realm, to be known as the *regnum Teutonicorum*, with a separate identity.[30] But of equal import-ance was the crucial symbolic role played by the French ecclesiastical hierarchy, notably the archbishopric of Rheims, where the cere-monies of anointing gave the Capetian kings an edge over their many rivals, lending the dynasty an aura and prestige even greater than the presence of the law schools in Paris or the military tenacity of successive kings. This sacral quality of French royalty going back to Papal legitimation of Pepin's usurpation of the throne in AD 754 and Charlemagne's Papal coronation is reflected in the myth of royal French election that was assiduously cultivated and that is echoed in the ethno-religious language of Pope Boniface at the end of the thirteenth century, when he declared that: '. . . like the people of Israel . . . the kingdom of France (is) a peculiar people chosen by the Lord to carry out the orders of Heaven'.[31]

Though the process was much slower and more drawn out than in England, the fact remains that the Capetian kings were able to establish a relatively effective and centralized kingdom, first in northern and central France, and then from the thirteenth century onwards to incorporate western, eastern and southern areas of the *pays d'oc* whose cultural heritage differed considerably from that of the north. With the gradual expulsion of the English and the annexation of southern kingdoms and Britanny the renaissance kings were able to unify the country by degrees, both in terms of administration and by elevating the French language into the official mode of communication and government. The quest for territorial and economic unification proceeded much more slowly, and legal standardization too had to wait for the Revolution despite the centralizing efforts of the Bourbons and their ministers. Indeed, regionalism persisted well into the nineteenth century; the large body of French peasants were not fully incorporated into the French nation until 1900, after the application of mass nationalist education and conscription by the 'Jacobin' state of the Third Republic.[32]

Spain provides an even more discontinuous and incomplete example of bureaucratic incorporation by a lateral ethnic state. Here it was the kingdom of Castile and Aragon that provided the main bulwark of Catholic resistance to Muslim conquests. In the later medieval period the rulers increasingly resorted to religion as an instrument of homogeneity, converting and ultimately expelling those who, like the Jews and Moriscos, could not be assimilated. Here, too, notions of purity of blood (*limpieza di sangre*) helped to determine membership of an Iberian Catholic lateral *ethnie*, which sought to penetrate outlying areas and middle classes through administrative and cultural regulation.[33]

But from the start the unity of the Spanish Crown was beset by demands on several sides from those who claimed ancient rights and retained their pre-existing cultural heritages. Quite apart from the Portuguese secession, Catalans, Basques and Galicians managed to retain their separate cultural identities into the modern era, even where, as after the Catalan revolt of 1640, there was considerable political integration of the regions they inhabited. By the seventeenth century the Spanish state and its empire had been considerably weakened and it was unable to extend and deepen the scope of its social and geographical penetration. The result was a less unified national community and a much more plural state than either France or Britain. By the mid-nineteenth century the Catalan renaissance paved the way for the reception and formulation of ethnic nationalisms, notably in Catalonia and Euzkadi, which in turn have repeatedly breached the unity of the Spanish state. At the same time most members of the minority ethnic communities also share on overarching Spanish political loyalty, in varying degrees, in addition to their often intense ethnic sentiments. But, then, this is the norm in most Western states today.[34]

THE FIRST NATIONS?

The formation of nations in the nineteenth and twentieth centuries has been profoundly influenced by the examples of England, France and Spain, and to a lesser extent Holland and Sweden. This is usually attributed to their possession of military and economic power during the period of the formation of nations in Western Europe. As the burgeoning great powers of the sixteenth and seventeenth centuries, these states were seen as models for imitation by those less fortunate, and their national format was increasingly regarded as a key to their success. In the case of England and France and to a lesser extent Spain this was hardly accidental. The relatively early development of their nations coincided with successive revolutions in the spheres of administration, the economy and culture. Indeed many would argue that in these and other cases the state actually 'created' the nation, that its activities of taxation, conscription and administration endowed the population within its jurisdiction with a sense of their corporate identity and civic loyalty. The state was the necessary condition and matrix for the gestation of the national loyalties so evident today. The extension of citizenship rights and the build-up of an infrastructure that linked distant parts of the realm and vastly increased the density of communication networks with the state borders drew more and more areas and classes into the national political arena and created the images of national community, of 'England', 'France', 'Spain', that evoke such powerful feelings of commitment and belonging to this day.[35]

In fact the criterion of *deep* state penetration of society and its several regions would postpone the realization of nations in the West by several centuries. Their temporal priority over other instances of the formation of nations would be a matter of a few decades, since the lower classes were not politically incorporated until the very end of the nineteenth century in France and England, and women not until the 1920s. But the influence of England and France in the wider world was exerted much earlier, so we cannot credit the mass mobilizing state with the rise of the first nations, as least not in the perception of others. It is, as we already saw, too simple an answer to claim that the state 'created' the first nations *tout court*. In so far as it bore any responsibility it did so in conjunction with (and in the context of) other processes.[36]

Two such processes or 'revolutions' are germane to our discussion. The first is economic: the movement to a market economy that began in a few core states of the late medieval West and spread outwards to other areas of Europe, Latin America, America, Asia and ultimately Africa. The capitalist revolution involved vastly increased trading networks in the West and then in selected peripheries, which in turn encouraged the accumulation of capital and the rise of wealthy urban centres and merchant capital. European states, often at war with one another, benefited from the activities of their bourgeoisies, who enabled larger and better equipped armies to be raised and more efficient administrations staffed by 'experts' to be built up.[37]

The second of these 'Western' revolutions was cultural and educational. Its centre was the decline of ecclesiastical authority in the wake of reforming movements in the Church and the wars of the Reformation. This in turn allowed the development of secular studies, notably classical humanism and science, of university learning, and ultimately of popular modes of communication – novels, plays and journals. An important role in these processes was played by the intellectuals and professionals (or intelligentsia), whom the expanding administrative state recruited to serve dynastic and political goals through their technical 'expertise' and 'rational' discourse.

Because of the relatively early development of the rational State in the West, despite its limited social penetration, the intellectual and professional strata were generally subordinated to the institutions of state and their bureaucratic procedures and personnel. Though some intellectuals operated outside state institutions (notably in the French Enlightenment), most were relegated to the ancient universities or co-opted into the royal or party administrations. This enabled the state to take the lead in identifying the boundaries and character of the national community, a process that revolutionary Jacobin patriotic regimes only served to reinforce.[38]

It was through these three revolutions – administrative, economic and cultural – that outlying regions and their *ethnies* and middle and lower classes were incorporated into the dominant lateral ethnic culture through the agency of the bureaucratic state. The creation of secular, mass nations was ultimately the outcome of a vigorous programme of political socialization through the public, mass education system. But it was long preceded by the more gradual dissemination of an aristocratic ethnic culture and its transmutation into a more truly national culture: one that was civic as well as ethnic, and also socially inclusive, in line with the extension of civil and legal rights to wider segments of the kingdom. Ultimately, however, the process could be traced right back to the presence of a core *ethnie* around which strong states could be built that made it possible to incorporate other strata and outlying regions and their *ethnies*. Because of the tenacity of certain ethnic myths, memories and symbols, embodied in customs, traditions, codes and styles, England from an early date, and France somewhat later, could be welded into kingdoms on the basis of fairly homogeneous (in the subjective sense) *ethnies*, which their strong states could extend and deepen, to create over the next few centuries the relatively novel concept of the nation.[39]

'VERTICAL' ETHNIES AND VERNACULAR MOBILIZATION

In contrast to the route of bureaucratic incorporation by an aristocratic ethnic community the process of forming nations on the basis of demotic *ethnies* is influenced only indirectly by the bureaucratic state. This is mainly because vertical *ethnies* were usually subject communities, and because the bond that cemented the membership in these cases was an exclusive and all-pervasive one. It was organized religion and its sacred scriptures, liturgy, rituals and clergy that acted as the chief mechanism of ethnic persistence among vertical communities. Here religion connotes a whole way of life; it is the social aspects of salvation religions that have shaped the character of demotic communities like the Byzantine Greeks, early Orthodox Russians, Monophysite Copts and Ethiopians, Gregorian Armenians, Catholic Irish and Poles, Sikhs, Jews and Druse. In all these *ethnies* myths of chosenness, sacred texts and scripts and the prestige of the clergy have helped to ensure the survival of the traditions and heritage of the community.

But religion-shaped peoples have problems peculiarly their own. As long as it is a question of quietist accommodation to an often hostile environment the symbols and organization of an ancient faith act as a protective shell, and one that is portable. But the moment the question arises of transforming the community into a nation it is far more difficult to break out of the habitual conceptual ethnic framework and its lifestyle. Moreover, there is no internal coercive agency, no bureaucratic state, to shatter the mould. The trouble is that so many of the members of a demotic community simply assumed that they already constituted a nation, and had always done so, possessing as they did the ethnic components of a nation – a common name, ancestry myths, historical memories, attachments to a homeland, and the like. Given an independent state, such communities felt they could be nations like any other.[40]

But a brief glance at the situation of the Arab 'nation' will suffice to show that matters are not that simple, and that the transformation of demotic *ethnies* into nations is often slow and traumatic. The Arabs, clearly, have been faced by adverse geo-political factors, including their far-flung geography, their division into states by colonial powers and the historic and economic differences between various regions of the Arab world. This alone has made it difficult to envisage a common Arab nation with a single division of labour and a unified economy. The very different historical legacies of the several Arab states have also made it difficult to envisage a common system of legal rights and duties, though here the *Shari'a* (the

Moslem legal code) may provide some basis for a unified approach to a common citizenship. There is also little sign of a common educational approach, let alone anything resembling a single public, mass education system for all Arabs. As for a common civic culture, the massive influence of Islam constitutes a source of weakness as well as strength. There is no reason why a common religious culture might not in principle act as the social cement of an Arab nation, were it not for the fact that the Islamic community of the faithful, the *umma*, by virtue of its very different inspiration and geographic extent, constitutes a rival. It creates a unity and destiny that is, from a purely Arab standpoint, ambiguous, reinforcing yet subtly negating efforts to rediscover an Arab past that is not universalistic and global. The difficulties of creating a 'compact' Arab nation are not only geo-political. [41]

Little wonder that Arab intellectuals have found the problem of Arab self-definition so insoluble. It is not that a distinctive Arab ethnic culture based on history, language and religious expression is lacking, only that it overlaps with the wider circle of Islamic culture and loyalty, and that an Arab intelligentsia finds it difficult to transform this ethnic culture into a truly national and civic mass culture. For this is the primary task of the new stratum of secular-minded intelligentsia: to alter the basic relationship between religion and ethnicity, between the community of the faithful and the community of historic culture. [42] Under the impact of a rationalizing 'scientific state', often of an imperial or colonial variety, the relationship between religious traditions and their demotic ethnic 'bearers' is eroded. The old accommodations between imperial or colonial states and their constituent minority *ethnies* are undermined, and westernization and the market economy throw up new social classes led by professional and intellectual strata who are drawn to various Western ideologies and discourses, including nationalist ones, by the pressure of the scientific state on traditional religious images and theodicies. [43]

In this situation various orientations appear among the intellectuals and their followers among the professionals: a conscious, modernizing return to tradition (or 'traditionalism'); a messianic desire to assimilate to Western modernity and all its works ('assimilation' or 'modernism'); and a more defensive attempt to synthesize elements of the tradition with aspects of Western modernity and revive a pure and pristine community modelled on a former collective golden age (or 'reformist revivalism'). Though they are also found in the lateral trajectory of the formation of nations, these orientations are particularly frequent and intense among demotic vertical communities on the road to forming nations. They are typical of communities with rich ethno-histories, that is, with well-documented and detailed histories.[44]

These orientations and debates among intellectuals are significant to the extent that they mirror and express fundamentally different directions in the transformation of demotic *ethnies* into political nations. It is important for the shape, pace, scope and intensity of that transformation whether it is conducted under the auspices of traditionalist, modernist or revivalist élites, or a combination or succession of them. In each case the intelligentsia attempts to provide new communal self-definitions and goals, involving the mobilization of formerly passive communities. These redefinitions should not be seen simply as inventions or constructs of intellectuals. Rather they are attempts to marry an understanding of Western processes of forming nations with a programme of rediscovering an ethnic past or pasts that will elevate the people and their vernacular culture to centre stage, often in place of (or reinterpreting) the old religious traditions. Instead of being merely a chosen vessel of religious salvation and passive recipient of divine ordinance, the 'people' now become the source of salvation and the saints and sages of old become manifestations of the people's national genius.[45]

Here then lies the main task of an ethnic intelligentsia: to mobilize a formerly passive community into forming a nation around the new vernacular historical culture that it has rediscovered. Beneath the different responses to westernization lies the imperative of a moral and political revolution, one which requires the people to be purified from the accretions of centuries, so that they can be emancipated into a political community of equal citizens. This revolution involves several interrelated processes. They include:

1. a movement from passive subordination of the community to its active political assertion
2. a movement to place the community in its homeland, a secure and recognized compact territory

3. a movement to endow the territorial community with economic unity
4. a movement to place the people at the centre of concern
and to celebrate the masses by re-educating them in national
values, memories and myths
5. a movement to turn ethnic members into legal 'citizens' by
conferring civil, social and political rights on them.

These were arduous undertakings, often bitterly opposed not merely
by the imperial or colonial power and its indigenous upper-class
allies, but also by the guardians of tradition, whose values and
leadership were jeopardized by the new definitions of community
proposed by the intellectuals. The success of these undertakings
hinged on a return by the intelligentsia to a living past, a past that
was no mere quarry for antiquarian research but that could be
derived from the sentiments and traditions of the people. This
meant a twofold strategy of furnishing 'maps' of the community, its
history, its destiny and its place among the nations, and of providing
'moralities' for the regenerated community, ones that could inspire
present generations to emulate the public virtues deemed to express
the national character. In these ways the new nation could be
endowed with a cognitive basis and moral purpose that would
ensure the continued renaissance of its distinctive cultural heritage
and vision.[46]

There were two main ways in which such maps and moralities
could be constructed out of a living ethnic past. The educator–
intellectuals found both in the life and symbolism of the people and
their popular historical traditions. The first way was through a
return to 'nature' and its 'poetic spaces'. This nature and these spaces
are quite specific; they constitute the historic home of the people,
the sacred repository of their memories. They have their own historical poetry, for those whose spirits are attuned to them. The
homeland is not just the setting of the national drama, but a major
protagonist, and its natural features take on historical significance
for the people. So lakes, mountains, rivers and valleys can all be
turned into symbols of popular virtues and 'authentic' national
experience; so the Jungfrau became a symbol of the Swiss virtues of
purity and natural beauty, and the *Vierwaldstättersee* the theatre of
an historical drama, the founding of the *Eidgenossenschaft* in 1291. In

this poetic history fact and legend are fused to produce inspiring myths of resistance to tyranny and of purity of soul.[47]

Conversely, the historical events and monuments of the homeland can be 'naturalized'. Castles, temples, tells and dolmens are integrated into the landscape and treated as part of its special nature. In the eighteenth and nineteenth centuries Stonehenge became a 'natural' symbol of British antiquity, as part of the romantic revival of history. Indeed, so much part of the 'British' (Briton) landscape did it become, that it became difficult to imagine that it was not natural and inherent in the British ethnic character, as much part of its original nature as the Wessex plains and hills around. A purely historical monument, of a particular time and context, had become 'naturalized'.[48]

The other way of constructing maps and moralities for present generations was through the use of history and, especially, the cult of golden ages. The purposes of nationalist educator–intellectuals are social and political, not academic; they aim to purify and activate the people. To do so, moral exemplars from the ethnic past are needed, as are vivid recreations of the glorious past of the community. Hence the return to that past through a series of myths: myths of origins and descent, of liberation and migration, of the golden age and its heroes and sages, perhaps of the chosen people now to be reborn after its long sleep of decay and/or exile. Together, these myth-motifs can be formed into a composite nationalist mythology and salvation drama.[49]

An example of the nationalist use of history and the nationalist's desire to return to a golden age is provided by the Gaelic revival of the 1890s. The vision here was as much pagan as Catholic, different cultural nationalists emphasizing different aspects of Ireland's golden age of St Patrick. For some, like O'Grady and Lady Gregory, it was the legends of Cuchulain and Fin Mac Coil in the golden age of the High Kings of Tara that they found in the rediscovered Ulster Cycle that they sought to propagate. Here was an aristocratic warrior society, but one that was rural and free and filled with spiritual wisdom, with its *fianna* bands and *filid* guilds of bards. For others, it was the era after the conversion by St Patrick, famed for its monasteries, its Celtic arts and its Christian learning and literature, when Ireland preserved, almost alone, the torch of intellect and civilization in a barbarian West. The dual cult of Celtic heroes and Christian scholar-missionaries suggested to a returning Irish intelligentsia what a free Ireland might have become, had its development not been thwarted by the Norman invaders, and then brutally cut off by the English Protestant conquests. The vision of an ethnic golden age told modern Irish men and women what was 'authentically theirs', and how to be 'themselves' once again in a free Ireland.[50]

In Finland, too, the past and its heroes was put to striking nationalist use. At the beginning of the nineteenth century the Finns formed a subordinate vertical ethnic community differentiated from the Swedish cultural élite and later from their Russian political masters that was a ready-made ethnic base for the national reconstructions of educator–intellectuals like Lonnröt, Runeberg and Snellman from the 1830s on. The doctor, Elias Lonnröt, in particular, captured the imagination of the Finnish intelligentsia and later of the people, by bringing back from the province of Karelia the ballads and poems that he formed into the *Kalevala* in 1835 (larger edition 1849). This epic of 'The Land of Heroes' bore only a partial resemblance to earlier 'Finnish' society of the first millennium AD (judging from the material remains), but it was enough to create for modern Finns a cult of the golden age of the heroes Väinämöinen and Lemminkainen, which was to inspire popular art and the genius of Sibelius and Gallén-Kallela.[51] Here was the ideal self-definition and exemplar for a regenerated Finland in its heroic struggle against Swedish cultural and Russian political domination at the end of the nineteenth century. The recovery of an ancient but apparently 'lost' period of Finnish history and culture restored to Finns that sense of community and dignity necessary for a small and relatively poor and despised society struggling to reassert its place through a 'high' culture.[52]

There are many other examples of the educator–intellectuals' uses of history and golden ages to promote a national revival. But, even when a rich vein of 'ethno-history' has been discovered and mined, the 'cultural wars' have only begun. These are normally of two kinds. The first is cultural resistance to an imperial cosmopolitanism or its colonial variant; or even to the cultural influence of more powerful neighbours, as the Slovaks did against a dominant Czech culture, or the Ukrainians against Russian culture absorption. The second is a cultural war of the 'sons against the fathers', when the secular intelligentsia turns against the older guardians of tradition, in order to mobilize the demotic *ethnie* and transform it into a political nation. This can be done by selective assimilation of foreign (usually 'Western') elements, as the Tatar education reforms of Ismail Bey Gasprinski or the borrowings of the Japanese Meiji reformers demonstrate. But it is also necessary to strengthen the indigenous ethnic base by a campaign of communication and socialization of new generations into the rediscovered ethno-history and revived language of the community. In these processes new self-definitions of community are forged, often in the teeth of resistance by guardians of the older ethno-religious self-definitions, so as to lay the basis for entry into the world of nations.[53]

MODERNITY AND ANTIQUITY IN THE NATION

I have traced two routes by which different kinds of ethnic community were transformed into nations. The first was state-sponsored. It set out from a lateral *ethnie*, the core of an ethnic state. As that state became more centralized and bureaucratic it attempted to incorporate middle classes and outlying regions through military, fiscal, judicial and administrative processes. If successful, it proved able to weld often disparate populations into a single political community based on the cultural heritage of the dominant ethnic core. If the intelligentsia played a part in this process it was a subordinate one. The chief actors were kings, ministers and bureaucrats, with the middle classes appearing later, and the aristocrats and clergy often ambivalent. For though it was, in a sense, *their* culture and heritage that was being diffused by the state, the result was a marginalization of aristocrats and clergy; *their* heritage and culture had become, in principle, everyone's. In the new political nation, they were often by-passed.[54]

The second route was more popular. It started from smaller, demotic communities whose ethno-religious self-conceptions had to be exchanged for more activist, political ones. The key to this transformation was the process of vernacular mobilization. Small circles of educator–intellectuals, despite their differential responses to westernization and modernity, were intent on purifying and mobilizing 'the people' through an appeal to the community's alleged ethnic past. To do this, they had to provide cognitive maps and historical moralities for present generations, drawn from the poetic spaces and golden ages of the communal past. In this way they hoped to transform a backward traditional ethnic community into a dynamic, but vernacular, political nation.

As the nineteenth century proceeded nationalists in both kinds of community came to see the nation as both modern and natural, as suited to the dawning industrial age but also going back to a primordial era. This dual orientation also underlies recent scholarly debates about the modernity of the nation and nationalism, as we saw. From the above account it is clear that nations are indeed modern phenomena in so far as:

1. they require a unified legal code of common rights and duties, with citizenship rights where the nation is independent

2. they are based on a unified economy with a single division of labour, and mobility of goods and persons throughout the national territory

3. they need a fairly compact territory, preferably with 'natural' defensible frontiers, in a world of similar compact nations

4. they require a single 'political culture' and public, mass education and media system, to socialise future generations to be 'citizens' of the new nation.

As we saw, it is rare to find most of these elements in any force in pre-modern ethnic states, however powerful they appear. Both in terms of technology and political will, as well as self-conception, the double drive to uniformity and uniqueness was lacking. There was neither understanding of these elements of the modern nation nor the incentive to create these prerequisites; or if there was such motivation it was overlaid by other more local, or more all-encompassing needs and visions, so that the village and the Church made the nation seem politically unnecessary.[55]

But there is another side to this picture. If the nation seems in many ways modern, it is also deep-rooted. The nationalists were guilty of telescoping history, but they were not altogether mistaken. They grasped that if a nation, however modern, is to survive in this modern world, it must do so on two levels: the socio-political and the cultural–psychological. What, after all, is the *raison d'être* of any *nation* (as opposed to state), if it is not also the cultivation of its unique (or allegedly unique) culture values? Ethnic distinctiveness remains a *sine qua non* of the nation, and that means shared ancestry myths, common historical memories, unique cultural markers, and a sense of difference, if not election – all the elements that marked off ethnic communities in pre-modern eras. In the modern nation they must be preserved, indeed cultivated, if the nation is not to become invisible.

There is another facet of the antiquity of modern nations: their location. They are where they are allegedly because of their long associations with particular stretches of territory. 'Nations have deep roots.' Even if those roots are not quite so deep, the claim must be made not simply for international recognition, but for the much more fundamental purpose of collective inner security and regeneration.[56] The severely practical aspects of nationality here join hands with the purely symbolic. Nationalism is about 'land', both in terms of possession and (literal) rebuilding, and of belonging where forefathers lived and where history demarcates a 'homeland'. Subjectively, therefore, locating the nation hinges on a reading of ethnic history, which presupposes links between the generations of a community of history and destiny in particular places of the earth. This does not mean that the nation is ancient; only that, subjectively, there are pre-modern elements within many nations.

CHAPTER 4

Nationalism and Cultural Identity

In the 'modernist' image of the nation it is nationalism that creates national identity. Gellner puts the matter succinctly when he declares: 'Nationalism is not the awakening of nations to self-consciousness; it invents nations where they do not exist – but it does need some pre-existing differentiating marks to work on, even if, as indicated, these are purely negative . . .'[1] In the same vein Kedourie argues that nationalism itself is an 'invented doctrine': 'Nationalism is a doctrine invented in Europe at the beginning of the nineteenth century.'[2] How shall we understand such 'invention'? In what sense does nationalism invent or create nations 'where they do not exist'?

We have already seen, in chapter 2, that we need to probe the configuration of ethnic *ties* and *sentiments* if we want to ascertain which units might emerge as nations (if and when they did so). Generally speaking, the stronger and more persistent the pre-existing ethnic identity, the more likely was any nation that might emerge to be based on that identity. In discussing the processes and routes of the formation of nations in chapter 3 it became equally clear that pre-modern ethnic identities formed the base-line in attempting to explain why and how nations emerged, at least in Europe.

I shall argue that the same is true of nationalism. Nationalism does, indeed, help to create nations, many of them apparently or in aspiration 'new'. As an ideology and a language nationalism is relatively modern, emerging into the political arena over a period in the late eighteenth century. But nations and nationalism are no more 'invented' than other kinds of culture, social organization or ideology. If nationalism is part of the 'spirit of the age', it is equally dependent upon earlier motifs, visions and ideals. For what we call nationalism operates on many levels and may be regarded as a form of culture as much as a species of political ideology and social movement. And, while a new era opens with the arrival of nationalism, it is impossible to grasp its impact on the formation of national identity without exploring its social and cultural matrix, which already owed so much to the presence of pre-modern *ethnies* and the gradual emergence of national states in the West. Hence the need to explore nationalism first as a form of culture and identity before going on to look at its political impact in the next chapter. Hence the need also to ask the question 'When and where did nations emerge?' in the context both of the impact of nationalism and its proponents *and* of the processes by which nations were formed on the basis of pre-existing ethnic ties, processes discussed in the last two chapters.

NATIONALISM: IDEOLOGY, LANGUAGE, SENTIMENT

The term nationa*lism* has been used in several ways. It can signify:

1. the whole process of forming and maintaining nations or nation-states
2. a consciousness of belonging to the nation, together with sentiments and aspirations for its security and prosperity
3. a language and symbolism of the 'nation' and its role
4. an ideology, including a cultural doctrine of nations and the national will and prescriptions for the realization of national aspirations and the national will
5. a social and political movement to achieve the goals of the nation and realize its national will.

We may, I think, dismiss the first usage from our consideration. It is much broader than the others, and it has already been discussed.

The second usage, that of national consciousness or sentiment, must be distinguished from the others. It is quite possible to find a population exhibiting a high degree of national consciousness without having much in the way of an ideology or doctrine of the nation, let alone a nationalist movement. England affords a good example of this, though even here nationalist ideologies have made their appearance from time to time, as in the period of Cromwell and Milton or at the time of Burke and Blake.

Conversely, we find nationalist movements and ideologies among populations with little or no national consciousness or sentiment. They may emerge among a small segment of the population but find no echo in the population at large. This was the case in much of West Africa, including the Gold Coast and Nigeria. Quite apart from ethnic and regional divisions, the novelty of these colonies meant that most of the inhabitants of these newly formed British colonies were unaware of a Gold Coast, later Ghanaian, or Nigerian nationality to which they were supposed to belong. Similarly, among Arabs and Pakistanis the vast majority saw themselves as Muslims rather than Arabs or Pakistanis, despite the vociferous campaigns of the small group of nationalists among them.[3]

The same could also be said about nationalism as a language and symbolism. As we shall see, this too begins as an élite phenomenon in which intellectuals play a preponderant role. It is not, however, the same as either nationalist ideology or national sentiment. A nationalist language and symbolism is broader than an ideology or ideological movement; it often connects that ideology with the 'mass sentiments' of wider segments of the designated population, notably through slogans, ideas, symbols and ceremonies. At the same time nationalist language and symbolism span both the cognitive and expressive dimensions, linking up with broader aspirations and feelings among both élites and wider strata. Notions of autonomy and authenticity and symbols of self-reliance and of natural community (for example, re-enactments of resistance events, or symbols of landscape and historical monuments or of local products, crafts or sports) exemplify the fusion of cognitive and expressive aspects and the links with wider sentiments and aspirations. The feeling for authenticity to be found among the exponents of the Gaelic Revival in late nineteenth-century Ireland, with its stress on native sports, nature, local crafts and ancient pagan heroes, illustrates the diffusion of the new language and symbolism of Irish nationalism.[4]

Finally, the last usage, that of nationalist movement, is closely linked with nationalist ideology. It is, in fact, inconceivable without it. Hence, I shall run the two together and, while recognizing that one can find and discuss nationalist ideology in the absence of a nationalist movement, I shall define national*ism* as *an ideological movement for attaining and maintaining autonomy, unity and identity on behalf of a population deemed by some of its members to constitute an actual or potential 'nation'.*[5] In fact, this definition embodies elements from both the ideology and the language-cum-symbolism of the nation, with references to wider sentiments and aspirations.

Let me start with the *ideology* of nationalism. We may define the central propositions of the ideology, or 'core doctrine', as follows.

1. The world is divided into nations, each with its own individuality, history and destiny.
2. The nation is the source of all political and social power, and loyalty to the nation overrides all other allegiances.
3. Human beings must identify with a nation if they want to be free and realize themselves.
4. Nations must be free and secure if peace and justice are to prevail in the world.[6]

I have deliberately avoided all mention of the state in this formulation of nationalism's 'core doctrine'. In a sense, such reference is implicit in propositions 2 and 4. But nationalism is an ideology of the nation, not the state. It places the nation at the centre of its concerns, and its description of the world and its prescriptions for collective action are concerned only with the nation and its members. The idea that nations can be free only if they possess their own sovereign state is neither necessary nor universal. Early nationalists, as well as cultural nationalists thereafter (such as Rousseau, Herder, Achad Ha'am, Aurobindo), were not particularly interested in the acquisition of a state, either in general or for the nation with whose aspirations they identified. Nor has every nationalist movement made the acquisition of a state for its nation a priority. Many Catalan, Scots and Flemish nationalists have been more concerned with home rule and cultural parity in a multinational state than with outright independence (though there are some nationalists who want outright independence in all these cases). The notion that every nation must have its own state is a common, but not a necessary, deduction from the core doctrine of nationalism; and it tells us that nationalism is primarily a cultural doctrine or, more accurately, a political ideology with a cultural doctrine at its centre. [7]

This cultural doctrine depends, in turn, on the introduction of new concepts, languages and symbols. Nationalism, I have argued, is an ideological movement for attaining and maintaining the *autonomy*, *unity* and *identity* of a nation. Each of these concepts derives from the new philosophical, historical and anthropological languages or discourses that emerged in the seventeenth and eighteenth centuries in Europe. There is, for example, a straightforward understanding of the concept of 'identity' as 'sameness'. The members of a particular group are alike in just those respects in which they differ from non-members outside the group. Members dress and eat in similar ways and speak the same language; in all these respects they differ from non-members, who dress, eat and speak in different ways. This pattern of similarity–cum–dissimilarity is one meaning of national 'identity'. [8]

But there is also a philosophical and anthropological concept that was developed in the eighteenth century. It stems from the idea of 'national genius' found in the writings of Lord Shaftesbury, among others; he speaks, for example, of the 'rising Genius of our Nation' (Britain) and prophesies that it will become the 'principal seat of the Arts'.[9] The idea of national identity or, more often, national character is common to eighteenth-century writers, notably Montesquieu and Rousseau. The latter, indeed, declared: 'The first rule which we have to follow is that of national character: every people has, or must have, a character; if it lacks one, we must start by endowing it with one.'[10]

Herder made this principle into a cornerstone of his cultural populism. For Herder every nation has its peculiar 'genius', its own ways of thinking, acting and communicating, and we must work to rediscover that unique genius and that peculiar identity, wherever it is submerged or lost: 'Let us follow our own path . . . let all men speak well or ill of our nation, our literature, our language: they are ours, they are ourselves, and let that be enough.'[11] Hence the importance of rediscovering the 'collective self' through philology, history and archaeology, of tracing one's roots in an 'ethnic past', in order to ascertain the authentic identity beneath the alien accretions of the centuries.

The concept of unity also has a plain and a more esoteric nationalist meaning. At the simplest level it refers to unification of the national territory or homeland, if it is divided, and the gathering together within the homeland of all nationals. Even here nationalists introduced a more philosophical idea: nationals outside the homeland were deemed to be 'lost', and the lands they inhabited, especially those contiguous to the homeland, were 'unredeemed' (*irredenta*) and had to be recovered and 'redeemed'. This sometimes produced nationalist movements of irredentism, such as the later Italian, Greek and pan-German movements of the late nineteenth and early twentieth centuries. Such movements are still in evidence: witness the Argentinian claim to the Malvinas or Falklands, the Somali claim to the Ogaden and the IRA claims to Ulster.[12]

But there is a further meaning to the nationalist ideal of unity. In nationalist language 'unity' signifies social cohesion, the brotherhood of all nationals in the nation, what the French *patriots* called *fraternité* during the Revolution. The family metaphor underlying the genealogical concept of the nation reappears here in secular, political guise: as the union of fraternal citizens, symbolized in David's celebrated *Oath of the Horatii*, the three brothers who swore on their father's sword to conquer or die (*vaincre ou mourir*) for their *patria* or fatherland.[13]

The nationalist ideal of unity has had profound consequences. For one thing, it has encouraged the idea of the indivisibility of the nation (*la république une et indivisible*) and justified the eradication, often by force, of all intermediate bodies and local differences in the interests of cultural and political homogeneity. This has spawned mass-mobilizing policies of social and political integration in which the state becomes the agent of the 'nation-to-be' and the creator of a 'political community' and 'political culture' that must replace the various ethnic cultures of a heterogeneous population. Here the nationalist concept of unity turns back on its ethnic roots and seeks a uniformity that will transcend cultural differences with the projected nation.[14]

Finally, with the concept of autonomy we have entered the Kantian world of 'self-determination'. Not that there was no concept of political freedom before the modern European philosophical tradition: as far back as Josephus, if not Thucydides, we find the appeal to freedom to preserve ancestral ways from foreign interference.[15] But with Kant autonomy becomes an ethical imperative for the individual, a principle of his being, not just a political ideal to be invoked at times of danger. Applied by Fichte, Schlegel and the other German Romantics to groups rather than individuals, the ideal of autonomy gave rise to a philosophy of national self-determination and collective struggle to realize the authentic national will – in a state of one's own. Only then would the community be able to follow its own 'inner rhythms', heed its own inward voice and return to its pure and uncontaminated pristine state. That is why nationalists must devote so much time and effort to instilling a genuinely national will, so that the members of the nation will be truly free of alien ideas and ways that are liable to destroy and stunt their development and that of the community as a whole. Nationalism signifies the awakening of the nation and its members to its true collective 'self', so that it, and they, obey only the 'inner voice' of the purified community. Authentic experience and authentic community are therefore preconditions of full autonomy, just as only autonomy can allow the nation and its members to realize themselves in an authentic manner. Autonomy is the goal of every nationalist.[16]

These concepts – autonomy, identity, national genius, authenticity, unity and fraternity – form an interrelated language or discourse that has its expressive ceremonials and symbols. These symbols and ceremonies are so much part of the world we live in that we take them, for the most part, for granted. They include the obvious attributes of nations – flags, anthems, parades, coinage, capital cities, oaths, folk costumes, museums of folklore, war memorials, ceremonies of remembrance for the national dead, passports, frontiers – as well as more hidden aspects, such as national recreations, the countryside, popular heroes and heroines, fairy tales, forms of etiquette, styles of architecture, arts and crafts, modes of town planning, legal procedures, educational practices and military codes – all those distinctive customs, mores, styles and ways of acting and feeling that are shared by the members of a community of historical culture.[17]

In many ways national symbols, customs and ceremonies are the most potent and durable aspects of nationalism. They embody its basic concepts, making them visible and distinct for every member, communicating the tenets of an abstract ideology in palpable, concrete terms that evoke instant emotional responses from all strata of the community. Symbols and ceremonies have always possessed the emotive collective qualities described by Durkheim, and nowhere is this more apparent than in the case of nationalist symbols and ceremonies. Indeed, much of what Durkheim attributes to the totemic rites and symbols of the Arunta and other Australian tribes applies with far greater force to nationalist rites and ceremonies, for nationalism dispenses with any mediating referent, be it totem or deity; its deity is the nation itself. The emotions it unleashes are those of the community directed to itself, self-consciously extolling itself. The virtues it celebrates are exclusively and solely those of the 'national self', and the crimes it condemns are those that threaten to disrupt that self. By means of the ceremonies, customs and symbols every member of a community participates in the life, emotions and virtues of that community and, through them, re-dedicates him- or herself to its destiny. By articulating and making tangible the ideology of nationalism and the concepts of the nation ceremonial and symbolism help to assure the continuity of an abstract community of history and destiny.[18]

What are the underlying sentiments and aspirations that nationalist ideology and nationalist language and symbols evoke? They relate to three main referents: territory, history and community. In the last chapter we saw how, particularly in demotic *ethnies* engaged in 'vernacular mobilization', intelligentsias sought to construct cognitive maps of a world of nations and to inculcate expressive moralities for collective emulation. To these ends they employed two main strategies: the use of landscape or poetic spaces and the use of history or golden ages. In fact, these strategies were rooted in popular attitudes to space and time and to popular attachments to home and fathers. It was these ancient beliefs and commitments to ancestral homelands and to the generations of one's forefathers that nationalists made use of in elaborating the new ideology, language and symbolism of a complex abstraction, national identity. The new concept of the nation was made to serve as a time–space framework to order chaos and render the universe meaningful by harnessing pre-modern mass aspirations and sentiments for local and familial attachments; herein lay a vital part of the wide appeal of an otherwise abstruse ideology and language.[19]

But perhaps the most fundamental sentiments evoked by nationalism were, paradoxically, those of family – paradoxically because real families can constitute an obstacle to the ideal of a homogeneous nation wherever nationalism embraces the ideal in that extreme form. That too was part of David's message in the *Oath of the Horatii*, mentioned earlier; the women on the right of the picture grieve for the loss of their loved ones and the imminent destruction of their family ties. At the same time the metaphor of family is indispensable to nationalism. The nation is depicted as one great family, the members as brothers and sisters of the motherland or fatherland, speaking their mother tongue. In this way the family of the nation overrides and replaces the individual's family but evokes similarly strong loyalties and vivid attachments. Even where local allegiances are tolerated and real families given their due the language and symbolism of the nation asserts its priority and, through the state and citizenship, exerts its legal and bureaucratic pressures on the family, using similar kinship metaphors to justify itself.[20]

TYPES OF NATIONALISM

So far I have considered nationalism as an undifferentiated whole in terms of its ideology and core doctrine, its language and symbolism and its sentiments and aspirations. When we move on to consider nationalist *movements*, however, we come up against clear differences in their goals, differences that reach back into the underlying conceptual divergence between the civic–territorial model and the ethnic–genealogical model of the nation, described in chapter 1.

This difference is so profound, and the kinds of nationalism to which these alternative models give rise are so varied, that some have despaired of finding any unitary concept of nationalism. Chameleon-like, nationalism takes its colour from its context. Capable of endless manipulation, this eminently malleable nexus of beliefs, sentiments and symbols can be understood only in each specific instance; nationalism-in-general is merely a lazy historian's escape from the arduous task of explaining the influence of this or that particular nationalist idea, argument or sentiment in its highly specific context. Though few would perhaps go as far as this claim implies, several historians would agree with the basic 'contextualist' argument and regard the differences between specific nationalisms as in many ways more important than any surface similarities. [21]

There are several difficulties with this argument. Nobody would deny the importance of social and cultural context in the rise, formulation and course of a particular instance of nationalism. But to describe it as an instance of nationalism presupposes some idea of a general family to which such instances belong or which they exemplify, albeit mixed with other elements. It is difficult to avoid recourse to a general concept of the nation and nationalism – even when we agree on the importance and uniqueness of each instance, a claim that nationalists, ironically, would gladly support.

Second, to deny the legitimacy of a concept of nationalism-in-general would prevent us from posing general sociological questions about the modernity of nations and the ubiquity of nationalism's appeal today and from making historical comparisons between different nationalist ideologies, symbols and movements. In fact, the same historians who insist on the specific context of each case of nationalism pose such general questions and make these historical comparisons; and this surely is desirable if we are to gain some understanding of so elusive and complex a phenomenon as nationalism.

Third, the 'contextualist' argument bypasses a fundamental task of the study of complex phenomena like nationalism: the provision of typologies of nationalist ideologies and/or movements. Such typologies recognize the importance of broadly differing contexts without sacrificing the possibility of more general comparisons. Arguing that nationalism exhibits a diversity within unity, they go on to pinpoint the main kinds of ideology and movement in terms of historical period, geographical area, level of economic development, philosophical assumptions, class context, cultural milieu or political aspirations. This is the strategy that I propose to follow here.

This is not the place to consider the various typologies that scholars have proposed. I shall mention one or two, and state briefly my own typology as a prelude to an analysis of the cultural matrix and impact of nationalism in Europe. Other typologies are enumerated in other earlier works.[22]

Undoubtedly, the most influential typology is that of Hans Kohn. He distinguished a 'Western', rational and associational version of nationalism from an 'Eastern', organic and mystical version. In Britain, France and America, he argued, a rational concept of the nation emerged, one that viewed it as an association of human beings living in a common territory under the same government and laws. This ideology was largely a product of the middle classes, who came to power in these states at the end of the eighteenth century. In contrast, Eastern Europe (east of the Rhine) had not developed a significant middle class. Instead a few intellectuals led the resistance to Napoleon and the ensuing nationalisms. Because they were numerically insignificant and excluded from power their versions of nationalism were inevitably shrill and authoritarian. For the same reason they saw the nation as a seamless, organic unity with a mystical 'soul' and 'mission' that only the vernacular intellectuals could fathom. Hence their often leading role in nationalist movements in Central and Eastern Europe as well as in Asia.[23]

This typology can be criticized on a number of grounds. Its geopolitical dimension overlooks the influence of both kinds of ideological nationalism in different European communities – the organic version in Ireland and later nineteenth-century France, the rational ideal in some versions of Czech, Hungarian and Zionist nationalism as well as in early West African nationalisms.[24]

It is also not clear that Western nationalisms are the product of the bourgeoisie. As we have seen, they owe much to earlier monarchical and aristocratic culture and activities. Similarly, the commitment of the bourgeoisie to rational versions of nationalism is a dubious assumption: witness the often mystical pan-German sentiments of the German industrial bourgeoisie or the support for an organic and 'primitivist' Russian nationalism by wealthy Russian merchants at the end of the nineteenth century.[25]

There is also the distinction drawn by Plamenatz between the culturally far more developed Italian and German nationalisms and the relatively underdeveloped Balkan and Eastern European nationalisms, with their lack of cultural and educational resources, which hampered their chances and produced weaker, but shriller, movements.[26]

Despite these criticisms, Kohn's philosophical distinction between a more rational and a more organic version of nationalist ideology remains valid and useful. It is implicit in the distinction drawn in chapter 1 between 'Western' civic–territorial and 'Eastern' ethnic–genealogical models of the nation. Here too we have to treat geopolitical labels cautiously. Both models can be found in the 'East', in the 'West', in Asia, Africa and in Latin America, as well as within many nationalist movements.

Nevertheless, the conceptual distinction has important consequences. Civic and territorial models of the nation tend to produce certain kinds of nationalist movement: 'anti-colonial' movements before independence has been attained and 'integration' movements after independence. Ethnic and genealogical models of the nation, on the other hand, tend to give rise to secessionist or diaspora movements before independence and irredentist or 'pan' movements thereafter. This overlooks a number of sub-varieties, as well as mixed cases; but it captures, I think the basic logic of many nationalisms.

On this basis we can construct a provisional typology of nationalisms around the distinction between ethnic and territorial nationalism, taking into account the overall situation in which particular communities and movements find themselves both before and after independence. These situations, together with the basic orientation, largely determine the political goals of each nationalism. Thus we find the following.

1. Territorial nationalisms
   (a) *Pre-independence* movements whose concept of the nation is mainly civic and territorial will seek first to eject foreign rulers and substitute a new state-nation for the old colonial territory; these are *anti-colonial* nationalisms.
   (b) *Post-independence* movements whose concept of the nation remains basically civic and territorial will seek to bring together and integrate into a new political community often disparate ethnic populations and to create a new 'territorial nation' out of the old colonial state; these are *integration* nationalisms.
2. Ethnic nationalisms
   (a) *Pre-independence* movements whose concept of the nation is basically ethnic and genealogical will seek to secede from a larger political unit (or secede and gather together in a designated ethnic homeland) and set up a new political 'ethno-nation' in its place; these are *secession* and *diaspora* nationalisms.
   (b) *Post-independence* movements whose concept of the nation is basically ethnic and genealogical will seek to expand by including ethnic 'kinsmen' outside the present boundaries

of the 'ethno-nation' and the lands they inhabit or by forming a much larger 'ethno-national' state through the union of culturally and ethnically similar ethno-national states; these are *irredentist* and *'pan'* nationalisms.[27]

This does not pretend to be an exhaustive typology. It omits several well-known kinds of nationalism, notably protectionist economic and 'integral' fascist nationalisms and racial nationalisms. But it can be argued that the latter constitute sub-varieties of post-independence integration or irredentist nationalisms, with which they are, in fact, historically associated, as in the case of Maurras' 'integral' nationalism in the period of French irredentist nationalism over Alsace-Lorraine, or Latin American protectionism at a time of populist integration nationalisms in Argentina, Brazil and Chile.[28]

Such a basic typology helps us to compare nationalisms within each category, and to place nationalisms in broad comparable contexts, while allowing the possibility of more general explanations. This is not to gainsay the unique features of particular instances of nationalism. On the contrary: the very fact that it has proved necessary to sketch a 'core doctrine' and the basic concepts and symbols of nationalism suggests the importance of those other features of a particular nationalism that are unique to each case. These specific doctrines and concepts (a better term than 'secondary' or 'additional') play a vital role in each instance and not just a supporting role. For it is the *specific* doctrines and ideas that provide the symbolism and ceremonial that arouse the deepest popular emotions and aspirations – notably when they are interwoven with much older symbols and ceremonies. The idea of Poland as the 'suffering Christ', a messianic figure of redemption that pervades the poetry of Poland's great poet, Mickiewicz, is allied to the redemptive power of the Madonna of Jasna Gora, still the object of a mass cult of devotion. The ethno-religious Catholic image of suffering and redemption is central to an understanding of the ideology, language and symbolism of Polish nationalism.[29] Similarly, the invocation of Hindu heroes and deities, like Shivaji and the goddess Kali, by Tilak and his followers, though remote from the secular ideology of nationalism-in-general, played a vital role in creating a Hindu Indian nationalism that singled out the unique, the incommensurable, elements of a genuinely Indian nation. For without such bonds of differentiation there can be no nation.[30]

The importance of specific doctrines and symbols of nationalism points towards the deeper meaning of nationalism – the ideology, the language, the consciousness. In a world of nations each nation is unique, each is 'chosen'. Nationalism is the secular, modern equivalent of the pre-modern, sacred myth of ethnic election. A doctrine of polycentric uniqueness, it preaches the universality of 'irreplaceable culture values'. Where once each ethnic community was a world unto itself, the centre of the universe, the light amid darkness, now the heritage and culture values from the storehouse of that same community, selected, reinterpreted and reconstituted, form one unique, incommensurable national identity among many other, equally unique, cultural identities. This means that every culture, even the least developed and elaborated, possesses some 'value' that is irreplaceable and may contribute to the total fund of human cultural values. Nationalism, as an ideology and symbolism, legitimates every cultural configuration, summoning intellectuals everywhere to transform 'low' into 'high' cultures, oral into written, literary traditions, in order to preserve for posterity its fund of irreplaceable culture values. Chosen peoples were formerly selected by their deities; today they are chosen by an ideology and a symbolism that elevate the unique and the individual and transform them into a global reality. In former days peoples were chosen for their alleged virtues; today they are called to be nations because of their cultural heritages.

THE CULTURAL MATRIX OF NATIONALISM

A world of cultural diversity, of many 'chosen cultures', is also a world of ethnic historicism. At first sight such a world appears remote from the world of territorial absolutism that saw the birth of nationalist ideologies, symbolism and movements. Nevertheless, it was in late seventeenth- and early eighteenth-century Western Europe that nationalist ideals, motifs and symbols first appeared. For, while sixteenth- and early seventeenth-century Europe witnessed powerful movements of messianic religious nationalism – notably in Holland and England but also in Bohemia and Poland – the concepts, ideals, symbols and myths of the nation as an ultimate end in itself had to wait till later and the 'core doctrine' and ideological movements later still. [31]

We are, of course, tracing complex processes that are never easy to periodize, let alone date. There is no fixed stage, let alone moment, when one can definitely point to the emergence of true nationalism. When historians debate whether nationalism emerged during the early Partitions of Poland (Lord Acton), during the American Revolution (Benedict Anderson), the English Revolution (Hans Kohn) or even Fichte's 1807 *Addresses to the German Nation* (Kedourie), this tells us a good deal about their different definitions of nationalism but not so much about its emergence. More important, it omits the much longer period of the gestation of nationalism as language-and-symbolism, and as consciousness-and-aspiration. Since it is extremely difficult to gauge consciousness and sentiment, except indirectly, I shall concentrate on the rise of nationalist concepts, language, myths and symbols, even though our sources are located exclusively among the small European educated classes of the eighteenth century. [32]

Already in the seventeenth century we find a growing interest in the idea of 'national character' and 'national genius'. We met the latter in Lord Shaftesbury's high opinion of British attainments, to which we may add Jonathan Richardson's comparison of the English with the ancient Greeks and Romans, in which he claimed: 'There is a haughty Courage, an Elevation of Thought, a Greatness of Taste, a Love of Liberty, a Simplicity and Honesty among us, which we inherit from our Ancestors, and which belongs to us as Englishmen: and 'tis in These this Resemblance consists.' [33] Similar sentiments can be found in early eighteenth-century France. Father Daniel linked France's greatness to its monarchy, declaring that 'antiquity itself would find much to admire in the endless productions of the several arts, the thousand marvels that France has produced in our time'; while Henri-François Daguesseau's oration to the Paris Parlement of 1715 praised the 'love of *patrie*' in which 'the citizens find a *patrie* and the *patrie* its citizens'. [34]

By the middle of the eighteenth century the concept of 'national character' was widely accepted. La Font de Saint-Yenne, an influential art critic, looked back with pride to the *Grand Siècle* of Louis

XIV, Colbert and Le Brun and prophesied the revival of 'le génie François', inspired, as he put it, by 'le zèle ardent et courageux d'un Citoyen, à exposer les abus qui déshonorent sa Nation, et à contribuer à sa gloire',[35] while across the Channel Reynolds preached the need for a national school of history painting worthy of the nation, and James Barry declared in 1775: 'History painting and sculpture should be the main views of every people desirous of gaining honour by the arts. These are tests by which the national character will be tried in after ages, and by which it has been, and is now, tried by the natives of other countries.'[36]

By the latter half of the eighteenth century this kind of language had spread to America (Noah Webster), to Germany (Moser, Herder), to Switzerland (Zimmerman, Fuseli), to Italy (Vico, Alfieri) and to Holland, Sweden, Poland and Russia. While their conceptual sources were various, including Shaftesbury, Bolingbroke, Montesquieu and the *philosophes*, they also looked to the practice of enlightened despotism, which was increasingly identifying 'its' states with 'its' populations and treating them, or at any rate their educated classes, as the nation. For by this period in the West it was no longer really possible to confine membership of the nation to the first two estates, as in parts of Eastern Europe. By the mid eighteenth century enlightened despots felt it necessary to take account of the sentiments and opinions of the wealthier and more educated classes, whose 'expert' services they increasingly required.[37]

The concept of national character and the idea of national genius became useful and necessary elements in the new outlook and language of a Europe of enlightened and competing states. Equally important was the new concern with history and social development. This had several sources. Perhaps the most important in this context was the common practice of comparing European with classical civilization, which came to a head in late seventeenth-century France in the *Quarrel of the Ancients and the Moderns*. Just as the discovery of new lands and cultures by eighteenth-century explorers opened up a new vision of space and spatial comparison, so the recovery of classical thought and art helped to create a new vision of time and to provoke historical comparison with the civilizations of the past.

It was a period that saw the growing power of the rational state to intervene in society and try to solve problems (of illness, famine, crime, even ignorance) that had previously been thought insoluble in this world. The growing confidence spurred by the economic revolution of capitalism, the administrative revolution of professionalized statecraft and the cultural revolution of secular, humanistic education and science inspired a belief in the possibility of progress rivalling the achievements of classical Greece and Rome and an evolutionary worldview in which states and civilizations could be ranged in a cultural hierarchy of national genius. 'Historicism', the belief in the birth, growth, efflorescence and decay of peoples and cultures, became increasingly attractive as a framework for inquiry into the past and present and as an explanatory principle in elucidating the meaning of events, past and present. By placing events and persons in their appropriate historical context, and seeking to portray the event and period 'as it really was', one could empathetically understand historical events and processes and thereby how things came to be in the present. For these reasons we find in Britain and France a significant increase in the number and range of works dealing with both classical and national history during the eighteenth century, including the histories of Rollin, Rapin, Hume, Gibbon, Buchanan, Campden, Abbé Velly, Villaret and Mably, and a much greater interest in questions of origin and descent of peoples and of their cultural distinctiveness and historical character.[38]

From this moment we can discern two parallel lines of development, though in practice they may cross and interweave at times.

From the early 1760s a new quasi-Grecian taste made its appearance in western European society, at first elegant and superficial in the manner of Pompeian frescoes but soon with a deeper, heroic intention. The suave refinement of Adam and Vien gave way to the starker martial visions of Fuseli, Canova and David, to the classical simplicity of Gluck and Haydn and the monumental classicism of Boullée and Ledoux, Soane and Jefferson. The neo-classical movement had both a primitivist and classical urban aspect: on the one hand, a return to primitive forms and states (Laugier's hut, Rousseau's noble savage), on the other hand, seeking inspiration from the ancient *polis* community in Sparta, Athens and republican Rome.[39]

This latter aspect was of particular importance for the growth of nationalism, the ideology and the language. Again it was Rousseau who anticipated and encouraged its dissemination, though he had precursors – Shaftesbury, Bolingbroke and especially Montesquieu's seminal concept of the 'spirit' of a nation. But it was Rousseau who made the idea of 'national character' central to the political life of a community and who sought to translate it into a practical programme of national preservation and restoration. In both his *Projet Corse* and his *Gouvernement de la Pologne* Rousseau insisted on the importance of national individuality and its maintenance through the cultivation and preservation of a nation's manners and customs: 'Ce ne sont ni les murs, ni les hommes qui font la patrie; ce sont les lois, les moeurs, les coutumes, le gouvernement, la constitution, la manière d'être qui résulte de tout cela. La patrie est dans les relations de l'état à ses membres: quand ses relations changent ou s'anéantissent, la patrie s'évanouit.'[40] For Rousseau, his heart in an idealized childhood Genevan republic, the models of national solidarity were the city-states of classical antiquity. He was by no means alone in these moral and political passions. Most of the Jacobin *patriot* leaders saw themselves and their roles as those of latter-day Romans and Spartans; Cato, Brutus, Scaevola, Phocion, Socrates and Timoleon were their heroes, the civic cults of the *polis* their ideal religion.[41]

But in this same period (1760–1800) a parallel trend opened up the way towards a very different vision. The 'history' that the neo-classical movement valued was essentially civic and political. It derived from a reading of classical antiquity as a plateau of civilization that was being realized again in modern Europe but on an even higher plane. It was a universal history, yet its constituents were city-states and their civic solidarities and patriotisms. Between the classical model and its modern realization there had been a falling away, characterized by a return to a more barbaric, rural (feudal) society. It was just this rural society of the age between the classical and modern epochs, the 'middle age', that became the source of inspiration for a very different reading of European origins and development.

'Literary medievalism', the return through medieval literature to that rural European past, was from the first much more particularistic. It depended, by its method of inquiry and its literary data, on the records of specific peoples and milieux in order that earlier periods of a community's history and culture were to be reconstructed as they had really existed. The movement began in poetry, mainly in Britain, with the cult of ancient British poetry, Ossian and the *Edda*, and soon spread to Germany in the 1770s, where Moser, Herder and the young Goethe presaged a romantic cult of medieval Germany during the *Sturm und Drang* period. For the first time Gothic cathedrals, medieval miniatures, stained glass, Christian romances, chivalry and aristocratic pedigrees came back into their own. Since they were 'rediscovered' by intellectuals from each emergent nation, and were viewed as objectifications of the underlying values and culture of each nation, manifestations of its unique 'genius', the cult of literary medievalism greatly strengthened the emerging consciousness of each nation's ethnic background and hence its ethnic nationalism.[42]

Britain and France, though open to neo-classical and medievalist developments, tended to diverge, at least for a time. France manifested a powerful movement of historical classicism in both politics and the arts, while Britain tended to move more quickly towards a literary medievalism that owed much to the revival of Shakespeare, Spenser and Milton, as well as Homer, the 'poet of nature'.[43]

At first, because of the impact of the Revolution, the French passion for moral drama and historical verisimilitude drawn from its reading of classical heroic patriotism swept through Europe in the wake of Napoleon's victorious armies, leaving in every city the architectural and sculptural marks of its classical triumphs. But soon other monuments speaking for a past nearer home, and recalling earlier periods of the community's history, appeared beside the classical temples, arches and chambers of commerce. Gothic churches, vaulted tombs, museums and houses of assembly, adorned with mementoes of medieval battles and national heroes, filled the *lacunae* of the nation's collective memory, and little children were taught to revere Arthur and Vercingetorix, Siegfried and Lemminkainen, Alexander Nevsky and Stefan Dusan as much, if not more than, Socrates, Cato and Brutus. For the medieval era and its golden age of ethnic heroes seemed to answer more fully to the historicist vision that underpinned the new language and ideology of nationalism, revealing in every corner of Europe the unsuspected glories of one national genius after another, each drawing inspiration from the golden age and poetic landscape of his or her ethnic community. Medievalist literary historicism spread the cult of national distinctiveness even to the most submerged community and cultural category of Europe's population.

Of course, it was not literary medievalism that stirred these communities to mobilize and demand national status. Many factors were involved in this process, not least the impact of rationalized states on outlying areas and market relations on subsistence economies. But medievalist literary historicism provided the concepts, symbols and language for the vernacular mobilization of demotic *ethnies* and a mirror in which members could grasp their own aspirations as they took shape amid the transformations wrought by the Western 'revolutions'. Here they could read of themselves as a unique community with a 'peculiar genius' and distinctive culture, and recognize a 'national character' that demanded its autonomy so that it could live authentically. Here too the members of each cultural community could discover why national unity was essential to a 'realization' of the true national identity and why only in an historic homeland could that community find its 'genuine self' and achieve autarchy and solidarity for its citizens. This was a language and a symbolism that sprang easily from the historicist vision that literary medievalism did so much to foster and disseminate throughout Europe.[44]

This language and this symbolism spread rapidly, first to Eastern Europe, then to the Middle East and Asia and, finally, to Africa, having already mobilized the educated classes in the United States and Latin America. In each case we can trace a definite cultural sequence, despite many variations in tempo, scope and intensity. First there is a concern with 'national character' and its necessary freedom of growth. This is swiftly followed by the rise of historicism, in which the 'national genius' is explained according to the laws of its own historical development. This gives rise to two cultural patterns. The first, which we may call 'neo-classical', is inspired by Western rationalism and enlightenment, which mediates the original classical sources outside Europe. Such Western neo-classicism is often associated with republicanism and its virtues. At the same time there is a growing interest in the vernacular past or medieval (or ancestral) heritage of the indigenous peoples. Sometimes this nativism or medievalism is counterposed to Western neo-classicism; sometimes it combines with it, perhaps in an 'official' nationalism propagated by particular ideological regimes, as was the case in Wilhelmine Germany and Meiji Japan. That such combinations were possible suggests the flexibility of these cultural patterns. For both neo-classicism and medievalism (or nativism) are variants of a wider romanticism, a yearning for an idealized golden age and a heroic past that can serve as exemplars for collective regeneration in the present. Yet the opposition between enlightenment and medieval romanticism also mirrors a deeper cultural and social cleavage between the two ethnic bases and routes in the formation of nations, from which two radically different concepts of the nation have emerged.[45]

THE INTELLECTUALS AND NATIONALIST CULTURE

From this discussion of the gestation of nationalism in eighteenth-century Europe we can begin to gauge the different levels of its operation.

There is, first, a strictly political level. Nationalism as an ideology is a doctrine of the units of political power and a set of prescriptions about the nature of power-holders. It is also a doctrine of the legitimate global relations of such units. There is too an economic level of nationalist activity. Nationalism ideally prescribes a self-sufficiency of resources and purity of lifestyle in line with its commitment to autonomy and authenticity; failing that, nationalists strive for maximum control over their homeland and its resources. Beyond that, nationalism operates at the social level by prescribing the mobilization of the 'people', their legal equality as citizens and their participation in public life for the 'national good'. Seeing the nation as a family writ large, it seeks to inspire a spirit of national solidarity and brotherhood in the members of the nation; hence it preaches the social unity of each nation.

But at the broadest level nationalism must be seen as a form of historicist culture and civic education, one that overlays or replaces the older modes of religious culture and familial education. More than a style and doctrine of politics, nationalism is a *form of culture* – an ideology, a language, mythology, symbolism and consciousness – that has achieved global resonance, and the nation is a type of identity whose meaning and priority is presupposed by this form of culture. In that sense the nation and national identity must be seen as a creation of nationalism and its proponents, and its significance and celebration too is the handiwork of nationalists.

This goes some way to explaining the role of the arts in nationalism. Nationalists, intent on celebrating or commemorating the nation, are drawn to the dramatic and creative possibilities of artistic media and genres in painting, sculpture, architecture, music, opera, ballet and film, as well in the arts and crafts. Through these genres nationalist artists may, directly or evocatively, 'reconstruct' the sights, sounds and images of the nation in all its concrete specificity and with 'archaeological' verisimilitude. It is not surprising, therefore, if in an era of burgeoning nationalism, in the late eighteenth century, Western artists were drawn to the 'archaeological drama' of recreated images of ancient Rome and Sparta, or medieval France, England and Germany, and to their political messages of 'moral historicism', the portrayal of examples of public virtue from the past in order to inspire emulation by present generations. In these 'golden ages', among idealized heroes and sages, they could recreate a vivid panorama of life *wie es eigentlich war*, which could suggest the nation's antiquity and continuity, its noble heritage and the drama of its ancient glory and regeneration. Who, more than poets, musicians, painters and sculptors, could bring the national ideal to life and disseminate it among the people? In this respect a David, a Mickiewicz and a Sibelius were worth more than several battalions of Father Jahn's *Turnerschaften* and a Yeats as much as the hurling societies of the Gaelic Association.[46]

There is a reverse side to this coin. Many artists, in Europe and outside, have been drawn into the world of nationalism, its language and symbolism. Among composers alone, we may mention Liszt, Chopin, Dvořák and Smetana, Borodin and Moussorgsky, Kodály and Bartók, Elgar and Vaughan-Williams, Verdi and Wagner, de Falla, Grieg and Sibelius; among painters, we may single out David and Ingres, Fuseli and West, Gros, Hayez, Maclise, Delaroche, Gallén-Kallela, Vasnetsov and Surikov, as well as many landscape and genre painters who contributed to a populistic nationalism in a manner that was more evocative than deliberate. For the language and symbols of nationalism helped to draw artists to seek outlets in motifs, genres and forms different from the traditional and classical in the tone-poem, the historical opera, ethnic dances, historical novels, local landscapes, ballads, dramatic poems, choral drama and the like. These forms, along with nocturnes, poetic fantasies, rhapsodies, ballads, preludes and dances, are characterized by a heightened expressive subjectivity that is well suited to the conceptual language and style of ethnic nationalism and to the rediscovery of the 'inner self' that is one of the chief ends of ethnic historicism.[47]

Expansion of the range and intensity of expressive language and subjectivity has gone hand in hand with the rise to prominence of circles of historicist intellectuals bent on uncovering the historical roots of collective identities and the inner meaning of ethnic distinctiveness in the modern world. Here I distinguish intellectuals proper from a much wider stratum of professionals as well as from the still wider educated public. Analytically, we may distinguish intellectuals who create artistic works and produce ideas from the wider intelligentsia or professionals who transmit and disseminate those ideas and creations and from a still wider educated public that 'consumes' ideas and works of art. Of course, in practice the same individual may produce, disseminate and consume ideas in the different roles of artist/intellectual, professional/interpreter and audience/public. Nevertheless, this tripartite distinction may help to clarify the seminal role of intellectuals in European, and later non-European, nationalisms.[48]

It is the intellectuals – poets, musicians, painters, sculptors, novelists, historians and archaeologists, playwrights, philologists, anthropologists and folklorists – who have proposed and elaborated the concepts and language of the nation and nationalism and have, through their musings and research, given voice to wider aspirations that they have conveyed in appropriate images, myths and symbols. The ideology and cultural core doctrine of nationalism may also be ascribed to social philosophers, orators and historians (Rousseau, Vico, Herder, Burke, Fichte, Mazzini, Michelet, Palacky, Karamzin), each elaborating elements fitted to the situation of the particular community for which he spoke.[49]

Critics of nationalism have seized on the seminal role of the intellectuals to explain the ideology's errors and lack of political realism. They argue that a doctrine of the national will must produce coercive fanaticism or else fall into anarchy in its delusionary dream of terrestrial perfection. Other scholars, for whom nationalism is primarily a type of *political* argument about seizing state power, while equally critical of the 'pseudo-solutions' that it provides, consider that the role of intellectuals has been overestimated, despite the importance of abstract ideology in the modern political world.[50]

There is a mass of evidence for the primary role of intellectuals, both in generating cultural nationalism and in providing the ideology, if not the early leadership, of political nationalism. Wherever one turns in Europe, their seminal position in generating and analysing the concepts, myths, symbols and ideology of nationalism is apparent. This applies to the first appearance of the core doctrine and to the antecedent concepts of national character, genius of the nation and national will. It is also true of that other tradition of social thought, namely the idea of collective liberty and popular democracy. Here too social philosophers played a major role, notably Rousseau, Siéyès, Paine, Jefferson and Fichte (at least in his early writings). The influence of Kant too cannot be overlooked, even though his major contribution, the idea that the good will is the autonomous will, applied to individuals rather than groups.[51]

It was the confluence of these two traditions, the cultural language of national character and the political discourse of collective liberty and popular sovereignty, that inspired the revolutionary fervour and excesses of the Jacobin *patriots* in 1792–4. But these cultural and political traditions also underlay the liberal 'bourgeois' Revolution of 1789–91 and its partial resumption under the Directoire.

Here one of the guiding forces was the ideology of nationalism, which made itself manifest, both in Siéyès' well-known pamphlet *Qu'est-ce que le Tiers Etat?* and in the *cahiers de doléances* of early 1789. The proclamation of the 'citizen-nation' and the mobilization and unification of all Frenchmen for a new, reformed social and political order, in the spring and summer of 1789, marked the moment of transition from 'nationalism as a form of culture', with which we have been concerned so far, to 'nationalism as a form of politics', to which I turn in the next chapter.[52]

For the present we need note only the vital role of intellectuals in the initial stages of both forms of nationalism. But, equally, we should be careful not to exaggerate that role in the later stages or even in the organization of more regular nationalist movements.

How shall we explain the seminal influence of the intellectuals in early nationalisms? Is it simply a function of intellectualism everywhere that any *ideological* movement requires its intellectuals to formulate a persuasive, abstract doctrine that will mediate the often conflicting interests of the groups supporting the movement? Is it simply a question of necessary skills and abilities, the need for every politically successful movement to have its trained advocates, constitutional experts, propagandists, orators and the like? Or should we characterize nationalism as a 'movement of intellectuals' excluded from power and bent on acquiring it through leadership of 'the people' whose cultural definition they have themselves supplied?

There is an element of truth in all these characterizations. Intellectuals and intellectualism are clearly needed for the purpose of propounding and elaborating the ideologies of most modern movements (though not all), and their skills, if they truly possess the required ones, will help to advance the movement's cause. But there is nothing specific to nationalism about such skills or intellectualism, and the relevant skills, as we shall see, are more likely to be the preserve of professionals (the intelligentsia) than of intellectuals proper; these are skills acquired in addition to their primary function of cultural creation and analysis.[53]

As for the notion that nationalism is a movement of 'power-seeking' intellectuals, though one may point to instances of excluded and resentful intellectuals, especially under a racialist colonialism, there is insufficient evidence to formulate a general proposition about the motives of nationalist intellectuals, and a considerable amount of contrary evidence showing that intellectuals proper rarely become nationalist *leaders*, though they may from time to time exercise advisory roles. Rousseau, Fichte, Korais, Obradovic, Karadžić, Gokalp, Achad Ha'am, al-Kawakibi, Banerjea, Li'ang Ch'i Ch'ao, Blyden, Cheikh Anta Diop, Gasprinski – these earliest propounders of their various nationalisms may have been secretly motivated by resentment, but they reaped no political reward. Indeed, they were often ignored, even temporarily forgotten, by their contemporaries, as was Marx's contemporary Moses Hess.[54]

How then shall we explain the attraction of nationalism for many intellectuals? The most popular thesis speaks of nationalism as the resolution of an 'identity crisis' of the intellectuals, and there is an important truth here, provided the thesis is properly formulated. Its validity is confined to intellectuals proper and should not be generalized to include other strata or classes, not even the intelligentsia. Moreover, the success and even the character of nationalism cannot be accounted for in these overly simple terms. A full-blown nationalism takes its character from a variety of circumstances and imprints, of which the intellectuals' is but one, albeit seminal, influence. Nor can the thesis explain the social thought and politics of the intellectuals *tout court*; after all, many intellectuals do not become nationalists or, if they do, it is only superficially and temporarily. What the thesis can try to explain is why nationalism has made a lifelong appeal to intellectuals in so many parts of the world and why their imprint on the ideology and language of nationalism has been so influential.[55]

The identity crisis of the intellectuals springs ultimately from the challenges posed to traditional religion and society by the 'scientific state' and the Western 'revolutions' that it promotes wherever its influence is felt. I have already described the different reactions of the intellectuals to this crisis of 'dual legitimation': of legitimation in terms of received religion and tradition versus legitimation by appeal to reason and observation, fostered by a state that makes increasing use of 'scientific' technique and attitudes. It is this profound challenge to traditional cosmic images, symbols and theodicies, a challenge felt first and most acutely by those exposed to rationalist and scientific thought and activity, that propels many intellectuals to discover alternative principles and concepts, and a new mythology and symbolism, to legitimate and ground human thought and action. Perhaps the most important of these principles and myths is that of 'historicism'. Its appeal lies exactly in its ability to present as (apparently) comprehensive a picture of the universe as the old religious world-views without appealing to an external principle of creation, while at the same time integrating the past (tradition), the present (reason) and the future (perfectibility). The question then arose: whose past and whose future? That of humanity as a whole, or that of its individual or collective parts? The answers to these questions provoked major divisions within the ranks of the intellectuals and led to the formulation of alternative, though often overlapping, social and political traditions and movements – to the traditions of liberalism and Marxism on the one hand and those of nationalism and racial fascism on the other.[56]

Hand in hand with this wider crisis of dual legitimation went a more specific crisis of the intellectuals as to *their* identity in a world torn by these challenges to their cosmic traditions. The questions then arose: who am I? Who are we? What is our purpose and role in life and in society? The answers to these questions were manifold, as one might imagine, and individual circumstances and choice often determined much of them. Nevertheless, the fact that the range of answers was neither unlimited nor random suggests lines of inquiry into why certain types of answer to this crisis of identity were particularly appealing. One such answer was certainly, and remains, the nationalist solution, which sinks or 'realizes' individual identity within the new collective cultural identity of the nation. The individual in this solution takes her or his identity from a cultural collectivity; she or he becomes a citizen, that is, a recognized and rightful member of a political community that is, simultaneously, a cultural 'community of history and destiny'. Ultimately, in this answer to the question of identity, 'we are who we are' because of our historic culture.

We are back to the image of nationalism as a form of historicist culture, which emerges out of the breakdown of earlier religious forms of culture. This has been, and remains, a large and vital part of both nationalism and national identity, that is, the identity solution proposed by nationalism. But, if we ask where this particular historicist solution comes from, we cannot simply appeal to the imagery and celebration of nationalists; we need to look deeper into the sources of their concepts and images. I have suggested that we look for those sources in the different kinds of ethnic base and political process in late medieval and early modern Europe, as well as in the wider sense of cultural community persisting in varying degrees in different parts of the world. Here, all around them, lay models and examples of collective identity that could serve both the intellectuals in their own private quest for an 'identity solution' and wider strata with different preoccupations and interests.

For we must never forget that the nationalist solution was adopted not only by many intellectuals in search of their roots but also by many others for whom a similar quest for roots, though it may have possessed other meanings, became equally paramount and for whom a similar solution, the nation, was equally necessary and attractive. It is to these others, and their national identity, that I now turn.

CHAPTER 5

Nations by Design?

As a doctrine of culture and a symbolic language and consciousness, nationalism's primary concern is to create a world of collective cultural identities or cultural nations. While it does not determine which units of population are eligible to become nations, nor why they do so, nationalism plays a large part in determining *when* and *where* nations will be formed. It is at this point that nationalism enters the political arena. As a doctrine and language of polycentric uniqueness, a modern, secular equivalent of the old doctrine of chosen peoples, nationalism might have remained a purely cultural and social vision and consciousness, largely divorced from the political realm, as was the case with many ethnic communities in premodern eras. The fact that nationalism often fails to recognize the boundary between the private realm of culture and the public one of politics suggests that other components of national*ism* discussed in chapter 4, as well as certain features of the modern world, have a direct political impact, irrespective of the intentions of particular groups and versions of nationalism.

In other words, what we mean by national identity comprises both a cultural and political identity and is located in a political community as well as a cultural one. This is significant because it means that any attempt to forge a national identity is also a political action with political consequences, like the need to redraw the geopolitical map or alter the composition of political regimes and states. Creating a 'world of nations' has profound consequences for the global system of states as well as for individual states.

The politics of national identity are complicated by the duality of concepts of the nation, the ethnic and the territorial model, described in chapter 1. This has led to attempts to create two very different kinds of national political identity and community. The first (in historical sequence usually) has been the territorial type of political nation; the second the ethnic type of political nation. In each case a rather different model of political identity and community is envisaged, drawing from the different neo-classical/rational and indigenous/romantic cultural sources discussed in the previous chapter. In this chapter I shall be concerned mainly with attempts to create *territorial* political identities and communities; in the next chapter, with the ethnic reaction that these attempts have provoked and the problems of polyethnic states.

EMPIRES INTO NATIONS

Historians commonly distinguish the growth of the 'old, continuous nations' of the West from the more deliberate creation of nations in Eastern Europe, Asia, Latin America and Africa. In Western Europe nations were to all intents and purposes in place before the rise of nationalism, the ideology, language and aspiration, during the eighteenth century. Outside the West the formation of nations followed the diffusion of nationalism in the relevant area. In Western Europe nations were largely unplanned. Outside the West they were largely the result of nationalist purposes and movements. The West acquired nations almost by accident; in other parts of the globe nations were created by design.[1]

From a Western standpoint this distinction has much to commend it. I have, in chapter 3, argued that Western nations, the first nations, did in part antedate the rise of nationalism, and emerged as an unintended consequence of processes of bureaucratic incorporation by aristocratic 'lateral' *ethnies*, whose ruling classes could by no stretch of the imagination be called 'nationalist'. But even here we need to exercise care. It remains an open question how much weight should be attached to royal centralization and homogenization from the fifteenth century, as opposed to Jacobin and subsequent nationalisms, in creating the French nation. The element of 'design' is not wholly absent even in the English, and later British, case; witness Tudor and Stuart centralization in opposition to papal Rome and Spain, the impact of Puritan ethnic 'nationalism' and the use of a rising tide of national sentiment in Britain from 1770 to 1820.[2]

Nevertheless, it remains true that, by comparison with non-Western cases, the rise of Western nations owed much less to nationalism and a movement to create a 'nation where none existed'. In non-Western instances of the formation of nations the specifically national*ist* element, as an ideological movement, assumes greater importance. That importance, and hence the role of 'invention' and 'construction' in the formation of national identity, varies considerably, depending in great part on the pre-existing local ethnic configuration. It is also influenced by the nature and activities of the preceding political system and institutions.

We distinguished in chapter 3 two routes in the formation of nations. One was the process of bureaucratic incorporation leading to the rise of territorial and civic political nations, the other a process of vernacular mobilization for the creation of ethnic and genealogical political nations. If we confine our attention to the first route, we can subdivide it outside the West into an 'imperial' and a 'colonial' route, according to the nature and activities of the political system preceding the formation of the nation. In the first case the unit in question is formally sovereign and independent; it requires not a movement of liberation from alien rule but rather a transformation of its political system and cultural self-definition. In the second case not only must a new cultural identity be forged but also the unit, as a dependent colony, requires to be liberated from rule by alien powers and become independent and sovereign.

Let me start with the independent states and the 'imperial' route. How is a national political identity forged in these cases? How was, or is, it possible to transform states and empires like Russia, China, Japan, Persia, Ottoman Turkey and Ethiopia into 'compact' political communities and 'territorial nations'?

The main characteristics of the polities that initiated the processes of forming nations, and the route by which this may be achieved, have included the following.

1. Their *aristocratic base* in a 'lateral' *ethnie*. Though they may include demotic elements (as in the Russian, Ethiopian, Turkish and Japanese cases), the state is suffused by an aristocratic culture and traditions, often permeated with religious and priestly influences.

2. Their *inclusion of significant ethnic minorities*. This varies considerably, with some empires including many large minorities (for example, Russia, Ethiopia, Ottoman Turkey), others only a few (Japan).

3. The *'modernizing' character* of their bureaucratic states.

Again, this varies in degree (compare Japan with Ottoman Turkey or Ethiopia), but it represents the consolidation of a dominant ethnic core and ruling class over subordinate *ethnies* and classes.

4. The frequent use of '*official*' *and institutional nationalism*. In order to consolidate their hold and homogenize the population into a compact nation, the ruling class seeks to assimilate ethnic minorities through an educational programme of nationalism, backed by major institutions. To this end, they promote official, establishment ideas and images of the nation, to which everyone must conform and which preclude the rise of any other ideas, symbols or imagery.

How successful has the imperial route and its programme of official nationalism proved in transforming ethnic states and empires into compact territorial political nations?

Success in this field has depended on both geopolitical and social changes. Broadly speaking, movement towards the goal of the nation-state has been swifter where the dominant *ethnie* and its rulers have been able to divest themselves of their imperial heritage, usually by redrawing their borders, as in the Turkish case, or where 'empire' did not include other, contiguous or overseas territories and their ethnically different inhabitants, as with Japan.

Socially, movement towards the goal of the nation-state has been swifter to the extent that the old ruling aristocracy has been replaced, though not necessarily by violence, by middle and lower classes, whilst simultaneously preserving and adapting their ethnic cultural heritage. Too sharp a repudiation of that heritage stores up problems of cultural, and political, identity for the future unless there is a vibrant alternative demotic community to hand within the dominant ethnic core.

Judged by these criteria, the imperial route for forming territorial political nations has had only partial success to date. This may be seen by considering a few empirical examples.

1. *Russia* The last century of tsarist rule saw both the attempted modernization (often interrupted) of social and political institutions and the use of an official nationalism to Russify large parts of the empire's populations and assimilate them through the imposition of

Russian culture and Orthodoxy. At the same time the gulf between rulers and ruled within the dominant Russian ethnic core widened, despite the abolition of serfdom in 1861; the westernized culture of the aristocracy and the Orthodox beliefs and rituals of the peasant masses expressed antithetical visions of 'Russia'.[3]

The October Revolution repudiated both visions for a Marxist 'proletarian' alternative that sought to turn the Russian empire into a federation of soviet republics for the most important peripheral *ethnies*. But the civil war, the building of 'Socialism in One Country' and especially the dangers of the Great Patriotic War against the Nazis brought a partial return to the traditional, even religious, heritage of Great Russian nationalism. Today that heritage is sought more openly at the cultural, if not the institutional, level. At the same time, even so partial a return under *perestroika* has been accompanied by growing nationalist demands of non-Russian demotic *ethnies*, demands that could imperil the socialist vision and its federal expression.[4]

In these circumstances it has been found necessary to delay the programme of greater cooperation between the socialist nations of the USSR and to postpone, perhaps *sine die*, the ideal of their fusion. We can no longer easily envisage the growth of a Soviet national identity or a Soviet political community except as a truly federal commonwealth of separate national identities and political communities.[5]

2. *Turkey* The last seventy years of Ottoman rule witnessed successive attempts to reform the basis of the empire (*Tanzimat*), including a resort to 'Ottomanism' through equality and citizenship for all subjects and to 'Islamism' under Abdul Hamid, which promoted the welfare of the Islamic inhabitants without abolishing citizenship for all.

But the modernizing attempts by an aristocratic Islamic élite failed amid the break-up of first the Christian and then the Muslim parts of the empire. At this point a new pan-Turkist ideology emerged among sections of the intellectuals, and it was taken up by some of the professionals and military after the *coup d'état* of 1908, hastening the alienation of the non-Turkic parts of the empire, including the Arabs.[6]

It was this Turkic ideal, shorn of its extra-Anatolian irredentism, that Kemal Ataturk made the basis of his secular, westernizing nationalism. In effect he engineered the secession of the Turkish heartlands from the Ottoman empire and caliphate, repudiating Ottomanism and Islam and pushing through a series of modernizing social and cultural reforms in the cities that would redefine the empire as a compact territorial political community aligned to the ethnic nation of Anatolian Turks. But, realizing that territorial and civic concepts of the nation require a solidary basis in a national cultural identity, the Kemalists attempted to furnish the necessary ethnic myths, memories, values and symbols by utilizing the theory of Turkish origins in Central Asia, their unbroken descent from Oghuz Khan and the antiquity of their (purified) original language (the Sun Language theory).[7]

Despite the apparent success of the territorial concept, its ethnic underpinning encountered serious problems. The small towns and villages continued to display strong Islamic loyalties and sentiments; Turkic theories and symbolism failed to replace this wider allegiance, even among the merchants. Pan-Turkism retained vociferous adherents, while Marxism also has a small following. Once again the *content*, if not the form, of Turkish national identity, proved elusive.[8]

3. *Ethiopia* It was only in the late nineteenth century that the Ethiopian state expanded into an empire under Menelik to include large numbers of Muslims, several ethnic communities and categories like the Galla, the Somali in the Ogaden and a variety of groups in Eritrea. For centuries the dominant *ethnie* on the Abyssinian plateau had been the Christian Monophysite Amhara, but it was only in this century that their rulers pursued an official Amharic nationalism that sought to create an Amharized 'territorial nation'. Modernizing policies were also begun under Haile Selassie in the 1960s but too late to overcome the serious economic problems and head off the intelligentsia's challenge. After a disastrous famine, the military revolt of 1974 deposed the Lion of Judah but continued his modernizing and centralizing policies against Tigréan, Galla, Somali and Eritrean ethnic separatisms with Soviet support and even fiercer determination. To their Marxist anti-Christian and land reform

programmes was allied an ethnic resettlement policy, one of whose aims was to promote the Dergue's vision of a socialist African territorial nation. Yet here too identity problems abound. Despite the attack on the Monophysite Church, the Amhara remain dominant, and Mengistu's regime combines Marxist with Amharic Christian symbolism; maintenance of Ethiopian borders owes more to Menelik than to Marx. Too sharp a repudiation of the aristocratic–clerical past may destroy Ethiopia's *raison d'être* if the borders are not to be redrawn.[9]

4. *Japan* Without doubt the most successful case of modernizing nationalism by the imperial route, Japan nevertheless suffers identity problems, at both the cultural and the political level.

More homogeneous and geopolitically rooted than most, the Japanese ethnic community was united in the early medieval era by the legacy of the Heian and Nara empires and by the emergence of successive feudal states (the Kamakura, Ashikaga and Tokugawa shogunates) despite long periods of civil war between feuding lords. By the early seventeenth century Japan had evolved into an ethnic state with only the small Ainu minority (later supplemented by Koreans) dwelling in the north. Tokugawa feudal absolutism cemented the congruence of state and *ethnie* by (almost) sealing Japan's borders with the outside world.[10]

The Meiji Restoration of 1868, led by some *samurai* factions, replaced the shogunal system by a modernizing Imperial one, open to necessary outside influences but bent on achieving political parity with the West through economic and political reform under imperial auspices.

To this end the Meiji élites utilized Confucian and peasant traditions of loyalty to one's lord, familism (*ie*) and the village community (*mura*) to reinforce the dominance of the emperor system, turn a politically passive and economically fragmented ethnic community into a more cohesive, economically centralized and mobilized political community and thereby create a Japanese national political identity. Here Meiji political nationalism created the modern Japanese nation on the basis of aristocratic (*samurai*) culture and its ethnic state, while also utilizing those demotic peasant traditions that could be integrated into the ruling imperial system.[11]

The results have been problematic despite the secure ethnic basis of modern Japanese national identity. The emperor system (*tennosei*), as the bulwark of aggressive nationalism and Fascism during the Second World War, has been deprived of its former mystique and position and remains under a cloud, at least for the time being. With that loyalty in abeyance, the foundations of Japanese national *political* identity have been shaken, though some advocate a prudent 'revivalist' political nationalism. In its place there has re-emerged the periodic Japanese preoccupation with national distinctiveness, notably in the literature known as *nihonjinron* (discussions of the Japanese), which is a vital element of any cultural nationalism concerned with redefining a national *cultural* identity. Though formulated by intellectuals drawn from various strata, this concern has been taken up by business élites in the large Japanese companies who stress the distinctive social and holistic culture of Japan. But how far this can prove a durable and comprehensive base for Japanese national identity, cultural or political, remains to be seen.[12]

In these examples nationalism, the ideology and symbolism, has grafted a new concept of national political identity on to a pre-existing 'lateral' ethnic identity. This process has met with only partial success, depending on the degree of cultural homogeneity of the state's population – that is, the degree to which it constituted an ethnic state – and whether it was able to divest itself of empire and hence of culturally different communities. Where the process has been relatively successful, nationalist ideals and symbolism have helped to redefine an imperial community as a fairly compact nation and political community.

COLONIES INTO NATIONS

By far the greater number of non-western states started out as colonies of outside (usually overseas) European powers. In most of these cases both cultural and political identities were lacking. Any identity or solidarity that a colonial population possessed was initially the product of the incorporation and changes brought by the colonial power. In the Gold Coast, Nigeria, Ivory Coast, Belgian Congo, Kenya, Egypt, Iraq, India, Burma and Indonesia, to take some examples, the nation that is (usually still) being forged has been defined, in its boundaries and character, by the colonial state.

There is a vast literature on the colonial state. Given the variety of European colonial policies – French, Belgian, Portuguese, British, Italian, German and Russian (in Central Asia and the Caucasus) – any generalization about the impact of colonialism is hazardous. But certain aspects, while not true of every instance, were widespread.

These include the following.

1. The overseas alien ethnic basis of the colonial state and its administrative élites. As Alavi highlighted, the colonial state was an outgrowth not of indigenous civil society but of metropolitan society mixed, however, with executive characteristics not tolerated within the metropolis. In other words, the colonial state was a hybrid: an alien executive instrument of a culturally different political community.[13]

2. The creation by treaty and political *fiat* of administrative boundaries that only partially took ethnic boundaries into account and the bureaucratic inclusion of previously separate ethnic communities and categories within a single political system. Not only did the colonial state vastly increase the scale of many units (even in India, which had only once been united for a brief period under the Mauryas); it also for the first time defined a *territorial space* for the interaction and loyalty of the included populations.[14]

3. The growth of a *territorial patriotism* based on this space and limited by these boundaries. This entirely novel territorial patriotism was directly encouraged by most administrative authorities (less so in French West Africa, where a policy of 'identity' with France was practised – by African élites); it was also the product of economic exchange and economic and legal regulation by the colonial regime within each territory. The upshot was an incipient sense of attachment to 'Nigeria', 'Kenya', 'Burma' among an élite.[15]

4. The rise to prominence of professional and educated strata in each colony, either through direct colonial policy or, in spite of colonial barriers, through higher-level educational provision (as in the Belgian Congo). This 'intelligentsia' normally played a key role in the subsequent nationalist movement.[16]

5. The provision by missionaries and missionary education,

but also by others, of ideals of emancipation and liberation from colonial rule. Here the link with the intelligentsia is most apparent; it was this stratum that became most imbued with such ideals and sought to realize them in practice.

6. The depreciation of indigenous peoples and their cultures even when they were preserved, by colonial bureaucrats, traders and soldiers – sometimes on a selective basis – and often with strong racial motives.[17]

The nationalisms that have characterized the colonial setting are, not surprisingly, termed 'anti-colonial' by many writers. The implication is that their potential is exhausted with the achievement of their goal of independence from the colonial power. They are not 'true' nationalist movements because there is no actual or potential nation available (with a few exceptions like Somalia). There is another aspect of this anti-colonialism: its westernizing orientation, coupled with the exclusion of its proponents, the intelligentsia. These nationalisms are literally anti-colonial in the sense that they originate with the exclusion of that intelligentsia from the colonial bureaucracy and are directed at correcting this state of affairs. We are back with 'resentment', the anger and frustration of the intellectuals – now the intelligentsia – at their unmerited exclusion, heightened in this case by the one-sided love affair of so many of the intelligentsia with the West and its values. Truly, colonial nationalisms are still-born; they are imitative 'nationalisms of the intelligentsia', unable to forge real nations.[18]

That there *was* exclusion of the intelligentsia from the upper echelons of many colonial bureaucracies is not in dispute. Such exclusion was structural and cultural, a combination of an excess of qualified graduates and educated personnel to posts in the colonial bureaucracies, often combined with racial discrimination against black or mixed-origin candidates, however qualified, notably in India and British Africa, much less so in French West Africa.[19] This helps to explain the earlier and more assertive politicization of sections of the intelligentsia in the British colonies. Yet, the fact that a strong cultural movement of Négritude emerged later in French territories in the West Indies and West Africa suggests that bureaucratic exclusion of the intelligentsia is only one, albeit important, factor in the genesis of colonial nationalisms. The depreciation of indigenous cultures must also be allowed its due, as must the attempts by a semi-Westernized intelligentsia to 'return' to the peasant masses.[20]

In fact, colonial nationalisms cannot be reduced to a single motor, however important and widespread. Their variety reflects the many differences in their backgrounds and influences. The degree of economic development of a colony and area, the extent to which capitalism has penetrated indigenous social structures, the nature of indigenous resources and infrastructure (ports, roads, etc.) the presence of settler communities, the thrust of colonial economic and political policies in each territory and the extent of urban growth and educational provision were among the many factors that influenced the timing, scope, direction and intensity of particular colonial nationalisms. Equally important was the nature of the cultural influences to which the intelligentsia and bourgeoisie in a particular colony were exposed. It has been shown that in British and French West Africa, for example, the influence of Rousseau and Mill helped to shape the aspirations, language and ideology of nationalist movements in the area, whereas in India to these influences were subsequently added those of Herder and the German Romantics, particularly in the thinking of Aurobindo and Tilak.[21] Arab nationalists were similarly drawn to German Romantic notions of language and national soul and mission, whereas Zionism was shaped by Russian populism and by Western liberalism (in Herzl's formulations).[22]

Even so brief a sketch of the factors involved in the genesis of colonial nationalisms reveals the limitations of the literal meaning of the term 'anti-colonialism'. But, by the same token, does it not also confirm their fundamentally 'imitative' and 'reactive' character? Have not the African and Asian intelligentsias imbibed their nationalisms abroad and used them to 'invent nations where none existed'?

Again, the fact that many members of the colonial intelligentsia were influenced in their nationalist thinking by European sources, whether through study or travel abroad or through libraries and books at home, is not in doubt. Nor is the profound influence of Western scholarship. It was the research of Jones, Müller, Renan, Cahun, Arminius Vámbéry, Zimmer, Rhys and other scholars that helped to define the character, boundaries and problems of the area or community in question, as well as spreading to non-European areas the language and concepts of nationalism, even if unintentionally.[23]

But such research fell on fertile soil. The 'diffusion of ideas' thesis deals with only a part of the explanation of the rise of nationalism; Its relevance, as we shall see, is more for demotic nationalisms based on 'vertical' *ethnies* than for the shaping of territorial cultural and political identities. The fact is that sufficient numbers of the African, Latin American and Asian intelligentsias were receptive to European romantic and nationalist influences at particular junctures, and this requires separate explanation. I shall return to this question in the next chapter.

THE 'INVENTION' OF NATIONS?

Our concern here is with the civic and territorial nationalisms that emerged from the colonial framework to provide one vehicle for the formation of new political identities in Latin America, Africa and Asia. How far were these identities the inventions of colonial intelligentsias and their successors? How, in fact, are the new nations of Africa, Asia and even Latin America being created?

There seem to be two main ways of creating civic, territorial nations outside Europe. The first is the 'dominant *ethnie*' model, in which the culture of the new state's core ethnic community becomes the main pillar of the new national political identity and community, especially where the culture in question can claim to be 'historic' and 'living' among the core community, as with the Javanese culture in Indonesia. Though other cultures continue to flourish, the identity of the emerging political community is shaped by the historic culture of its dominant *ethnie*.

Egypt presents a striking example. Though the Coptic minority continues to flourish, it is the Arabic-language, Islamic culture of the majority of the community that predominates as the official national identity. On one level Egypt affords a prime example of the compact territorial nation; at another, its cultural identity reveals different historical layers, so that in this century a purely Egyptian 'pharaonism' can be counterposed to a broader, dominant Islamic

Arabism. These cultural differences have spilled over periodically into the political realm: an earlier political sentiment of 'Egypt for the Egyptians' gave way under Nasser to an expansionist demotic Arabism, only to return in muted form to a narrower Egyptian focus under his successors. How far Egyptian leaders can integrate their civic, territorial model with the Islamic popular aspirations of the majority remains to be seen. But in practice 'invention' of an Egyptian nation is heavily circumscribed by pre-existing ethno-religious communal ties and sentiments.[24]

In Burma too, despite a high level of conflict, the vivid and historic nature of the dominant Burman culture reduced the scope for the territorial 'invention' of a Burmese nation. It is the Burmans and their historic culture who are likely to shape the nature of any Burmese political identity, if only for demographic and historical reasons. The conflicts with Karen, Shan, Mon and other *ethnies* are the more protracted because of the vivid, active quality of Burmese ethnicity and historic culture, even if overlaid by the ideology of the present regime and the equally vibrant quality of ethnicity among the minority communities.[25]

In Kenya too a process of Kikuyization is apparent. Here, however, the dominant ethnic community is periodically challenged by other communities, especially the Luo. Nevertheless, the nature of a 'Kenyan' territorial nation is heavily influenced by the aspirations, needs and culture of the dominant Kikuyu community. Similarly in Zimbabwe it is Shona culture and historical memories that are likely to shape any emerging sense of Zimbabwean identity, despite the need to accommodate the aspirations of the important Ndebele minority community.[26]

In these cases the process of constructing the nation is less one of 'invention' than of 'reconstructing' the ethnic core and integrating its culture with the requirements of a modern state and with the aspirations of minority communities. In this respect it resembles, to a certain extent, the situation of late medieval kingdoms in Europe. They too were built up, as we have seen, around ethnic cores and expanded to embrace adjacent lands and ethnic communities, which it then became necessary to suppress or accommodate. In the African and Asian cases, however, the time span is quite different, and so is the ideological context. Given the geopolitical situation, regimes in the new states are under considerable and immediate pressure to create nations such as exist in Europe and America, if only to be able to compete in the international arena. Besides, ideologically they are committed to 'nation-building', which in practice means state-building combined with national integration and mobilization; this too requires the formation of a national cultural and political identity that clearly differentiates it from its neighbours. It is tempting to use the cultural distinctiveness of the dominant *ethnie* to hand to forge the political and cultural identity of a new nation and at the same time opt for a popular mass-mobilizing solution to the problem of creating a 'new' nation in a post-colonial framework.

The second way to create civic, territorial nations in the colonial setting is to find ways of creating a supra-ethnic 'political culture' for the new political community. In these cases there is no acknowledged dominant *ethnie*; either the new state contains a number of equally small ethnic communities and categories, none of which can dominate the state, as in Tanzania, or a number of rival *ethnies* as in Nigeria, Uganda, Zaire and Syria.

Nigeria affords the classic instance. With some two hundred and fifty ethnic communities and categories, and the three major regional *ethnies* accounting for some 60 per cent of the total population locked in political and economic competition, the colonial territory of 'Nigeria', created relatively recently by the British, furnished one of several bases for the formation of nations in the aftermath of independence. Given the near-parity and rivalry of the three main ethnic communities, the Hausa–Fulani, the Yoruba and the Ibo, the construction of a Nigerian cultural and political identity was bound to be an arduous task. In the event it required two coups, massacres of the Ibo and a ruinous civil war to create the conditions for moving towards the vision of a civic, territorial Nigerian nation. Continuing unease over the political predominance of any Hausa–Fulani ethnic coalition must render doubtful any attempt to forge a pan-Nigerian identity by political means. Given the deep cultural and religious differences, the 'trapped' minority status of some large *ethnies* (Efiks, Tiv, Ibibio) and the ability of the three largest communities to 'amass' the new administrative states created by the government (to secure larger shares of federal benefits), the chances of creating a common 'political culture' out of recent West African

colonial experiences and the nationalist struggle must remain problematic.[27]

In other cases post-colonial regimes have tried to forge consciously
supra-ethnic 'civil religions'. Zaire and Syria furnish examples of
this strategy. In Zaire the regime of Mobutu has inculcated and
propagated a common 'Zairian' symbolism and religion in a conscious effort to weld disparate *ethnies* and ethnic categories into a
new nation of Zaire, free of the ethnic strife that marked the hasty
departure of the Belgian colonial power and Katanga's secession.[28]
In Syria Assad's regime seeks to forge a new socialistic Syrian
political identity on the twin bases of army and Ba'ath Party ideology. But that ideology remains strongly pan-Arab and Islamic in
character, drawing on symbols and memories of early Arab glory
under the Umayyads and seeking to revive Damascus as the seat of
a regenerated Arab nation, thereby surmounting ethnic and sectarian
differences within Syria.[29]

The position is rather more complicated in the Indian subconti-
nent. Though the Punjabis provide the dominant ethnic community
in Pakistan, there are a number of competing *ethnies*; yet Islam
provides a rationale for a wider territorial 'political culture' and the
basis for a possible national identity, albeit heavily Punjabi in character. In India Hinduism functions in a similar manner, despite the
presence of large religious minorities and even more competing
ethnies and regions. Here the modern bureaucratic state imposed
by the British was captured by northern and central Hindi-speaking
and Hindu élites; and they have been trying to weld the many
Indian regions and ethnic communities into a single secular, territorial nation by means of a series of interlocking institutions and
cross-cutting ties and through Hindu myths, symbols and customs. A
social religion is used paradoxically to create a measure of cultural
homogeneity above the tolerated diversity of castes, regions, languages and ethnic groups. The revival of Hindu mythology and
values by the mass-mobilizing nationalists became part of the overall
strategy of forging a territorial political identity based on the achievements and boundaries of British rule and an all-India civil service.[30]

The Indian example reveals the importance both of manufactured
political ideology and identity and of pre-existing ethno-religious
ties and symbols from which such an identity could be constructed.

The process involved both cultural and political levels of identity. On the one hand a new cultural concept of 'India', based on the rediscovery of a heroic Indo-Aryan past and its Vedic and Hindu legacy, had to be formulated and disseminated. On the other hand this 'Indian' population had to be mobilized as a single political force, not only against the British but also against persisting local caste, regional and linguistic—ethnic identities. A civic and territorial nationalism had to provide the framework in which a more demotic, vernacular Hindu mass-mobilization could be encouraged. Here the two routes to the formation of nations coexist, sometimes unhappily, providing alternative models of inspiration and visions of 'India'.[31]

How far, then, may we legitimately speak of the 'invention of nations' from colonies by the intelligentsia? In the majority of such cases the element of 'invention' is doubly circumscribed: first by the 'sanctity' of colonial units and boundaries as the basis of the new civic-territorial nation and, second, by the presence of a dominant *ethnie* whose culture and political identity necessarily shapes the character of the state and regime and hence of the emerging nation.

This pattern is found in Indonesia, the Philippines, Malaysia, Burma, Sri Lanka, to some extent in India, Pakistan, Iraq, Egypt, Algeria, Sudan, Kenya, Guinea and Zimbabwe ... The fact that many of these dominant-*ethnie* states encounter fierce opposition from ethnic minorities within the state reveals the failure to 'invent' a new political culture and mythology, one that can encompass or transcend the ethnic identities of both dominant and minority *ethnie* at a time when ethnic nationalism is mobilizing the peripheral, demotic communities and giving them a new, self-aware political assertiveness.

The attempt by dominant *ethnies* – and nations – to use the modern state to incorporate other ethnic communities in the manner of West European state-making and nation-forming processes provoked often determined opposition from many demotic *ethnies*, which the fragile new state could barely contain, let alone subdue.[32] The record to date does not lend support to the view that such territorial 'creations' possess the resources and stability, let alone the ability, to furnish acceptable political cultures that transcend ethnicity or to gain legitimacy for the political domination and culture of the predominant ethnic community.

What about new states in which no one *ethnie* was dominant? Were the chances of creating an acceptable political culture and political community higher in these cases?

The record to date has not been encouraging. Detaching individuals from their primary loyalties to their ethnic communities, at least to the extent of inculcating a larger, public loyalty to the 'state-nation', has been attempted in a number of cases but has had variable results. In Tanzania, where there have been no larger ethnic communities to compete for domination, the inculcation of a Tanzanian national identity has gone farthest, aided by the drive to a particular version of agrarian socialism and by the dominance of a single party and its highly respected leader. In other states, like Nigeria and Uganda, ethnic rivalries persist despite determined centralizing policies and administrative measures designed to depoliticize the major competing *ethnies*. But there has also been progress in securing a measure of attachment among the more educated middle class for the post-colonial territorial units through the state's determined use of political symbolism in the schools, press, radio and TV. At the same time some early post-colonial regimes sought to mobilize their polyethnic populations for participatory sacrifices through the agency of a vigorous 'political religion', in which the nation was viewed as sinless and seamless and the state (and leader) was seen as its political expression, as in Nkrumah's Ghana and Nasser's Egypt. This had the effect of legitimating a relatively novel concept, the territorial nation, and its accompanying political identity – legitimation that was reinforced by the strong stand taken by continental organizations like the OAU (in 1964) to uphold the colonial partition of Africa in the form of existing colonial boundaries.[33]

This commitment to the sanctity of colonial boundaries has been maintained, despite some signs of a less rigid interpretation of the concept of the unitary territorial state, at least within its boundaries, as revealed in the Nigerian Constitution's nineteen states and the 1980 Sudanese experiment with six main regions, though this has not allayed southern suspicions of northern Islamic hegemony.[34]

Such evidence, however, as well as the relative failure of ethnic secession movements to date, is negative. It illustrates at most the coercive and economic power of the state in its role as one of the main employers and the fiscal manager. It tells us little about the growth of a clear cultural and political territorial identity among the population at large. As we shall see, attempts to mobilize the population for greater participation run considerable risks of ethnic fragmentation, particularly where the state apparatus is not equal to the task of containment.

Even in those states that have adopted a socialist or Marxist route towards transcending ethnicity, success in creating a mass 'political culture' has been partial to date. In Mozambique a unitary, territorial concept has been created in the absence of any dominant *ethnie* and in the wake of the political unification of the movements of resistance to Portuguese rule in the 1960s. But in Angola (as in Ethiopia and Burma) ethnicity has provided a base for political divisions leading to civil war, as the rival movements of resistance to Portuguese rule, based on the BaKongo, Ovimbundu and Akwambundu, failed to unite in their guerrilla struggles. Hence any progress towards creating a primary Angolan territorial political identity is bound to be slow and shaky.[35]

More generally, the spate of periodic ethnic movements in non-Western states, whether they originated as parts of old empires or as colonies, is evidence of the revitalization of ethnic ties among demotic communities and the ethnic politicization of ethnic categories, all of which hamper efforts to 'invent' territorial nations where none existed. It is where the new state is built up around a dominant *ethnie*, as in the West itself, that, paradoxically, the best chance of creating a 'territorial nation' and political community exists.

THE 'CIVIC NATION' OF THE INTELLIGENTSIA

Can we characterize more fully the nature of the territorial political identity that non-Western nationalists have been striving to create? What type of community is it that their nationalism seeks to realize?

The answers to such questions will, of course, vary considerably in detail, and they must not be confused with a reality that is frequently a grotesque caricature of nationalist aspirations. Nevertheless, we can, I think, single out recurrent features of these territorial nationalisms and the political identities that they aim to forge. These include the following.

1. *Territorialism*   I mean by this a political commitment not simply to particular boundaries, however they originated, but to a particular spatial and social location among other territorial nations. The basis of this commitment is a belief in the importance of residence and propinquity, as opposed to descent and genealogy. 'Living together' and being 'rooted' in a particular terrain and soil become the criteria for citizenship and the bases of political community. Often such criteria are wedded to notions of return to agrarian simplicity and self-sufficiency and to the rustic virtues corrupted by urban luxury.

The nation is conceived of as a territorial *patria*, the place of one's birth and childhood, the extension of hearth and home. It is also the place of one's ancestors and of the heroes and cultures of one's antiquity. Hence from the standpoint of a territorial nationalist it is quite legitimate to annex the monuments and artefacts of earlier civilizations *in the same place*, appropriating their cultural achievements to differentiate and glorify the territorial nation, which may (to date) lack achievements of its own. Contemporary Iraqis may therefore appropriate the ancient Babylonian culture from Hammurabi to Nebuchadrezzar; Ghanaians may appropriate the glories of the medieval empire of Ghana many miles to the north; and Zimbabweans may seek to incorporate the mysterious monument and civilization of Great Zimbabwe into their political self-image. In other words, the *patria* must become an historic territory.[36]

2. *Participation*   Of course, all nationalisms presuppose the active participation of all citizens, at least in theory. In practice such participation is often heavily circumscribed. What is important to territorial nationalists is the active participation of all citizens *on a territorial and civic basis*. It is a form of territorial populism that is often practised, an appeal over the heads of chiefs, elders, religious leaders, village headmen and the like to every potential citizen of the nation (or 'nation-to-be'). In the Gold Coast Nkrumah's Convention People's Party appealed, through its rural branches, to members of different ethnic communities and categories to form a populist following for the party and its leader. The basis of that appeal was not ethnic, religious or familial but to the individual as a resident, and hence citizen-to-be, of the territory and hence nation-to-be.[37]

Similarly, the one-party system, which allows debate within the organization, is organized on a territory-wide basis and seeks to involve in its activities every citizen throughout the territory of the state. (There are some exceptions to this rule, and we shall return to them in the next chapter.)

3. *Citizenship* This again is not unique to territorial nations (legal citizenship being a concomitant of any nation), but it assumes a peculiarly prominent role in territorial nations and nationalisms. For here citizenship is used not simply to underline membership of the nation and differentiate 'us' from 'them' but even more to outbid the claims of competing allegiances and identities, notably ethnic ones. Given the frequent salience of the latter, legal citizenship carries strong moral and economic overtones, becoming the main device for exclusion but also the chief agency of inclusion and benefits (in jobs, education, health care, etc.), irrespective of ethnic origins.

Again, this is a conception more honoured in the breach than the observance, but it remains the touchstone for progress towards the nationalist ideal of the civic-territorial nation and the basis on which individuals can claim legal rights in the political community.

4. *Civic education* This is potentially the most significant feature of territorial nationalism and the identity it seeks to create. Observers often remark on the seriousness with which the regimes of new states embark on campaigns for literacy and primary education of the whole population and, sometimes, for (some) secondary education. Equally important is the content of that education in the territorial nations. If the curriculum is secular and Western (except in some Islamic states), its spirit is largely 'civic' in character. That is to say, education is as much for the benefit of the national community as for the individual. There is far greater emphasis on the service to the community that the individual can provide, and the debt that he or she incurs, even if this is conveyed indirectly by social approval rather than by indoctrination.[38]

A 'civic' emphasis in the education system is not confined to non-Western or territorial nationalisms. It may be traced back to the Jacobin *patriots* of the French Revolution and was a feature of the French Third Republic and of the education systems in the modern

United States. The point is only that, in the absence of a stress on vernacular education of ethnic members, the civic element plays a greater role exactly because of the weight placed on training for citizenship in territorial nations. If ethnic cleavages are to be eroded in the longer term, it is argued, this can be done only by a pronounced emphasis on inculcating social mores in a spirit of civic equality and fraternity. Part at least of the contents of that education may be termed civic too. For it may be used to convey, through language (assuming there to be a *lingua franca*), history, the arts and literature, a political mythology and symbolism of the new nation (or the 'nation-to-be') that will legitimate its novel, even revolutionary, directions in the myths, memories, values and symbols of its anti-colonial struggle, its movements for social and political liberation and its visions of distant heroes and 'golden ages' that may inspire similar self-sacrifice today.[39]

Cui bono? Whose interests do all these aspirations and ideals of territorial nationalists ultimately serve?

It would be tempting to answer: the interests of the bourgeoisie, the middle classes, even the intelligentsia – there would be some truth in each characterization depending on how one defined each social category – tempting, but ultimately misleading.

It may be true that, at the cultural level, national*ism*, the ideology and language, is a product of intellectuals and that intellectuals tend to be attracted to its promise. At the political level, however, intellectuals proper are much less in evidence. Their place is taken, variously, by other groups. And, to complicate matters, the 'same' social category can possess different meanings in different societies.

This is relatively clear in the case of the bourgeoisie. The term can, of course, be specified precisely in the context of Marxist theory. But then its relevance is limited to capitalist or semi-capitalist societies. To enlarge it by including officers, police, top bureaucrats and politicians, traditional élites and leading members of the liberal professions, to make up what Markovitz calls the 'organizational bourgeoisie', is to dilute it to the point of destroying its explanatory power.[40] Similarly with the ubiquitous middle class(es) and the intelligentsia, which is variously described as 'free-floating' (Mannhein), 'modernizing' (J. H. Kautsky), the rising 'New Class' (Gouldner).[41]

In fact, the social composition of nationalist movements, viewed comparatively, is both cross-class and highly variable depending on the historical juncture and the phase of the movement. Not only 'workers' and 'peasants' (or segments thereof) but also officers, lower clergy, minor (sometimes major!) aristocrats, as well as intellectuals proper, merchants and industrialists, technicians and members of the liberal professions, can be found among their adherents. This should not surprise us. We have seen how complex, abstract and multi-dimensional is the concept of national identity – so much so that different social groups can at different historical junctures feel that their needs, interests and ideals are served in and through identification with the abstract but emotionally very concrete nation.[42]

The question may, with these cautions, still be legitimately posed: *cui bono?* Whose interests, in particular, are served by national identifications on a territorial and civic basis at different times?

Once again it appears that one group in particular plays a prominent role in *early* territorial nationalisms, though other social groups are also frequently active. That group is often called the intelligentsia (here distinguished from the much smaller circles of intellectuals) if by that term we mean simply the professionals.

It was among these professionals (lawyers, doctors, engineers, journalists, teachers, etc.) that early civic and territorial nationalisms found their primary support – though in certain instances a number of businessmen, managers and traders were also attracted to the promise of a centralized, regulated and territory-wide market in the new civic nation, wherever, of course, some degree of capitalist enterprise was permitted.

We should exercise caution in making such an assertion. The professionals do not usually originate the ideology of the civic nation. Theirs is a more practical role: that of disseminating the idea and realizing it in political institutions and activities. Nor do most of the intelligentsia – the professionals – usually participate in these activities. Many are concerned with their own career prospects. But then many people do not join social movements, save in exceptional circumstances.[43]

In the ex-colonies, however, the lack of a developed civil society, the dominance of the state and its bureaucratic institutions and the need for communication skills in the development of anti-colonial nationalisms placed the professionals in positions of leadership on the eve and the morrow of independence. In the early post-independence African legislatures the leading social category was that of the professionals, followed some way behind by the entrepreneurs, managers and traders. Many of the leaders of the Asian and African states were also drawn from the professional strata immediately after independence, and several studied in Western institutions of higher education, including Kenyatta, Nkrumah, Ho Chi Minh, Manley, Senghor and Gandhi. They were part of wider circles that, disappointed by the gulf between Western, Christian ideals and colonial political practice, sought to return to their communities and fulfil their messianic dreams through their own peoples. Yet most of them did not return all the way to those peoples; they took from the West its model of the civic and territorial nation and sought to adapt it to their communities. In other words, theirs was not a real 'ethnic solution', for it was not the particular *ethnie* to which they necessarily or primarily returned. Even when circumstances compelled them to seek their power base in one of the ethnic communities that made up the colonial state they still aspired to rule over the whole of the territory once the colonial power was ejected, and to create a new territorial nation and civic political identity above or in place of the various smaller ethnic communities.[44]

There is, in fact, an 'elective affinity' between the adapted model of a civic, territorial nation and the status needs and interests of the professionals (and, to a lesser extent, of the commercial bourgeoisie). The demand of the professional is for a 'career open to talent', for an income worthy of his or her skills and for a status commensurate with the dignity of the vocation. These demands are most easily satisfied in a territorial nation with a civic ideology, albeit one tailored to local communal beliefs and needs. The equality of rights and duties embodied in a common citizenship, the lack of barriers to mobility, geographical and social, inherent in a residential territorialism, the summons to active participation in public affairs, and above all the emphasis upon a standardized, public, civic education, often with considerable secular and rationalist content – all these features of the civic-territorial model of the nation are conducive to the realization of the interests and status demands of aspiring professionals.

This is not the only, perhaps not the major, reason for the persistence of the territorial-civic model of the nation. It is, after all, a fundamental assumption of the inter-state order and its juridical definition of the state. But the leading role of local intelligentsias must not be overlooked. It helps to flesh out the bare structure of the inter-state system and its components by its pressure for social integration and cultural homogeneity in the public realm and by its holding up of a different image of political community from that offered by ethnic nationalists. Though the reality usually falls far short of that image, though many populations fail as yet to identify with a territorial and civic community, the pressures to do so – and thereby to achieve a measure of integration and homogeneity – remain powerful.

That such images and pressures bear different connotations in different societies, that homogeneity, civic education or territorial participation may mean somewhat different things in Angola, Nigeria and Pakistan, is undeniable. Yet there remains for many of the professionals, merchants and bureaucrats of non-Western states a common language – common concepts and symbols – of civic-territorial nationalism that underlies many of the actions of such states and their élites in the inter-state systems and by means of which they make sense of their relations and actions.

But it is only one of the nationalist ideologies and languages in the contemporary world. It faces challenges from many sides, not least from a rival form of nationalism and national identity. It is to that rival and its political consequences that we must now turn.

CHAPTER 6

Separatism and Multi-nationalism

The impact of nationalism on the rise and incidence of national identities is not confined to the creation of territorial nations. Perhaps even more significant, and certainly more explosive, has been its role in the formation of ethnic nations. It is the challenge of ethno-nationalism to the world order of states that has brought nationalism, and nations, into such disrepute in so many quarters. To assess the validity of this judgement, we need to look more closely at the impact of ethnic nationalism today and in the recent past.

We need first to recall our distinction between the two models of the nation, the civic–territorial and the ethnic–genealogical, and the two routes of the formation of nations, that of bureaucratic incorporation and that of vernacular mobilization. Those nations created by aristocratic élites from a lateral community by using a strong state to incorporate lower strata and outlying areas have predictably manifested a fervent territorial nationalism, both towards minorities within the politically demarcated territory and to enemies outside its boundaries. In contrast, those nations created 'from below' by excluded intelligentsias and some middle strata from a vertical community, using cultural resources (ethno-history, language, ethnic religion, customs, etc.) to mobilize other strata into an active, politicized 'nation', have equally predictably evinced a powerful ethnic nationalism directed both inwards to galvanize and purify the 'true' nation and its members, and outwards against alien oppressors and competitors for political power. It is this latter kind of nation and nationalism that accounts for the vast majority of active nationalisms today.

RECURRENCE OF DEMOTIC ETHNO-NATIONALISM

We can, in fact, distinguish several waves of ethnic nationalisms since the late eighteenth century. The first is the classic period of ethnic self-determination in the early to late nineteenth century, with its main centres in Eastern Europe and a little later the Middle East. Generally speaking, movements of ethnic self-determination mobilized some of the middle and lower strata into a vernacular politicized culture and then attempted to secure the secession of that community and its 'historic' territory from large, unwieldy empires. Essentially such movements were directed against regimes that were both modernizing and autocratic. The regimes generally ruled over a medley of ethnic communities and categories whom the rulers sought to integrate and, usually fitfully, homogenize. Hence, classic ethnic nationalism can be seen as both provoker of, and response to, an 'official' imperial nationalism of the dominant *ethnie*'s ruling élites, as in the case of the Habsburg, Romanov and Ottoman empires.[1]

A second group or wave of ethnic nationalisms emerged in the overseas territories of European colonial empires in the early to mid-twentieth century. Such movements continue to challenge the peace and stability of post-colonial states in Africa and Asia today. We find early intimations of such demotic ethno-nationalisms in Bengal at the turn of the century, and among Kurds, Karen, Ewe, Somali and BaKongo before and after the Second World War. Such movements, like their European predecessors, aim at outright secession from the (colonial and) post-colonial state that is seen, in a manner analogous to the earlier European empires, as an alien intrusion or imposition, despite the fact of its claim to be autochthonous. Demotic ethno-nationalisms bring the contrasts between state and nation into sharp focus; all across Africa and Asia they mobilize distinct ethnic communities in the name of submerged and neglected, but irreplaceable, culture-values, threatened with extinction by the forces of modernization and the bureaucratic state that in turn is often at the service of a dominant *ethnie* and its élites. For Tamils, Sikhs, Moros, Baluchis, Pathans, Uzbeks, Kazhaks, Armenians, Azeris, Kurds, Georgians, Palestinians, South Sudanese, Eritreans, Tigre, Oromo, Luo, Ganda, Ndebele, Ovimbundu, BaKongo, Lunda, Ewe, Ibo and many others, the new states into which colonialism incorporated them are viewed with sentiments that range from reserve to outright hostility, which may spill over into protracted wars of ethnic liberation threatening the stability of whole regions.[2]

Even in the West and the 'old, continuous nations' of Europe, ethno-nationalism has renewed itself. Since the 1960s a third wave of ethnic movements for autonomy or separation has swept through much of Western Europe, reaching Yugoslavia, Romania, Poland and the Soviet Union. Perhaps the earliest manifestations of this particular wave could be found in Canada, among the Quebecois, and in the United States, among the Southern Blacks and later the Indians and Hispanics. On the other hand a good many of the European ethno-nationalisms (for example, the Catalan, Basque, Breton, Scots, Welsh and Flemish movements) were pre-war in origin, with cultural antecedents reaching back in some cases to the 1880s.[3]

It is this third wave of ethno-nationalisms that has prompted a critical reassessment of theories of the national identity. For the earlier diffusionist models of historians and socio-demographers like Deutsch and Lerner failed to explain why members of particular ethnic communities are available for vernacular mobilization and political activism. Besides, they too readily assumed a secular tendency for smaller communities with 'low' cultures to be assimilated by their dominant ethnic neighbours, a prediction that events in the 1960s and 1970s clearly disproved.[4]

The place of diffusionist models has been largely taken by dependency models, which stress the processes of 'internal colonialism' by which peripheral communities are economically and politically subordinated to core *ethnies*, especially during and after industrialization. But here too there have been problems. Approaches that emphasize the dependence of the 'periphery' on the 'core' fail to explain the incidence and timing of recent ethno-nationalisms. Industrialization often long antedated the rise of such movements, and ethno-nationalism appears to correlate with no specific type of socio-economic background. We find vigorous ethno-nationalisms in economic settings as diverse as Slovenia and Catalonia on the one hand and Corsica and Brittany on the other, with Wales and Flanders occupying an economic middle ground. As Walker Connor has demonstrated, there appears to be no correlation between degrees of ethno-nationalism and economic factors of any kind.[5]

For these reasons we need to look more closely at the significance of Western 'neo-nationalism' against the background of the wider global movement of ethnic mobilization. For on the success or failure of such movements hangs much of the shape and meaning of national identity in the future, as well as the stability of the various regional systems of states in the world.

In fact all these demotic ethno-nationalisms exhibit remarkable similarities in their goals and meanings for the participants, despite changes in the social composition and consumption of these nationalisms. These similarities stem from the basic processes of vernacular mobilization and cultural politicization that are the hall-marks of the route by which demotic vertical *ethnies* are transformed into ethnic nations. As a result, the type of national identity that they generate is quite different from the territorial civic identities examined in the last chapter, and it poses a radical challenge to the plural nature of most contemporary states.

ETHNIC SEPARATISM FROM OLD EMPIRES

The classic cases of ethnic self-determination in the last century were those of Eastern Europe and the Middle East. But, even then, there were instances of ethnic separatism on the western, northern and southern fringes of Europe: in Ireland, Norway, Finland, Brittany, Catalonia and the Basque country. The links and overlappings of classic and later ethnic 'neo-nationalisms' are typical – they reveal the kinship of the various 'waves' of separatist ethnic nationalisms and their common cultural groundwork.[6]

What was this common cultural basis? The goals of all these movements were remarkably similar. They included:

1. the creation of a literary 'high' culture for the community where it was lacking
2. the formation of a culturally homogeneous 'organic' nation
3. securing a recognized 'homeland', and preferably an independent state for the community
4. turning a hitherto passive *ethnie* into an active ethno-political community, a 'subject of history'.

The cultural basis for the pursuit of these aims was the presence and/or rediscovery of a distinctive 'ethno-history'. Where that history was deficient it would have to be reconstructed and even 'invented' in places. In either case the uses of ethno-history were always selective: it was as important to forget certain things as to remember others.

The uses of ethno-history were essentially social and political. Nationalists were interested not in inquiring into 'their' past for its own sake, but in the reappropriation of a mythology of the territorialized past of 'their people'. Throughout, the basic process was one of vernacular mobilization of a passive *ethnie*, and the politicization of its cultural heritage through the cultivation of its poetic spaces and the commemoration of its golden ages.

Cultivating poetic spaces meant, first of all, identifying a sacred territory that belonged historically to a particular community, and that was thereby sanctified by the association. Such a sacred homeland held within its domains places of pilgrimage and reverence – Mount Zion, Mount Ararat, Mount Meru, Croag Patrick, Qom, Yasna Gora – places of historical collective salvation and redemption, where saints and sages had inspired their followers or the deity had appeared to the community or its representatives. From these sacred historic centres the light of ethnic election shone forth to consecrate the whole land.[7]

Cultivating poetic spaces also signified a process of turning natural features of the homeland into historical ones, and naturalizing historical monuments. Rivers like the Danube and Rhine, mountains like Zion and Olympus, lakes like the Vierwaldstättersee and lake Peipius, have become humanized and historicized by their associations with communal myth and endeavour. Conversely, historical monuments like Stonehenge, the Breton dolmens, megaliths, tells and ruined temples, have all become part of a particular ethnic or regional landscape, an inseparable component and memorial of older civilizations absorbed by the flow of time into their natural habitats. It was just these natural and monumental features that struck so rich a chord in the ethnic nationalism of the returning intelligentsia when they sought to rediscover their ethno-history and mobilize their peoples through vernacular culture. For composers, artists and writers, the nationalist myth of poetic landscapes evoked powerful sentiments of nostalgia and identification, which they amplified and diffused through their art. For Smetana and Dvořák in Bohemia, Sibelius in Finland, Bartók and Kodály in Hungary, and Borodin and Moussorgsky in Russia, their country's landscapes and changing seasons, legends and monuments, stirred strong nationalist passions that through their music they were able to communicate to large and receptive publics.[8]

Equally important was the celebration and commemoration of the heroic past. Max Weber remarked on this aspect of demotic ethnic nationalism, apropos of the Alsatians whom the German Reich had annexed, when he wrote of their sense of community with the French (despite the fact that many Alsatians were German-speakers): 'This can be understood by any visitor who walks through the museum in Colmar, which is rich in relics such as tricolors, *pompier* and military helmets, edicts by Louis Philippe and especially memorabilia from the French Revolution; these may appear trivial to the outsider, but they have sentimental value for the Alsatians. This sense of community came into being by virtue of common political and, indirectly, social experiences which are highly valued by the masses as symbols of the destruction of feudalism, and the story of these events takes the place of the heroic legends of primitive peoples.'[9]

These historical memories and heroic legends are not, in fact, confined to 'primitive peoples'. We find them throughout the first great wave of classic Eastern European and Middle Eastern nationalisms – among Poles and Czechs, Finns and Armenians, Germans, Turks and Arabs. In each case nationalists rediscovered and often exaggerated the heroism of past ages, the glories of ancestral civilizations (often not 'their own') and the exploits of their great national heroes, even when those heroes belonged more to the realm of legend than history and, if they lived, knew nothing of the nation which was so busy reclaiming them from obscurity. Siegfried, Cuchulain, Arthur, Lemminkainen, Nevsky, Agamemnon, formerly heroes of ancient sagas, were now elevated into exemplars of national virtue and prototypes of the regenerated 'new man' extolled by ethnic nationalists everywhere.[10]

Whom did these rediscoveries and reconstructions serve? In the first place a deracinated intelligentsia, seeking entry into the 'living past' of their resurrected *ethnie* in order to mobilize its members in the quest for social status and political power. By placing their professional skills at the service of their newly-found community, the returning intelligentsia attempts to bridge the gulf between themselves and the majority of 'their' ethnic populations generated by the rationalist 'culture of critical discourse' that they have imbibed through their increasingly secular education.[11]

But, equally important, the beneficiaries of this return to a reconstructed ethno-history are the members of the mobilized *ethnie* at large. For their status is reversed through the process of vernacular mobilization: not simply in the sense of being activated, and no longer passive objects of external domination, but more particularly because it is a form of *their* folk culture that is appropriated by the historicist intellectuals and elevated into a literary 'high' culture. For the first time the masses become the subject of history, under the slogan of popular sovereignty. At the same time in *their* culture is sought the individuality, the uniqueness, and hence the *raison d'être*, of the community-turned-nation.[12]

In the process of vernacular mobilization quite new 'relations of communication' are forged. Where familial and ethnic modes of communicating values, symbols, myths and memories, and of socializing new generations in these traditions, had prevailed in many areas, the effect of vernacular mobilization by a returning intelligentsia was to create a new mode of 'national' communication and socialization, in which ethnic values, myths and memories became the basis of a political nation and a politically mobilized community. Under the aegis of different kinds of intelligentsia in conjunction with certain classes (usually bourgeoisie, but sometimes lower aristocracy or even workers) a new and distinctly national identity is created, which diffuses a reconstructed ethnic folk culture to all classes of the community. That identity has its civic elements, too; members are now legal citizens of the political ethno-nation, and they begin to define themselves in territorial terms as well. But the basis of their kind of national identity remains true to its demotic roots; the national identity created by intellectuals and intelligentsia among formerly vertical *ethnies* strives to stay close to its putative ethnic culture and boundaries. Mass mobilizing ethnic nationalism creates a political nation in the image of its presumed ethnic roots.

Hence the very different form that national identities take among communities created by the mobilization and transformation of formerly demotic *ethnies*, at once more intense and often more inward-looking than territorially-based national identities. The deep preoccupation of many Irish nationalists with the revival of a Gaelic culture, or the powerful sentiments evoked among Finns by the rediscovery of Karelia, its landscape, history and poetry, are typical of this intense rediscovery and spiritual mobilization of a lost ethnic past in the service of a newly politicized community, where every member must be re-educated into the new vernacular culture that claims to be the only authentic voice of the people.[13]

The consequences of this intense preoccupation with an 'authentic' vernacular culture and history are well known. In Eastern Europe and parts of the Middle East it inevitably brought populations that had long lived side by side in stable, if sometimes uneasy, relations into competition and even conflict. In ethnically mixed areas the quest for a homeland in which the authentic culture could be explored and realized helped to create antagonisms or exacerbate pre-existing rivalries. By the late nineteenth century these areas in particular became the scene of the most intense conflicts and terror.[14]

Terror and instability were aggravated, not only by the passions aroused by the process of vernacular mobilization, but also by the slow but visible decline of the old empires in which most demotic *ethnies* had been incorporated. For centuries the only source of political legitimacy in these areas had been the imperial state and its monarchs. There was no obvious and accepted alternative. To locate an alternative source in the historic culture–community was not only to create a new type of political identity, but also to elevate that identity into the underlying principle of a new political order, one that derived political authority from the doctrine of a sovereign people. Hence the importance of repeated 'French revolutions' in lending credence to the idea of a sovereign culture–community as the sole legitimate source of political authority, within that exemplar of a compact nation in the very heart of the prestigious West. Only that example and that prestige could have given political legitimacy to the intelligentsia's programme of vernacular mobilization, and turned a moral and cultural transformation into a political and social revolution. The reverberations of the French Revolution in the hinterlands of the Habsburg, Ottoman and even Romanov empires, were felt well into the twentieth century.[15]

But the fusion of French ideals of the sovereign people and

vernacular mobilization of pre-modern demotic *ethnies* by the intelligentsia produced a rather different model of 'national identity' among these folk communities. Popular participation, rather than civil and political rights; populist organization, more than democratic parties; intervention by the people's nation-state, rather than protection of minorities and individuals from state interference: these became for many decades the hallmarks of the newly formed ethno-political nations erected on the basis of pre-modern demotic *ethnies*. This attempt to fuse the civic ideals of the territorial nation with the genealogical attachments of the ethno-political nation, usually in the wake of a secessionist struggle from large empires, has provided the model for subsequent waves of vernacular mobilization and the creation of separatist ethno-political communities in the new states of Africa and Asia, as well as the old states of the West.

ETHNIC SEPARATISM IN POST-COLONIAL STATES

The vast majority of ethnic separatist movements after the Second World War have occurred in the newly formed states of Africa and Asia. In other words, they have sprung in a double sense from colonialism: first, because it was the colonial state that brought many quite separate and distant ethnic communities and categories under a single political jurisdiction, increasing both the scale of politics and the chances of conflict over centrally distributed resources; second, because it was during the process of decolonization, during the years of decline and handover, that ethnic separatisms emerged to challenge the civic order of the future post-colonial state and its territorial national identity.

The basic processes at work in these post-war ethnic separatisms are similar to those of classic ethnic nationalism. But their order is often telescoped or even reversed. Instead of the politicization of the *ethnie* and its heritage succeeding the process of vernacular mobilization by an intelligentsia, as in Eastern Europe and the fringes of that continent, we often find the two processes occurring together or even changing their usual sequence. Whereas in Europe the nationalist movement emerged from a preceding cultural 'reawakening' over some decades, in Asia and Africa the two kinds of nationalism were often conjoined or simultaneous. Among the

Kurds, for example, the first cultural and literary organizations sprang up in the wake of the Young Turk *coup* in 1908. Apart from a short-lived Kurdish journal founded in 1898, the first Kurdish cultural organization (*Taali we Terakii Kurdistan*, Recovery and Progress of Kurdistan) was formed in the autumn of 1908, publishing a lively cultural gazette in Istanbul, and young intellectuals set up Kurdish clubs in the main Kurdish cities. By 1912 the first Kurdish political association, *Kiviya Kurd* (Kurdish Hope), created in 1910, was legalized. The First World War interrupted Kurdish political activity, as did the ensuing deportations and massacre of Kurds; but new political organizations, notably *Kurdistan Taali Djemiyeti* (the Society for the Recovery of Kurdistan), took up the struggle. The campaign to standardize the script and modernize the Kurdish language is an offshoot of the wider nationalist political struggle and proceeds *pari passu* with politicization of a tribally divided ethnic community in the various guerrilla campaigns against the Turks, Iraqis and Iranians, notably in the 1960s and 1970s.[16]

In the case of the Baluchi in Pakistan, though their intellectuals can look back to a long history and a rich and ancient folklore, it is clear that the process of vernacular mobilization developed as an outgrowth of a Baluchi political nationalism from 1947 onwards. It is only recently, for example, that a distinctive Baluchi alphabet, based on a modified form of the Persianized Nastaliq style of the Arabic alphabet, was used in a Baluchi textbook produced in Canada in 1969, but many Baluch nationalist works are written in Urdu and English. In this case recurrent wars with the central authorities in Pakistan have engendered widespread Baluch national consciousness, cutting across tribal divisions, while gradual urbanization and education has produced a literate class that is providing a new nationalist leadership.[17]

In still other cases, such as those of the Palestinians and Eritreans, the process of vernacular mobilization must first discover an ethnic past that is serviceable for present needs and then create a unified and distinctive consciousness and sense of ethnic community out of a politicized common culture. In the Palestinian case this means accentuating a separate Palestinian cultural personality and distinguishing it from the wider Arab identity. In the case of Eritrea cultural unity must be created out of the common fate of regional unity and political struggle. In both cases it is the military and political struggle itself that will provide the crucible of vernacular mobilization, though here too it presupposes some measure of cultural symbolism held in common.[18]

Current cases of separatist ethno-nationalisms, whatever their origins, seek autonomy or secession from relatively new states whose boundaries and *raison d'être* are part of the colonial legacy. The primary source of their disaffection lies in the plural nature and fragile legitimacy of the post-colonial state itself. While economic grievances provide the catalysts of rebellion in most cases, as the new state fails to deliver its promises or favours certain ethnic communities and categories at the expense of others, it is the very nature of the post-colonial state that creates the underlying conditions for the possibility of a resort to secession. Given the considerable power of the state and its offices, not only is ethnic competition for political power in the new states sharpened but victory and defeat carry with them far higher rewards and penalties than in the developed and more unified states of the West. Because social classes are less developed and ethnic ties more pronounced, especially in conditions of urban competition, the political constituencies of leaders and parties are much more likely to be composed of one or more ethnic community or category, distinguished as such in the party's slogans and programmes. Fierce political competition between ethnically defined constituencies tends to harden the boundaries and promote the self-awareness of *ethnies* and ethnic categories; moreover, failure in that competition, particularly if repeated, may drive the defeated community to contemplate secession, especially where its leaders have internalized negative stereotypes or where, as in the Biafran case, such stereotypes helped to create conditions of terror and massacre. Unless, therefore, the leaders of new states take active measures to defuse ethnic cleavages through economic and administrative measures, as the Nigerian leadership since 1975 has attempted to do, or is prepared to use the dominant *ethnie* to repress ethnic opposition by force, the latent tendencies of the new polyethnic states to generate ethnic instability must always be reckoned with.[19]

There is, of course, a close relationship, perhaps a dialectical one, between attempts to create a civic and territorial national identity and movements aiming to separate from that 'territorial nation' one or other ethnic community or category and fashion it into an 'ethnic nation'. The more the leaderships of the new states strive to create integrated territorial nations out of a polyethnic mosaic, the greater the chances of ethnic dissent and even attempted secession wherever colonialism and nationalism have roused a returning intelligentsia to rediscover their ethnic past and its cultural heritage.

Where such pasts can no longer be recovered, or where an intelligentsia that could recover them is absent, neither colonialism nor an integrative territorial nationalism will be able to ignite ethnic dissent, let alone a separatist movement. This is true of many small ethnic categories in sub-Saharan Africa, where it is possible to speak of 'failed nationalisms' in the sense that movements of ethnic nationalism never got off the ground, despite the colonial presence, the beginnings of Western capitalist penetration and the example of other nationalisms near by. In these cases the necessary 'internal' conditions − a stratum of secular intellectuals, a wider intelligentsia and a recoverable ethnic past − were lacking.[20]

This is not to deny the importance, in many cases, of the degree of relative economic and cultural development of different ethnic communities and categories or of the regions in which they are located. The burden of Horowitz's argument turns on just these developmental relationships. Movements of ethnic separatism, he contends, emerge most quickly and frequently among backward ethnic groups in backward regions, like the southern Sudan, Kurdistan, the Karen and Shan of Burma and the Bengalis of Pakistan. They have too little to gain from inclusion in the new states with their project of creating integrated territorial nations. On the other hand, advanced ethnic groups in backward regions are reluctant to secede. They do so only when, as population exporters to other regions of the new states, their position becomes untenable and the costs of remaining become too high. For advanced groups in advanced regions, like the Yoruba, Baganda and Sikhs, secession is likely only if its economic costs are low, and usually it is more profitable for the community to remain within the undivided state. Backward ethnic groups in advanced regions may contemplate secession more easily, but they are rarely preponderant within the region; the anticipated economic benefits of secession are not matched by sufficient political control, with the exception of southern Katanga. In general, economic interest combines with group anxiety to explain the paths to ethnic separatism, but in the greater number of cases group anxiety outweighs perceived economic gains.[21]

Horowitz's matrix of secession is intended to be only a guide. There are too many intervening variables – the severity of ethnic discrimination, civil-service representation, the extent of migration into regions and so on – to be able to deduce the incidence and timing of secession from the relative development of groups and regions. Nevertheless, the fact that it highlights the numerical preponderance of secession movements among backward ethnic groups in backward regions suggests the utility of relating secession to the relative position of groups and regions within the new states.

The problems of this kind of matrix are twofold. First, there is the difficulty of pinning down terms like 'advanced' and 'backward', given the possible combinations of indicators and the fluctuating evaluations and conflicting stereotypes in each case. The Eritrean and Biafran cases illustrate the difficulty of applying such terms to whole groups or deducing outcomes from hypotheses based on these terms. Recent events in the Baltic states also cast doubt on predictions about the reluctance of 'advanced' groups in 'advanced' regions to secede. Second, as these cases suggest, entirely different factors need to be fed into any such matrix, making it far more complex and difficult to use. I am thinking of factors like the degree of political repression (as Horowitz concedes in the Basque case) and democratic freedom, the opportunities for cultural and political mobilization and the presence or absence of an intelligentsia, as well as a usable ethnic past, however recent. The existence of ethnic antagonisms in the past is also a relevant factor in the aftermath of colonialism and in the context of a fragile new state.[22]

But perhaps the most potent factor, and the one that most influences the chances of creating new ethnic nations, is the determination and power of the élites who control the apparatus of the new states to resist movements of ethnic secession, often with considerable force. In fact, very few ethnic separatisms have achieved their goals since the Second World War. Most new states were created through the process of decolonization, not secession. The exceptions – Bangladesh and Singapore – were the products of exceptional circumstances; the separation of Singapore, with its overwhelmingly Chinese population, was an agreed process, whereas that of Bangladesh was the result of an unusual geopolitical constellation of regional power. In every other case, notably Biafra, Eritrea, Kurdistan, Kalistan and Tamilnad, neither agreement nor an unusual regional geopolitical constellation exists. While each of these (and other) ethnic separatisms has had its external backers, at least temporarily, none has been able to count on a degree of external support that would force significant concessions from a state whose ruling classes are drawn from the dominant *ethnie* and have set their faces against even a measure of ethnic autonomy. The ensuing political instability has taken many forms, ranging from simmering ethnic discontent to open protracted wars of secession, as in Ethiopia, Angola and Sri Lanka, with little prospect of an early peaceful resolution.[23]

What does this instability bode for the creation of ethno-national identities within the context of post-colonial states? Do the integrative and sometimes discriminatory pressures of these states erode or reinforce the processes of vernacular mobilization and cultural politicization that are the hallmarks of the transformation of demotic *ethnies* into ethno-political nations? It is difficult to be categorical here. It is clear that the pressures of integration have undermined the structures and eroded the cultures of many smaller ethnic categories that lacked literary traditions, as in Siberia and Africa, or had partially lost them, as in parts of Latin America. In these cases the failure to develop or maintain literary 'high' cultures and specialist communications groups has lowered the resistance of these ethnic categories to cultural integration in the post-colonial states. Such categories, perhaps for these reasons, also lacked the political will and military resources to counter acculturation and integration.[24]

On the other hand, where there existed a living cultural and literary tradition that could be adapted to modern conditions, the integrative pressures of the post-colonial state, following on as they often did the divisive policies of colonialism, frequently reinforced the processes of ethnic mobilization and politicization. Growing conflict has itself crystallized a sense of ethnic identity in what was before often only a linguistic or ethno-regional category and may still be divided by religion and ethnic origin, as is the case with

Eritreans and southern Sudanese. Even such well-known ethnic groups as the Kurds and Ibo knew little unity and cohesion until after the Second World War, the former being divided to this day into mountain tribes that were often in dispute, the latter into villages and districts that were drawn together, in competition with non-Ibo and non-Christians, only by the changes wrought by British colonialism and the fierce ethnic competition after 1960. It is the conflicts with states and other communities in which Kurds and Ibo were involved that have given the members of both groups a wider self-awareness and a sense of their common history and destiny. In this respect the endemic instability of the post-colonial state has fuelled the regional and ethnic conflicts that over the years tend to promote a heightened sense of ethnic identity and strengthen the aspirations for separate ethno-national identity.[25]

Ethnocide and ethnic mobilization, then, are equally possible outcomes of the often fragile but coercive nature of the post-colonial state and its attempts to integrate into a 'territorial nation' a poly-ethnic society. This is true in many cases, despite the efforts of regimes in several states to accommodate, and even satisfy, the economic and political demands of minority *ethnies* and regional ethnic categories. Where this balance no longer holds, where disaffected *ethnies* become alienated enough to resort to terror and revolt, their ethnic nationalism may become the vehicle for a new national identity that draws many members of the community involved in the conflict into a new type of politicized vernacular culture and creates a different kind of participant society. In these cases the movement itself is the prototype and harbinger of a new society and culture. Its cells, schools, guerrilla units, welfare associations, self-help groups, women's societies and labour unions, as well as its songs, flags, dress, poetry, sports, arts and crafts, all presage and create the nucleus of the future ethnic nation and its political identity, even where secession is prevented and the community fails to obtain its own state. In these cases the movement has helped to create a proto-nation out of a demotic *ethnie*, for the nation is not to be equated with the state, even when it aspires to have a state of its own.[26]

SEPARATISM AND AUTONOMISM IN INDUSTRIAL SOCIETIES

A third wave of demotic ethnic nationalisms has been sweeping industrial societies since the late 1950s. This is a new phenomenon: the renewal of nationalism in states that had experienced nationalism before the Second World War and were thought to be immune from its influence. The difference between the ethnic nationalisms of developing societies and those of the developed states is apparent: in the former we are witnessing a straightforward trajectory in which the drive to create territorial nations in the new states evokes a reactive ethnic separatism, whereas in industrial societies we have entered a second cycle in the drama of nationalism, re-enacted on the ashes of former national hatreds. In North America, Europe and the Soviet Union undergoing *perestroika* the interventionist state has rekindled among its ethnic minorities those aspirations for autonomy and even separation that had previously been muted or repressed. No wonder many observers were surprised by the vigour of this nationalist renewal.[27]

What are the new features of this renewal? First, they are, for the most part, autonomist rather than separatist: the majority of followers of the ethnic movement prefer to have cultural, social and economic autonomy while remaining part of the political and military framework of the state into which they were incorporated, often centuries ago. There are exceptions to this generalization. More radical wings of the movement, such as ETA among the Basques and the SNP in Scotland, have opted for outright independence from Spain and Britain; a few movements, as a whole, have expressed separatist aspirations, as with Sajudis in Lithuania. But, on the whole, most ethnic movements in industrial societies have preferred autonomy to separation.[28]

Second, movements of ethnic autonomy recognize the possibility, perhaps desirability, of dual identities, a cultural–national and a political–national identity or, as they would see it, a national identity within a territorial state identity, a Breton nation within France, a Catalan nation within Spain and so on. In other words they recognize the duality of historical memories and political sentiments that cannot easily be severed, not to mention the economic benefits to be gained by remaining within an existing state framework, as for example, the Scots realized during the devolution debate in the 1970s.[29]

Third, movements of ethnic autonomy in industrial societies take place in well-established states enjoying a generally higher standard of living than that of most developing states. They may occur among relatively less advanced groups in less advanced regions, but few of these groups, or their regions, are poor in the manner we encounter in developing societies; Bretons and Brittany cannot be compared with the southern Sudan. In some cases, indeed, both *ethnies* and the regions they occupy are more advanced than the dominant group and the centre; Basques and Catalans, and Slovenes and Croats, enjoy higher levels of economic development than Castile or Serbia. But in all these cases the states of the developed world are less precarious and novel, and their economic base is more advanced, than those of the developing world.[30]

Fourth, with one significant but partial exception, movements for ethnic autonomy in industrial societies are directed against modern 'nation-states', that is to say, states that had for some time been regarded and regarded themselves as 'nations', even though from the standpoint of a strict interpretation of nationalism, they were national hybrids, a mixture of *étatiste* and nationalist principles. The partial exception, of course, is the Soviet Union, which represents a federation of nations preserving borders roughly similar to those of a former empire and held together by a command structure based on Russian national preponderance. So ethnic nationalism in the Soviet Union today wears a double aspect: a movement of ethnic autonomy from the Soviet state, as in the West, and a more separatist rejection of Russian imperial preponderance, a reaction to an older imperial tradition of incorporation. In this sense ethnic nationalism in the Soviet Union is closer to the classic nationalism of the nineteenth century than Western 'neo-nationalisms', which are directed as much against neglect by the 'nation-state' as against its bureaucratic interference.[31]

But there are also more fundamental similarities between the renewal of ethnic nationalism in industrial societies and the earlier waves of ethnic nationalism in nineteenth-century Europe and twentieth-century separatisms in Africa and Asia. For one thing, they are all movements of 'subject peoples' against dominant *ethnies* and 'alien' states and their ruling élites. Theirs are movements of popular mobilization, at least in their rhetoric and slogans, if not always in deed. They are directed against the *status quo*, the existing distribution of power within the polyethnic state, its systematic exclusion or relegation of certain ethnic categories and its denial of their collective culture and rights. In this they contrast sharply with the territorial nationalisms of dominant *ethnies* and their bureaucratic states.[32]

Second, all these demotic movements involve processes of vernacular mobilization and cultural politicization. They are bent on creating a new kind of individual in a new kind of society, the culturally distinct ethnic nation. This means returning to an idealized image of 'what we were', which will serve as an exemplar and guide for the nation-to-be. By returning to an ethnic past the community will discover a cognitive framework, a map and location for its unfocused aspirations. Similarly, 'our past' will teach the present generation not only the virtues of their ancestors but also their immediate duties. It will disclose to the community its true nature, its authentic experience and hidden destiny. From its past the community will discover the inner morality that defines its unique character. Hence the underlying impetus of all these demotic ethnic nationalisms is to rediscover their communities (even where that means 'inventing' large parts of the 'self') through the uses of landscape and history and the resuscitation of dying customs, rituals and languages. It is not enough simply to mobilize the masses; to sustain that mobilization, to turn 'masses' into 'nations', it is first necessary to 'vernacularize' them and thereby bestow a unique identity and destiny upon them.[33]

Third, in all these movements intellectuals and intelligentsias play an important role. The extent, and exact nature, of that role, as we saw, varies according to context; in different societies and periods the meaning of the term 'intelligentsia' may vary, but it varies within definite limits. For it is nevertheless possible to discern the strong influence, and often leadership, of intellectual and professional groups both in the process of vernacular mobilization and in the cultural politicization of wider strata of the community or category. The intellectuals and professionals not only revive customs and

languages, rediscover history and (re-)establish ceremonies and traditions; they also give these activities and rediscoveries a national
political meaning they never previously possessed. From the rediscovery of epics like the *Edda* and *Kalevala* to the revival of
hurling in Ireland and folk singing in Brittany, the leading role of
educators, artists and journalists is evident; and this remains true of
the latest surge of demotic ethnic nationalisms in industrial societies.[34]

The renewal of nationalism in industrial societies must, therefore,
be understood not as something new and *sui generis* but as a new
phase of the whole process of demotic vernacular mobilization that
has been sweeping various parts of the world since the eighteenth
century and possibly earlier, if we include the Puritan Dutch and
English movements in the early and mid seventeenth century.[35]

The kinship between all these movements is also historical. In fact,
several of the 'recent' movements for ethnic autonomy in the West
are really not at all recent; they merely experienced an upsurge of
support in the 1960s. But that upsurge built on pre-existing vehicles
and ideals formed before 1939 and in some cases – Wales, Scotland,
Catalonia, Euzkadi, Brittany – before 1914. In all these cases a
cultural renaissance, literary, linguistic and historical, preceded the
formation of political movements demanding ethnic autonomy.[36]

There is really nothing surprising about this upsurge of ethnic
nationalism among minorities within old-established, industrial
states, just as there is no cause for wonder at the subsequent revival
of nationalism in the communist states of Eastern Europe and the
Soviet Union. In each case we are dealing with perceptions of
neglected or suppressed identity, and in each case it is the centralized
state itself that is held to blame. One has to admit that in this matter
the state can do no right; benign neglect is as much cause for
grievance as crass intervention.[37] That is why it is perhaps wiser to
treat the state's role as that of powerful catalyst of underlying
conditions and sentiments that must be sought elsewhere. This is
not to absolve it of all responsibility for ethnic unrest. Clearly, state
policies can greatly exacerbate (as well as determine the timing and
intensity of) underlying sentiments and conditions, particularly when
the state acts in an ethnically partisan manner, as not infrequently
happens and not only in the developing states.[38]

Where then should we look for the causes of those conditions and sentiments that so often fuel movements of ethnic autonomy and separation? Obviously the answer to such a broadly framed question will vary with the period and area under consideration. But we can, I think, usefully single out certain recurrent factors that together create the conditions and promote the sentiments that underlie the proliferation and renewal of ethnic nationalisms all over the world. It is these factors, and the prospects for 'national identity' in the next century, that we need finally to address.

CHAPTER 7

Beyond National Identity?

Of all the collective identities in which human beings share today, national identity is perhaps the most fundamental and inclusive. Not only has national*ism*, the ideological movement, penetrated every corner of the globe; the world is divided, first and foremost, into 'nation-states' – states claming to be nations – and national identity everywhere underpins the recurrent drive for popular sovereignty and democracy, as well as the exclusive tyranny that it sometimes breeds. Other types of collective identity – class, gender, race, religion – may overlap or combine with national identity but they rarely succeed in undermining its hold, though they may influence its direction. Governments and states may muzzle the expression of national aspirations for a time, but it is likely to be a costly and ultimately fruitless expedient. For the forces that sustain national allegiances have proved, and are likely to prove, stronger than any countervailing trends.

Why have national identity and nationalism become so fundamental in the modern world? First, because of their ubiquity. If any phenomena are truly global, then it must be the nation and nationalism. There is scarcely an area of the world that has not been marked by ethnic and national conflicts or witnessed the rise of movements claiming national independence for their chosen populations. The nationalist dream of a world of nations, each homogeneous, united and free, even if far from realization, has been taken up by peoples across the globe, and has inspired popular resistance, effort and conflict. The globalization of nationalism, if not yet of the homogenous nation, is a powerful reality, one that conditions our cultural outlook and political endeavours.[1]

But national identity today is not only global, it is also pervasive. Though there are some situations in which it is felt to be more important than in others, it may also be said to pervade the life of individuals and communities in most spheres of activity. In the cultural sphere national identity is revealed in a whole range of assumptions and myths, values and memories, as well as in language, law, institutions and ceremonies. Socially, the national bond provides the most inclusive community, the generally accepted boundary within which social intercourse normally takes place, and the limit for distinguishing the 'outsider'. The nation may also be seen as the basic unit of moral economy, in terms both of territory and of resources and skills.

In political terms national identity today determines not only the composition of the regime's personnel, but also legitimates and often influences policy goals and administrative practices that regulate the everyday lives of each citizen. Finally the nation and national identity, by commanding the basic political allegiance of citizens, have become the only recognized source of 'inter-national' legitimacy, of the validity of a system of states in each region and continent, and ultimately in the world as a whole. Such order as may be found in the community of states is premissed on the norm of the nation as the sole unit of political loyalty and action.

Third, there is the sheer complexity and variety of the 'nation' and 'national identity'. As we saw in the first chapter, national identity is an abstract and multidimensional construct that touches on a wide range of spheres of life and manifests many permutations and combinations. Historians today tend to curtail the range of 'nationalism', reacting to the tendency of an earlier generation of scholars to inflate the concept. But the nation and nationalism should not be regarded as conceptual refuges of the 'lazy historian', nor should we underestimate their chameleon-like nature and their facility in combining with, and often subsuming, other issues and ideologies. Chinese communism was at first treated as a genuine variety of western Marxism, until it was realized how much Mao's movement owed to Chinese nationalism, both doctrinally and in practice. Today it is the nationalist component of Maoism that is stressed, and the way in which Mao accommodated his Marxism to the national outlook of the Chinese peasantry in its resistance to the Japanese invasion in 1937. Conversely, the anti-communist movements in Eastern Europe in 1989 were at first treated as western-style movements of political and economic liberalism, until it was realized how powerful were the nationalist dimensions of popular mobilization.[2]

The point that is often missed is that national aspirations tend to combine with other non-national economic, social or political issues, and the power of the movement often derives from this combination. It is not that nationalism feeds on other 'rational' issues and interests, as is sometimes assumed. Rather, neglected, oppressed or marginalized ethnic communities or categories fuse their national grievances and aspirations with other non-national aspirations and grievances; so that at a particular point in time there is often a single set of interests being pursued by a given population, which we divide for analytic purposes into 'national' and 'non-national' categories, to isolate the 'national factor'.[3]

SUPRA-NATIONALISM: FEDERAL AND REGIONAL IDENTITIES?

Ubiquitous, pervasive and complex, national identity and nationalism remain powerful and explosive global forces as we approach the third millennium. But are they strong enough to resist the trends of increasing global interdependence? May we not look forward to an early 'supersession of nationalism'?

This was undoubtedly the hope and expectation of liberals and socialists from the early nineteenth century till today. From Comte and Mill to modernization theorists, the evolutionary perspective promised both the attainment of nationhood and its overcoming, as humanity forged ever larger, more inclusive and more powerful units of resource. The erosion of familism, localism and religion would allow the state to oversee humanity's progress towards a global society and culture. Similarly, Marxists envisaged the 'withering away' of the state and the 'transcendence' of nations and nationalism; though national cultures might remain, they would be infused with proletarian values, retaining only their national form.[4]

In support of these hopes liberals and socialists, including many scholars, have pointed to two sets of evidence. The empirical evidence is drawn from various experiments in multinational states, as well as various kinds of regional federation. The theoretical support is sought in the consequences of the new transnational forces and technologies that are spawning a 'post-national' world. Let us consider the two kinds of argument and evidence in turn.

We may start from the oft-remarked fact that most states today are ethnically heterogeneous and plural. For some this means that a new kind of nation is in the making, a 'multinational nation'; for others it means that the nation is being superseded. Clearly, the view one takes will depend largely on the definition of nation adopted, or at any rate the premise of 'homogeneity' of the nation. Even if one assumes that the concept of the nation is a construct exclusively of the nationalists (and I have argued that nationalists were constrained by particular ethno-histories), it is not clear that the demand for a 'homogeneous nation' possessed the same meaning for all nationalists. What all nationalists demanded was autonomy, unity and identity; but neither unity (meaning social, territorial and political union), nor identity (meaning distinctiveness and historical individuality) entailed complete cultural homogenization. Not only have the Swiss managed to achieve political unity; they have also retained a clear sense of historical individuality, despite their linguistic, religious and cantonal divisions. The Swiss have resisted cultural homogenization, despite powerful sentiments of national identity amounting to armed neutrality. Nor are the Swiss entirely alone in this. In both Germany and Italy regionalism has been permitted to flourish, often with strong local institutions, but in neither case has there been a diminution of the sense of national identity and periodic surges of national sentiment.[5]

This means that while some Romantic nationalists have called for complete cultural homogeneity, many others have been content with unification and identification around core values, myths, symbols and traditions, expressed in common customs and institutions, as well as a common homeland. This in turn allows for the possibility of constructing 'territorial nations', as we saw, from polyethnic populations, as so many Third World national élites seek to do.

But if the nation need not be culturally homogeneous, can there be such a thing as a nation that subsumes several incorporated nations? How flexible can the concept of the nation be without losing its fundamental features, particularly those of common culture and history?

Here the Yugoslav model springs to mind. Yugoslavia was built around two concepts: a federation of nations, and a common cultural–historical experience. The latter was sometimes dubbed 'Illyrianism'; but as even its ideologues conceded, it was less the *political* history that held South Slavs together than cognate languages and geographical proximity, and perhaps foreign occupation (albeit by different powers). On the other side the separate histories of Slovenes, Croats, Serbs, Macedonians and Montenegrins, as well as religious differences, have suggested the possibility of Yugoslavia providing a model of the 'transcended nation' in the form of a federation of nations, which could be replicated on a larger scale elsewhere.[6]

Unfortunately, the history of Yugoslavia to date has not lived up to the hopes entertained for it and for other federations. The division of the Communist Party into national parties, the centrality of the nations in constitutional arrangements and in economic allocation, and the history of national antagonisms, especially during the Second World War, have all undermined the fragile unity of the Yugoslav state, first under Tito and now under his successors. The Croat Spring, the conflicts in Kossovo and the dispute with Slovenia suggest the abiding power of the constituent nations that compose the federation rather than the supra-national institutions or any Yugoslav sentiments.[7]

Similar components and experiences, but on a much vaster scale, mark the history of the Soviet Union. Founded on the ruins of, but within much the same boundaries as, its predecessor, the tsarist empire, the revolutionary communist state felt it necessary to make important concessions to the principle of nationality within both the Party organization and the Constitution. Following Lenin's decision to recognize the right to, if not the practice of, national self-determination and secession, the Soviet leadership set about restructuring the Soviet state as a federation of national republics, each based on its language and culture, organizing all categories of population into recognizable *ethnies*, selecting, fusing, even inventing appropriate languages and ranking them all in a hierarchy of ethno-national size and strategic importance. Thus small groups like the Udmurts or Evenki were classified as peoples, while much larger and more developed communities, like the Georgians or Uzbeks, were treated as nations with their own sovereign territorial republics, administrations, Party organizations, languages and cultures. In this way cultural and territorial bases of ethnicity were maintained and constitutionally safeguarded, while political and economic decision-making was removed to the political centre.[8]

The Soviet Union, therefore, had till the era of *perestroika* operated on two levels. On the military, political and economic planes there was a high degree of centralization, with the Party in Moscow holding the levers of power over the republics and their Party organs. But in the spheres of culture, education and social welfare the individual republics enjoyed considerable autonomy. This was reinforced by the policy of drawing administrative recruits for each republic from the dominant ethnic community (*korenisatzia*) that emerged in the 1920s but has been heavily eroded in the era of *perestroika* and *glasnost*. The effect was to separate potential conflicts through the bifurcation of spheres of relevance and even mutually to reinforce national and Soviet allegiances. But even before the lifting of tight Party control the nationalities problem was barely contained, erupting from time to time in riots and repressive measures and calling forth policies of Russian settlement and the elevation of the Russian *lingua franca* in all areas. The non-Russian demographic increase, the potential for Muslim instability on the southern borders, the distribution of resources and posts between the republics and the centre, the nationalist dimensions of dissent and the effects of education in activating ambivalent ethnic intelligentsia, above all the postponement of the ideal of national fusion (*sliyanie*) and questioning of the present stage of national cooperation (*sblizhenie*) – all these developments revealed profound anxiety over the divisive potential of the 'national question' in the decades after Stalin's death.[9]

In the era of *glasnost* and *perestroika* under Gorbachov ethnic divisions that have lain concealed have become salient. Ethnonationalism has mobilized mass support in the Baltic states, the Caucasus and Central Asia, and Russian neo-nationalism has aligned itself more closely with Orthodox religious resurgence, from which it draws much of its moral and aesthetic inspiration and part of its ethno-history. In large measure all this follows from the structure of the Soviet state and Party organization and from Lenin's historic compromise with the tide of East European ethno-nationalisms, including the Great Russian variety that he so condemned. Although the federal principle institutionalized national sentiments and cultures, it also afforded bases for the revival of active nationalism wherever those sentiments and cultures appeared to their members to be threatened by neighbours or by the centre. Given the long exclusion of a genuine popular voice from political organization, the most likely beneficiary of pent-up resentments and aspirations for real participation was the nation or ethnic community. As a result the attempt to encourage more open political participation carried with it a content of self-expression that was national as well as democratic, revealing once again that, as in other communist states, ethnic ties and nationalist aspirations have proved more durable and resilient than Marxist ideologies and parties.[10]

What the Soviet experience suggests is that even revolutionary 'invented traditions' must harness or forge (often both) a national cultural and political identity if they are to strike deep popular roots.

It is instructive to compare the American experience in this respect. There too national aspirations have been continental but have had to operate in a polyethnic environment. In the United States, however, what is often termed 'neo-ethnicity', though often vital, has remained (or become) symbolic and organizational. Unlike their Soviet counterparts, American ethnic communities and categories have been largely divorced from any territorial dimensions and have instead been transformed into the most effective vehicles of mass mobilization and some of the most powerful pressure groups in the American political system. With rare exceptions, ethnic aspirations are at most 'communal', in the sense of demanding a controlling voice for *ethnies* in cities and localities. Blacks, Chicanos and Native Americans apart, 'national' goals and symbols have been reserved exclusively for the all-American political community and its culture.[11]

What is this community and culture, and has it managed to transcend the nation and nationalism, as Soviet man and society was intended to? The content of the all-American identity and culture clearly reveals its ethnic roots in the Anglo-American Protestant traditions of the original settlements. By the late eighteenth century we may describe the dominant myth and culture in the colonies as a 'vernacular ancestralism' that looked back to the Americanized forefathers against the 'wicked British step-mother' and proclaimed a unique destiny for the new 'chosen people' in the New Jerusalem.[12]

This Anglo-American myth of Puritan election was reinforced by the secular Romanizing myths of the Revolution, the Constitution and the heroic age of the Founding Fathers. It was only after the content of the new nation's cultural identity had been formed by stages that the great influx of European immigrants began, and it was into this underlying but flexible cultural pattern, founded on the supremacy of Anglo-American language and culture, that they were required to integrate themselves. But this 'supersession of ethnicity' did not entail a transcendence of the nation. Quite the contrary: the United States became a prime example of the territorial national type of political community and of the power of territorial nationalism. In these respects it has been, so far, more successful than the Soviet Union, whose own attempt to forge a 'territorial nation' had to fall back *in extremis* on the evocation of the very Great Russian nationalism that it wished to transcend. Even before that, during the Civil War and in the period of 'building socialism in one country', the language and symbolism of nationalism had to be appropriated by Lenin and Stalin to mobilize the 'masses' to make the necessary sacrifices to realize the new socialist and supranational society. So where the Soviet experiment was flawed by an historic compromise with the forces of national identity and nationalism, the United States has attempted to move, with some hesitancy, to a state of full acculturation on the basis of an Anglo-American culture and providential myth and its territorial political community.[13]

Neither the Soviet Union nor the United States can be said to have transcended the nation or superseded nationalism, though for different reasons. As a result, cosmopolitans have recently shifted their hopes to another, more 'regional', groupings of states – from the Scandinavian experiment in cooperation to the inter-African, -Arab and -Latin American regional blocs. Perhaps the most promising of these experiments in regional cooperation has been the move towards a European Community, based originally on the Treaty of Rome signed by six West European states in 1956, after an earlier, successful but more limited experiment in cooperation, the European Coal and Steel Community of 1950. As has often been pointed out, these origins betray the functional grounds for inter-state cooperation in Europe and the incremental and institutional mode of European unification, punctuated by periodic crises over conflicts of interest. The economic content of the Community's basis has also frequently been underlined and a sharp dividing line drawn between a 'customs union' and a 'political community'. Memories of an earlier *Zollverein* leading to national unification, however, raise doubts about such 'boundaries'; do they not conceal more than they illuminate?[14]

For many the prime motivation for European unification was, from the first, political, even military: the rejection of war as an instrument of state policy and a reading of recent European history as the futile carnage of civil wars unleashed by the blind forces of unbridled nationalism, culminating in the holocaust of Nazism. On this reading the European Community will represent the triumph of political reason over national passions and selfish interests; the economic dimensions are seen as means rather than contents or goals. It was just this reading that de Gaulle resisted with his concept of a *Europe des patries* from the Urals to the Atlantic (excluding Britain) and that the European movement, founded in The Hague in 1948, set out to promote in the European Parliament, in the Commission and in popular sentiment.[15]

Even after, perhaps because of, the opening up of Eastern Europe under the influence of Soviet *perestroika* these two political currents remain at the heart of the debate over 'Europe'. For the proponents of the concept of the European Community as a customs union of associated nation-states, national identity remains the natural form of modern political and cultural community, the nation-state the most beneficial and cohesive type of political unit and a moderate, 'healthy' nationalism the sole means of achieving solidarity and collective prosperity. An economic association of European *patries* will enable each to realize these ends, or it is worth nothing. For those who press for a political union of European states the national type of collective identity has ceased to be viable and desirable. The nation-state is fast becoming obsolete, and nationalism, which brought humanity to the brink of ultimate catastrophe, must be expunged from human consciousness or at least rendered forever harmless. Instability in the East can only make the political unification of Europe more necessary and more urgent.

But what kind of community and culture is the European project likely to realize? I shall return later to the question of a European culture, though it is intertwined with the problems of community. How shall we envisage a European political community? As a 'super-state'? A 'super-nation'? Something entirely different and *sui generis*? Let us take each of these in turn.

1. There is little prospect of a European 'super-state' until each European state surrenders its control over its military forces and arsenals and its claims to exercise the monopoly of violence within its own territory, and that self-denial is popularly accepted. But it is as yet NATO and the Warsaw Pact that limit the legitimate exercise of force in the two halves of the continent, not the European Community. The latter's institutions specifically exclude any military organs or jurisdiction. Besides existentially, so long as each European state has the military means to resist external measures or even to back up a threat of political withdrawal, its sovereignty is ultimately assured. In such circumstances a European 'super-state' would be a political impossibility.

2. There is equally little prospect of a European 'super-nation' until the majority of each European nation's population becomes infused with a genuinely European consciousness. (This may be compatible with remaining national sentiments and consciousness, but another wider circle of loyalty and belonging would need to be added to the existing national ones.)

    But here lies a dilemma. Might we not be witnessing thereby the growth of a new 'super-nation' of Europe? And a new, even more powerful, nationalism – an expectation and a fear entertained by some?[16]

    As yet there is little sign of any diminution of the nationalisms and national identities of individual European nations or a growth in a truly European political nationalism, despite the aspirations of members of a more influential European Parliament. But, on the cultural level, there are signs of a wider pan-European sentiment; I shall return to this later.

BEYOND NATIONAL IDENTITY?

3. If the shape of the European project is neither of a 'super-state' nor of a 'super-nation', is it a new form of political association that is *sui generis*? Might we perhaps speak of a 'condominium' of powers, a voluntary agreement to hand over certain powers to a series of central institutions, with overlapping jurisdictions, empowered to take binding decisions for all within carefully circumscribed spheres? If so, could such a condominium have a profound effect on the European pattern of individual national identities?

It is difficult to answer such questions with any degree of confidence. A condominium of this kind, were it to describe the political pattern of an emerging Europe, would be able to coexist with individual national identities within Europe. It might even help to reinforce them, for the conflicts that a condominium must settle but will be unlikely ever to erase will probably accentuate existing national aspirations and consciousness, just as cultural cross-fertilization is likely to provoke vigorous renewals of national culture and national identity. On the other hand, depending on the kinds of condominium leadership, we might see the addition of a new circle of European allegiance and aspiration in a poly-centric world of regional associations and power blocs. But this in turn will hinge on the rise of a sense of specifically 'European' heritage and on the growth of an accepted 'Euro-pean mythology'.

There is another problem. Could the European experiment become a model for other areas and associations? Clearly, the specific institutional arrangements of the new 'Europe' could not be trans-planted to other continents in the manner of the ill-fated 'Westminster model'. But the European Community may well serve as a generic example if and when conditions elsewhere are ripe; and, as I shall argue, that ripeness may well depend, paradoxically, on the progress of certain cultural conditions, notably certain kinds of nationalism.

THE NEW TRANSNATIONAL FORCES

If it is as yet unclear what the European project presages and how far large-scale polyethnic states and regional groupings have taken

153

root, where else may we look for that global interdependence that can underpin a cosmopolitan culture that transcends national limitations? Here it is customary to invoke the new transnational forces that have become so prominent since the Second World War: regional power blocs, transnational economic corporations and global telecommunications systems. Let us consider each in turn.

The Second World War saw the growth of vast power blocs springing out of military confrontations on an unprecedented scale. At first two great blocs, communist and capitalist, confronted each other in Europe and elsewhere, drawing various client states and regions into their orbit. This in turn spawned looser and weaker regional blocs in Latin America, Africa and the South-east Asia, but militarily and economically they remained dependent on the two main industrialized power blocs. In the 1970s and 1980s this polarity was relaxed, first by the economic and political weight of members of the two blocs – West Germany, Japan, China – and latterly by the quickening of the pace towards European economic union and by the impact of *perestroika* on both the Soviet Union and Eastern Europe. The power blocs remain, but their binding ideologies have become nationally diversified and, in some cases, have lost any mobilizing power they once possessed. We have clearly forsaken a bipolar for a polycentric, and shifting, geopolitical configuration, one in which the right of 'nation-states' to choose their own destinies is once more apparent.[17]

The power of the transnational corporations is equally familiar and recent. With huge budgets, sophisticated technologies and the ability to plan long-term strategies over several continents these corporations have proved remarkably flexible instruments of accumulation and control. In many cases they have been able to bypass or override governments, many of whose budgets and technical levels are much lower than those of the corporations they confront. They have also been able to use domestic operations and workers to supplement their own skilled personnel in many Third World countries; such operations enable them to ignore cultural differences and secure the markets they seek. The result is the formation of an international division of labour in which states at different levels of development are inserted, often through the operations of the transnational corporations, into the world capitalist economy in a comprehensive economic hierarchy.

Finally, and perhaps most pervasive of all, there has been a rapid growth in the range and power of mass telecommunications systems and a vast expansion of computerized information networks. The scope and sophistication of such systems make it impossible to limit information networks to even the largest of national units; at the same time they provide the material basis for an amalgamation of national into regional cultures and even for the formation of a global culture. It is now possible to put out and package global information and imagery that can swamp more local information networks and the national messages they emit. In the hands of vast power blocs and transnational corporations these telecommunications systems and computerized information networks can act as powerful vehicles of a new cultural imperialism.

These new transnational forces, to which we may add massive population movements and the growing importance of environmental pollution and disease on a regional or global scale, figure in two parallel arguments. The first claims that advanced industrial capitalism has given birth to giant economic and political units that render the 'nation-state' obsolete. The agent of such obsolescence is held to be primarily the enormous transnational corporation, with its highly diversified capital-intensive operations and sophisticated technologies able to provide complex computerized networks and package imagery in a flexibly specialized but effective manner. The second argument sees the supersession of the nation as part of the move to a 'post-industrial' society. While nations were functional for an industrial world and its technological and market needs, the growth of the 'service society' based on computerized knowledge and communications systems overleapt national boundaries and penetrated every corner of the globe. Only continental cultures, ultimately a single global culture, can fulfil the requirements of a post-industrial knowledge-based society.[18]

To each of these claims, and the observations on which they are based, there is a standard reply. We have been witnessing the crumbling of even the most powerful of political and military blocs in a manner that has been both sudden and decisive. Even before that their ideologies, in both the West and the East, had become muted, ossified and diversified in the face of rapid change and new demands, such as those of the feminist, ethnic and ecology movements. The latter had created new nodes of collective action and organization that absorbed the spiritual and political energies of many people for whom the slogans of capitalism and communism had become meaningless. Hence the vitality of these blocs had already been sapped from within.[19]

Not only new movements but also reformulations of older ones re-emerged, notably the 'neo-nationalisms' that we discussed in chapter 6. This renewal fits well Richmond's thesis that the greater intensity of small-scale communications networks facilitates the proliferation of linguistic and ethnic nationalisms in a post-industrial era. This resurgence of minority or 'peripheral' ethnic nationalisms may well provoke a renewal of the majority nationalisms of *ethnies* that are dominant in a given state – among Serbs, Czechs, Germans, Poles and Russians – often through a reactive and liberating process. The overall result may well be to strengthen those very 'state-nations' that had been thought to be obsolete and to give them a new, more powerful lease of life.[20]

The same may well be true in the sphere of international economic relations. Quite apart from the economic competition of 'state-nations' in the Third World and between them and Western state-nations, the effects of both demographic and economic developments have, if anything, accentuated national divisions and aspirations. As populations explode and emigrate, as wars bring mass death or refugee influxes, the barriers between nations are raised by immigration policies, nationality laws and dire warnings of population explosions. Similarly the impact of the transnational corporations has been contradictory. They may girdle the world through their networks of commodities, investments and operations, but they also provoke national opposition (or partnership) wherever governments are strong enough to make bargains or impose terms. Even if we cannot wholly assent to Warren's contention that political independence gives Third World countries real political leverage against the great capitalist corporations, it does allow the more tenacious and skilful Third World leadership to play the superpowers and the transnational corporations off against one another and thereby to increase the chances of more favourable terms. But, more important for our purposes, it helps to foster a growing sense of national identity and purpose in the face of external pressures and to locate the new 'state-nation' in an international hierarchy of similar political 'communities-in-the-making'. Paradoxically, therefore, these transnational economic forces may end up reinforcing the nations and nationalisms they were expected to supersede.[21]

COSMOPOLITANISM AND A 'GLOBAL' CULTURE?

But it is in the cultural sphere that the claims of theorists of advanced capitalism or post-industrialism are most questionable. Are these undoubtedly sophisticated and massive telecommunications and computerized information systems fusing national cultures or at least overlaying them with a new cosmopolitan culture? And what exactly would be the content of this global culture?

The answers to such questions must be largely speculative, but the Western experience of post-modern cultures may provide important clues. Broadly speaking, recent cultural developments in the West combine a veneer of streamlined modernism with a pastiche of post-modern motifs, themes and styles. This is essentially an eclectic culture. On the one hand we are deluged with a torrent of standardized mass commodities uniformly packaged for mass consumption; on the other hand these commodities – from furniture and building to TV films and advertising – draw their contents from revivals of earlier folk or national motifs and styles, torn from their original contexts and anaesthetized or treated in whimsical or satirical vein. From Stravinsky and Poulenc in the 1920s to Hockney and Kitaj today, this pastiche of parodied styles and themes has come to stand for the possibility of a post-modern, even a pseudo-classical, mass culture.[22]

A global culture would therefore be composed of a number of analytically discrete elements: effectively advertised mass commodities, a patchwork of folk or ethnic styles and motifs stripped of their context, some general ideological discourses concerned with 'human rights and values' and a standardized quantitative and 'scientific' language of communication and appraisal, all underpinned by the new information and telecommunications systems and their computerized technologies.

This post-modern global culture would differ from all previous cultures not only in its worldwide diffusion but also in the degree of its self-consciousness and self-parody. Indeed, believing there to be no place for the 'self' outside the particular discourses and language conventions in which every human being is enmeshed and no vantage points of reference, no 'centre' beyond these conventions, the new cosmopolitanism is inherently eclectic and in motion. Its shape is constantly changing. Hence it can be 'described' only in very general terms.

Unlike previous cultural imperialisms, which were rooted in an ethnic time and place of origin, the new global culture is universal and timeless. Being eclectic, it is indifferent to place or time. It is fluid and shapeless. Though currently more advanced in the West than elsewhere, a post-modern cosmopolitan culture has been carried by the mass media and telecommunications around the world. It is here and now and everywhere. It boasts no history or histories; the folk motifs it uses are quarried for surface decoration of a present- and future-oriented 'scientific' and technical culture.

It is also a fundamentally artificial culture. Its pastiche is capricious and ironical; its effects are carefully calculated; and it lacks any emotional commitment to what is signified. Craft-like and shallow, the new cosmopolitanism is more interested in means and in re-formulating dilemmas of value into technical problems with purely technological solutions. In this it is true to its technological character, in which intersecting systems of communication and information create networks of interdependence expressed in a universal quantitative and scientific discourse and operated by a technical intelligentsia, whose culture of technical discourse replaces the earlier, purely critical, discourse of the humanist intellectuals.[23]

There is little doubt that the lineaments of such a technical global culture can be discerned, though it is rather unevenly spread across the planet at present. But can such a cosmopolitan culture survive and flourish? Can it put down roots among the populations of the world?

Again, there is little in the past to guide us. In the past there was never culture, only cultures, that were particular, expressive and historically specific. Even the most imperial and widely diffused were bound to the time and place of their origins – be it Rome or Byzantium or Mecca – as were their imagery and sense of identity, which were based on concrete historical traditions that had popular resonance over long periods, like the imagery of Caesar and Tsar in Rome and Russia. It may be possible to manufacture traditions and to package imagery, but images and traditions will be sustained only if they have some popular resonance, and they will have that resonance only if they can be harmonized and made continuous with a perceived collective past. All those monuments to the fallen – ceremonies of remembrance, statues to heroes and celebrations of anniversaries – however newly created in their present form, take their meaning and their emotional power from a presumed and felt collective past.[24]

Now, in the modern world, that felt and perceived collective past is still pre-eminently ethnic and national. Identities, images and cultures remain similarly and obstinately plural and ethnic or national. This is only to be expected, given the centrality of memory in forging identities and cultures, which is why the basic motifs, ideas and styles of post-modern cosmopolitanism are folk or national in origin. There is to date no other, except a synthetic neo-classicism (itself harking back, however tenuously, to antique forebears). There is no global 'identity-in-the-making'; a global culture could be only a memory-less construct or break up into its constituent national elements. But a memory-less culture is a contradiction; any attempt to create such a global culture would simply accentuate the plurality of folk memories and identities that have been plundered in order to constitute this giant *bricolage*.

Here at last we stumble on the limits of human 'construction' and 'deconstruction', for behind the project of a global culture stands the premise of culture as a construct of human imagination and art whose 'text' we have to 'read' and whose assumptions we have to deconstruct. Just as the nation itself may be regarded as an 'imagined community', the construct of rulers and intelligentsia, so a global culture that is a pastiche of the past underpinned by science and telecommunications is humanity's most daring, all-embracing act of the imagination. Yet the texts of which such cosmopolitanism is necessarily composed, the satirized components of this patchwork, are just those myths, memories, values, symbols and traditions that form the cultures and discourses of each and every nation and ethnic community. It is these nations and *ethnies* that set historical limits to our discourses. To penetrate their ethno-national forms and to challenge their assumptions does not in itself undermine their power or destroy the hold of national discourses. Bound up, as they are, with the realities of state power and cultural communication, ethnic and national discourses and their texts set limits to human imaginative construction, for the *longue durée* of ethno-histories have furnished the very languages and cultures in which collective and individual selves and their discourses have been formed and continue to bind and divide human beings. It is not enough to imagine the global community; new and wider forms of political association and different types of cultural community will first have to emerge. It is likely to be a piecemeal movement, disjointed and largely unplanned.[25]

THE USES OF 'ETHNO-HISTORY'

So far I have suggested one set of reasons for the failure to extinguish, and the improbability of superseding, nations and nationalism: the inherent implausibility of the project to construct a global culture, even so eclectic and technical a culture as 'post-modernism' offers us with its promise of new 'post-national' styles and languages.

But there is another even more powerful reason for this failure, namely the continuing hold of ethnic styles and national discourses themselves over the vast majority of the planet's populations. This is quite easy to verify on the ground. Most political conflicts, most popular protests and most state projects have a powerful nationalist dimension, unless they are specific expressions of national aspirations and consciousness. Nationalism figures prominently in the most bitter and intractable of such conflicts and protests, even when it is linked with other issues of gender, class, race and religion.

The question is: why does national identity remain so ubiquitous, multifaceted and pervasive, as we said at the beginning of this chapter? We have seen how nations and nationalism emerged and spread across the globe. The question now is, what functions does national identity continue to serve that other types of identity either fail to cover, or address rather inadequately?

Perhaps the most important of its functions is to provide a satisfying answer to the problem of personal oblivion. Identification with the 'nation' in a secular era is the surest way to surmount the finality of death and ensure a measure of personal immortality. Even the Party cannot make so unequivocal a promise; it too must ultimately fall back on the nation. For the Party has only its short, revolutionary history; the nation can boast a distant past, even where much of it must be reconstructed or even fabricated. Even more important, it can offer a glorious future similar to its heroic past. In this way it can galvanize people into following a common destiny to be realized by succeeding generations. But these are the generations of 'our' children; they are 'ours' biologically as well as spiritually, which is more than any class or Party can promise. So the promise of life immortal in our posterity seems genetically vindicated. Can we not take comfort in the memorials of our posterity, and do these not assure us of the after-life that secular doubt appeared to destroy? So the primary function of national identity is to provide a strong 'community of history and destiny' to save people from personal oblivion and restore collective faith.[26]

To identify with the nation is to identify with more than a cause or a collectivity. It is to be offered personal renewal and dignity in and through national regeneration. It is to become part of a political 'super-family' that will restore to each of its constituent families their birthright and their former noble status, where now each is deprived of power and held in contempt. Nationalism promises a 'status reversal', where the last shall be first and the world will recognize the chosen people and their sacred values. This is where ethno-history is so vital. Not only must the nation boast a distant past on which to base its promise of immortality; it must be able to unfold a glorious past, a golden age of saints and heroes, to give meaning to its promise of restoration and dignity. So the fuller and richer that ethno-history, the more convincing becomes its claim and the deeper the chord it can strike in the hearts of the nation's members. The felt antiquity of a community's ethno-history, irrespective of its truth-content, as nationalists have long understood, is the criterion of national dignity and the bar at which they must make their appeal for national restoration. That is why Finnish intellectuals like Lönnröt and Snellman, Gallén-Kallela and Sibelius, felt they had to recreate Finland's lost past, its distant golden age in the land of heroes, the *Kalevala*, from the ballads of the Karelian peasants, and present it as authentic history, so that they and all

Finns might re-enter the living past of their community and thereby restore their collective dignity and bind themselves into the chain of generations that alone could confer immortality. It was under the abstract construct of 'Finland' that they could renew themselves, but that construct took its meaning and popular resonance from a perceived kinship with a much longer presumed ethno-history with which most Finns could identify and that seemed to promise release from oblivion.[27]

A third function of national identity is the prominence it gives to realizing the ideal of fraternity. The ideal itself suggests the close relationship between the family, the ethnic community and the nation, at least on the ideological plane. *Ethnie* and nation are seen simply as families writ large, a sum of many interrelated families, brothers and sisters all. But nationalists also prescribe rituals and ceremonies to rehearse and reinforce the ideal. By means of parades, remembrance ceremonies, anniversary celebrations, monuments to the fallen, oaths, coinage, flags, eulogies of heroes and memorials of historic events, they remind fellow-citizens of their cultural bonds and political kinship through reaffirmations of identity and unity.

In many ways this ceremonial and symbolic aspect is the most decisive to the success and durability of national identity – it is the area in which individual identity is most closely bound up with collective identity. There is more than one reason for this affinity. We should not underrate the importance of aesthetic considerations – the feelings of beauty, variety, dignity and pathos aroused by the skilful disposition of forms, masses, sounds and rhythms with which the arts can evoke the distinctive 'spirit' of the nation. No doubt this helps to explain why so many poets, composers, painters, sculptors and other artists have found the idea of national identity so potent and evocative for themselves and their art. But the chief reason why the symbolic and ritual aspects of nationalism impinge so directly on the sense of individual identity today lies in its revival of ethnic ties and ethnic identification, and especially its commemoration of 'the forefathers' and the fallen in each generation of the community. In this nationalism resembles those religious faiths that, like Shintoism, set great store by communion with the dead and worship of ancestors. Like those religions, nations and their remembrance ceremonies bring together all those families that have lost kinsmen in war and other national disasters, and all who look back to common forefathers, so as to draw from their example that strength of purpose and spirit of self-sacrifice that will inspire in them a similar heroism.[28]

Transcending oblivion through posterity; the restoration of collective dignity through an appeal to a golden age; the realization of fraternity through symbols, rites and ceremonies, which bind the living to the dead and fallen of the community: these are the underlying functions of national identity and nationalism in the modern world, and the basic reasons why the latter have proved so durable, protean and resilient through all vicissitudes.

There are also other historical and geo-political reasons. Historically, the nation-state has proved its worth, ever since the hegemony of France and Britain showed its efficacy in war and peace. It became a universal model, albeit one often copied more in externals than in spirit. Similarly, the success of Germany and Japan suggested the power and efficacy of ethnic nationalism and an 'ethnic' type of national identity. The diffusion of Herderian and Fichtean concepts is evidence of the wide influence of the German model. Given the demotic nature of many *ethnies*, this ethnic model of the nation has proved even more successful; there are few areas of the world that have been free of often violent ethnic nationalisms.

Ethnic violence, though it has several causes, is also a function of the uneven distribution of 'ethno-history'. There are considerable differences in the nature, depth and richness of each community's historical memories. Some communities claim a long, well-documented and powerfully evocative ethno-history; others can find few records of communal exploits, and of those most are recent; for still others, mostly ethnic categories, only a recent history of oppression and struggle is available for collective use, and perhaps some fragments of memory of earlier cultures in the area, which can be appropriated. In early modern Eastern Europe, for example, we could have found distinctive *ethnies* such as the Poles, Hungarians and Croats in their historic states, boasting long and rich histories; submerged ethnic communities like the Serbs, Romanians (Wallachians and Moldavians) and Bulgarians, whose medieval histories had to be rediscovered and aligned with their recent memories of Ottoman oppression; and ethnically mixed areas and categories of

Macedonians and Ruthenians, the major part of whose memories are fairly recent and who, together with the Slovaks, had to dig deep into the past for genealogical filiation and shadowy ancestor-heroes.[29]

Now a rich ethno-history can be a significant source of cultural power and a focus of cultural politicization. Communities able to boast such histories have a competitive advantage over others where that history is scanty or doubtful. In the latter case the intellectuals have a double task: they must recover a sufficiently large quantity of communal history to convince their own members that they have an illustrious past, and they must authenticate it sufficiently to convince sceptical outsiders of its merits. Nationalist intellectuals have, rightly, been more concerned with the first of these tasks than the second; the truth-content of the unearthed memories is less important culturally and politically than their abundance, variety and drama (their aesthetic qualities) or their example of loyalty, nobility and self-sacrifice (their moral qualities) that inspire emulation and bind present generations to the 'glorious dead'.

Generally speaking it is the smaller, submerged communities and categories that have to offset their lack of a long, rich, continuous ethno-history through 'cultural wars' in which philology, archaeology, anthropology and other 'scientific' disciplines are used to trace uncertain genealogies, to root populations in their native terrains, to document their distinctive traits and cultures, and to annex earlier civilizations. So Iraqis appropriated much earlier civilizations like those of the Sumerians and Babylonians because they flourished in Mesopotamia, and Turks laid claim to the Hittite empire of the second millennium BC. Greeks and Bulgarians engage in dispute over the 'national' provenance of the royal tombs of ancient Macedonia, while Jews and Palestinians wage war over the area of Nablus and Samaria, and Hungarians and Romanians over the mixed area of Transylvania.[30]

More generally, the cultural competition fostered by the uneven distribution of ethno-history has been a driving force in the widespread processes of vernacular mobilization and cultural politicization traced in earlier chapters. The example of other successful ethno-nationalisms, together with the fear of domination by culturally more advanced neighbours, has helped to inspire ethnic movements and promote ethnic conflicts all over the globe, from Fiji and Sri Lanka to the Horn of Africa and the Caribbean. Given the number of ethnic communities and categories that can be mobilized through the recovery of even indistinct ethno-histories, the likelihood of an end to the cultural wars of *ethnies* and nations, and of the supersession of nationalism, seems remote.

GEO-POLITICS AND NATIONAL CAPITALISM

To these cultural and psychological reasons for the pervasive and ubiquitous nature of national identity must be added equally powerful economic and geo-political grounds, whose combined effect is to intensify existing ethnic and national differences and globalize their impact. We often hear that advanced capitalism has rendered nationalism obsolete and that, by overleaping national boundaries, it is creating a single, interdependent world. This is sometimes coupled with the Marxist assertion that nations and nationalism were products (and instruments) of early capitalism. Yet, in a world of transnational corporations and the international division of labour, nations and nationalism continue to flourish. Clearly, careful analysis is not served by continuing to see nations and nationalism as phenomena dependent upon changes within the capitalist mode of production.

In fact the two trajectories of the rise of capital and the emergence of the nation are better kept apart, even though they often crossed each other's paths in specific historical instances. Capitalism, after its early banking phase in northern Italy and Flanders, soon became merchant capital, becoming gradually dominant through its role in the competition of a few 'core' states in northwest Europe from the late fifteenth century. By the eighteenth century it had drawn considerable areas of Western and Central Europe, as well as coastal areas and enclaves in Asia, Africa and Latin America into its periphery even before the Industrial Revolution gave it world hegemony in the late-nineteenth and twentieth centuries. Meanwhile the first modern (rationalized, professional bureaucratic) states had emerged in the same area of northwest Europe in the fourteenth and fifteenth centuries, on the basis, as we have seen, of pre-existing ethnic communities in the heartlands of France, England, Spain, Holland and Sweden. It was in these areas, on the basis of these 'ethnic states' (never homogenous, however), that the first modern nations arose, soon to be emulated in different parts of Europe and the globe from the late eighteenth century onwards, to become the political norm in the late nineteenth and early twentieth centuries.

There is, indeed, a close parallel in the periodization of the rise both of the nation and of capital to world hegemony, and it is not an accidental one. The fact is that the new forces of bourgeois capitalism operated within a pre-existing framework of ethnic communities and states that were frequently locked in rivalry and warfare. The advent of first merchant, then industrial, capitalism intensified and expanded these rivalries. War in turn cemented both the state and its dominant ethnic population into the compact, territorial and legally unified nation. The impact of expanding capitalism, then, was to strengthen the existing inter-state system in Europe, and through its wars and rivalries to help the process of crystallizing national sentiment in the state's dominant *ethnie*.[31]

There were at times, in fact, close links between the operations of capital and the rise of particular nations. If trade rivalries sharpened the sense of national difference, and provided economic content for national conflicts, so equally the rising national sentiment of the bourgeoisie gave a new edge to their competitive drive overseas. If capital furnished the economic instruments of the modern states, so the framework of ethnically based states and their loyalties often dictated the direction of trade and the competition between merchants and (later) industrialists.

The prime contribution of capitalism to the nation has been to furnish states with new classes, notably the bourgeoisie, workers and professionals, which can exercise leadership and promote its interests in the face of rival states and nations. It does so, however, within the confines of pre-existing ethnic communities and state systems.

Capitalism creates a new class structure, often superimposed on the old agrarian ones, which furnishes the rising nation with the necessary complement of occupational skills and diversified economies. But the nation should not be seen as the 'product' of the new classes. Rather, different classes become the agents of the formation of nations out of pre-existing lateral or vertical *ethnies*; or, in the case of the intelligentsia in ethnic categories, the promoter of a new ethnic community in the image of neighbouring *ethnies*.

During successive historical periods different classes and strata took the lead in turning the old ethnic community into a modern nation. In the early modern West the monarch and aristocracy, and later the gentry, were the prime agents of the bureaucratic incorporation of the lower classes and outlying communities into the 'national state' that they, along with the Church, helped to create. This was a long, slow and discontinuous process, which can be traced back to the twelfth and thirteenth centuries in England and France. Later, as diaspora ethnic communities – Catalans, Germans, Armenians, Jews – helped to spread early merchant capitalism, the indigenous merchant and trading classes in France, Spain, England, Holland and Sweden helped the Crown to continue the task of bureaucratic incorporation, often in conflict with aristocratic and clerical interests.

In Eastern Europe, on the other hand, with the exception of Poland and Hungary, the role of the aristocracy and gentry was taken by a small professional and intellectual stratum, sometimes as in Greece or Serbia in conjunction with a merchant class, but often with very little backing from a tiny commercial stratum. In most cases it would be premature to speak of the penetration of capitalism when the wage-earning element was so minute a fraction of the population. Outside Europe, with a few exceptions like India and southern Africa, both territorial and ethnic nationalisms pre-dated the penetration of capitalist relations of production, though coastal trade often acted as a catalyst and facilitated the rise of an educated urban class in the late nineteenth and early twentieth centuries. But here, too, the parameters of capitalist influence were set by the political and administrative framework of European colonialism, and by territorial boundaries dictated by strategic and prestige requirements.[32]

If capitalism *per se* can be credited with only a powerful contributory role in the rise of nations and nationalism, the same cannot be said for the role of bureaucratic states and regional inter-state systems. If the bureaucratic state and inter-state system was decisive for the rise of capitalism, it was equally vital for the diffusion of national identity and nationalism, both through the wars it generated and through its impact on diverse ethnic populations and classes. That impact was often fraught with conflict, as centralizing states provoked protest and opposition, sometimes revolution. Here the role of alienated intellectuals was often crucial. They alone could formulate the ideals of a 'genuine' national community, which would replace the despotism of élites and the absolutism of the state. At the same time they were able to attract a following among the educated 'public' in the middle classes, notably the very professionals whom the state needed, recruited and trained for its purposes.[33]

As a result the sovereign bureaucratic state increasingly set the boundaries of territorial and political units, as well as economic and military forces. By the early twentieth century it had become the recognized norm of political association in most parts of the world, under the aegis of nationalist principles. As guardian of national identity the state derived its legitimacy from the nation it sought to embody and represent; just as only nations with states of their own could feel secure and autonomous in a world of 'nation-states'. In this way state and nation became fatefully confused.

But, though this confusion has brought much conflict and misery in many lands, it has only served to strengthen both the state and the nation. Their symbiosis has proved irreversible. It has entrenched the hold of national identity and the ideals of nationalism as firmly as any nationalist could wish and any cosmopolitan must lament. But it has also strengthened the legitimacy of the state and its bureaucratic apparatus; regimes that play the nationalist card effectively can survive for long periods, despite growing unpopularity. Together, state and nation (under the frequent misnomer 'nation-state') have marched forward in triumphant unison as the sole acknowledged constituents of the equally misnamed 'inter-national' community.[34]

Today, the world is divided into 'nation-states' loosely grouped in regional inter-state systems. These systems and their constituent states put a premium on the solidarity and political commitment of their citizens, and on the sovereign jurisdiction of the nation-state within its own boundaries. Despite infringements (Czechoslovakia, Grenada, Panama), the international community generally rejects external intervention in the domestic affairs of sovereign states, on the grounds that such affairs are the province of the citizens and subject to the national 'will of the people'. In this respect *étatisme* reinforces the nation and its moral boundaries. So increasingly do the various regional inter-state systems. For these systems the only collective actors are nation-states, states that are legitimated by clear expressions of the national will and of national identity. To be legitimate in these terms a nation-state must show that its citizens are sharply differentiated from 'foreigners', but equally undifferentiated from each other internally, as far as is possible. In other words legitimation in a world of 'nation-states' requires a measure of internal homogenization; geo-political demarcations now take priority over other differences.

But, while geo-political demands can reinforce ethnically relatively homogenous states, they are just as likely to undermine the cohesion of ethnically plural states. The very demands for solidarity, commitment and homogeneity that the inter-state system presents often provoke just that ethnic resistance that was to be suppressed for the sake of the system's stability. Given the prior existence of *ethnies* and ethnic categories in many areas, the drive to superimpose on surviving ethnic mosaics and patchworks a system of compact, rational, bureaucratic states is bound to produce grave instability and deep ethnic conflicts wherever such states fail to fit the pre-existing ethnic map. As the interventionist bureaucratic state tends to provoke protest from suppressed classes and regions in any case, protests that are often led by alienated intellectuals, it is not difficult to see how suppressed ethnic communities and categories can be roused in opposition to the homogenizing demands of the new type of state and inter-state system. And once the conflict between centralizing territorial 'nation-states' and ethnic communities has erupted, the geo-politics of the modern state can only make the claims of two (or more) nationalisms in perpetual, if sometimes latent, conflict more intractable.[35]

So, contrary to much current thinking, it is the very political configuration of states into wider regional systems that helps to entrench the power of the nation and fan the flames of nationalism everywhere. It is therefore not to any new regional alignments or 'supra-national' blocs of 'nation-states' that we must look for the super-session of nations or nationalism; for such inter-state groupings, be they Leagues, Communities or Organizations, only help to perpetuate, if they do not inflame, the hold of national identities and nationalist aspirations, as do the new classes of international capitalism.

NATIONALISM BEYOND NATIONS?

Today national identity is the main form of collective identification. Whatever the feelings of individuals, it provides the dominant criterion of culture and identity, the sole principle of government and the chief focus of social and economic activity. The appeal of the nation and nationalism is global; there is no area free from ethnic protests and nationalist uprisings. Praised or reviled, the nation shows few signs of being transcended, and nationalism does not appear to be losing any part of its explosive popular power and significance.

There is nothing random or recent in this state of affairs. It is rooted in a long history of ethnic ties and sentiments that reach back long before the birth of our modern world, but that have been unexpectedly and powerfully revitalized by modern bureaucratic state systems, capitalist class structures and the widespread longing for immortality and dignity in a community of history and destiny in a secular age. Through the rediscovery of an ethnic past and the promise of collective restoration of the former golden age, national identity and nationalism have succeeded in arousing and inspiring ethnic communities and populations of all classes, regions, genders and religions, to claim their rights as 'nations', territorial communities of culturally and historically cognate citizens, in a world of free and equal nations. Here is an identity and a force with which even the strongest of states has had to come to terms, and it is one that has shaped, and is likely to shape, our world in the foreseeable future.

For many this is a bleak conclusion. It suggests no way out of the world of nationalism, no possibility for transcending the nation and surmounting the many bitter conflicts that nationalism helps to generate. The conflicts between nation-states, and between states and their constituent *ethnies*, are likely to continue and perhaps proliferate, mobilizing tomorrow ethnic communities and categories that are dormant today. From the standpoint of global security and a global culture this conclusion offers no way out of the impasse of endemic division, mistrust and war.

But are we justified in delivering such a harsh and unmitigated verdict? Did not our earlier remarks about the significance of the new global forces (trans-national corporations, telecommunications systems, etc.) point in a quite different direction? Was our discussion of recent federal systems in some states, and of the European project, really so negative? If the wilder dreams of cosmopolitans must be discounted, if a memory-less global culture lacks conviction, may there nevertheless not remain some sober expectations for a gradual remaking of our collective identities at the regional level? I think there are grounds for such more limited hopes, in the sphere of culture rather than politics and in ways that are something of a paradox.

The burden of my argument throughout has been the interplay between the forces that shape not only modern collective identities, notably ethnic ties and ethno-history, but also states and classes, and the ways in which human beings, usually nationalist intelligentsia, have tried to reconstruct and reshape their heritages into 'old-new' national identities. This duality continues to inform recent visions and endeavours to reshape national identities into something 'beyond the nation'. It means that serious attempts to move beyond the nation have to start from its principles and use them to go further. The principles of the nation are those of nationalism. Hence it may only be possible to transcend the nation through a form of nationalism, one that is paradoxically broader than the compact nation that has usually been the object of its endeavours.

There is a form of nationalism that is broader in extent and scope than the 'normal' compact nation. I refer to 'Pan-nationalisms'. These can be defined as movements to unify in a single cultural and political community several, usually contiguous, states on the basis of shared cultural characteristics or a 'family of cultures'. Yugo-slavism was one of the earliest examples of Pan-nationalism, and it was soon followed by various irredentist movements (Pan-Germanism, Pan-Bulgarianism, -Italianism, etc.) that usually aspired to include certain ethnically similar parts of other states, and by the larger-scale 'Pan' movements proper, like Pan-Turkism, Arabism, Africanism, Latin Americanism, etc., which range from serious attempts at political unification to looser political associations on the basis of common colonial experience and culture.

None of these movements has been politically successful (except the smaller-scale irredentist movements, to varying degrees). But their importance lies elsewhere. Pan-Slavism got nowhere near unifying the Slavs in a single political community, let alone a single territorial state. But it did inspire a cultural renaissance among speakers of Slavic languages, and promoted various common ideas and sentiments, as well as meetings of writers and artists, in a wide culture area.[36]

Pan-Arabism was never strong enough to prevent internecine Arab wars, let alone convey the sense of a political community for all Arabs. Yet it has inspired some inter-Arab projects, as well as broader cultural and philanthropic links. Similarly, Pan-Turkism, though it had a disastrous military end, did manage to foster a cultural renaissance among Turks both in Turkey and outside, a renewed interest in Turkic languages and history, and various links between Turkic-speaking peoples.[37]

The importance of Pan-nationalisms lies in their ability to counteract, or at least suggest an alternative to, the fissiparous tendencies of proliferating ethnic nationalisms. While Pan-Africanism did not manage to restrain a succession of minority ethnic nationalisms from staking their claims in the new post-colonial states, it did give them a new sense of pride in past African achievements and a sense of wider community in which all Africans could share. Hence its importance lies less in the political endeavours of the Organization of African Unity that it helped to create than in raising the horizons and restoring the dignity of Black Africans, so often scorned by their colonial masters, through the rediscovery of a shared African past and 'family of cultures'.[38]

The concept of a 'family of cultures' is significant here. Whereas political and economic unification today is willed, constructed and institutional, a 'culture area' containing a family of related cultures is usually a product of long-term processes, and is mostly unanticipated, unintended and undirected. Whereas political and economic unities are planned and organized, families of cultures and culture areas appear inchoate and uninstitutionalized but are no less real and potent for those in their orbit. Islamic, American and Soviet Russian identities and cultures possess an attraction for their members far beyond the political and social institutions that are their official mouthpieces.

One reason for this appeal is the re-emergence of the *lingua franca*. In the high middle ages, Latin and Arabic achieved a genuinely trans-territorial and trans-cultural sway. But, in those cases, there was a corporate identity – the medieval clergy and ulema – with a transterritorial function that a *lingua franca* could serve. Today, with many oral 'low' cultures turned into literary 'high' cultures for mass, standardized public education, national languages have replaced the earlier *lingua franca*. But not entirely – the extension of certain prestige languages to facilitate communication and exchange over wide areas has promoted a sense of loose cultural kinship within culture areas and sometimes even beyond them. The importance of English in North America, Spanish in Latin America, Arabic in the Middle East and Russian in the Soviet Union, though not unchallenged or unproblematic, does afford new vehicles for remaking identities on a broader scale than existing compact national identities, if and when other conditions prove favourable.[39]

Another reason is the new perception of common regional problems, notably in the ecological sphere. Geo-political location and proximity, made visible by the mass media, help to forge a new awareness of dangers beyond national frontiers yet common to all nations in the region and culture area. Often the impact of an ecological disaster is wider still; a Chernobyl, Sahel famine or Brazilian rain forest decimation penetrate human consciousness far beyond the culture areas they immediately affect. In other cases the problems are regional (Mediterranean pollution, Californian earthquakes, floods in Bengal), and they help to evoke a cultural awareness of the region's common needs.

Yet a third reason for the growing attraction of culture areas and families of cultures is the frequent kinship in their social and political mores and institutions, including their basic political values. In certain areas military dictatorships with low levels of civil rights and political freedoms have become the norm, reflecting not just levels of economic development but also cognate political cultures based on a family of political values. In other areas processes of mobilization and democratization may sweep away previous authoritarian, single-party regimes; and while economic explanations can be proffered, the importance of related historical experiences and political cultures should not be underestimated.

These are some of the historical processes that have created the context for the European project in the western half of Europe.

Though the will to European cooperation has been mainly economic in content and political in form, it is of course premised on wider cultural assumptions and traditions. A single *lingua franca* may be lacking (though French and English may well serve that function), but both ecological awareness of common dangers and kinship of political mores and institutions help to buttress a sense of related European cultures within a distinctive culture area. The boundaries of that area have been notoriously difficult to demarcate; defined negatively at first by the Cold War's divisions, they have become more fluid and open as political changes have swept through Eastern Europe. The motive for unity has also subtly shifted towards the political federation favoured by the Pan-Europeans. But what has remained fairly constant has been the conviction of a European pattern or patterns of culture.

These patterns of European culture – the heritage of Roman law, Judeo-Christian ethics, Renaissance humanism and individualism, Enlightenment rationalism and science, artistic classicism and romanticism, and, above all, traditions of civil rights and democracy, which have emerged at various times and places in the continent – have created a common European cultural heritage and formed a unique culture area straddling national boundaries and interrelating their different national cultures through common motifs and traditions. In this way an overlapping family of cultures has been gradually formed over the centuries, despite many breaks and schisms. This is not the planned 'unity in diversity' beloved of official Europeanism, but a rich, inchoate *mélange* of cultural assumptions, forms and traditions, a cultural heritage that creates sentiments of affinity between the peoples of Europe. It is here, rather than in the mythology of medieval Christendom (despite current ecumenical efforts) or a Rhine-based Holy Roman Empire (despite the location of Strasbourg), that we must look for the basis of a cultural Pan-European nationalism that may paradoxically take us beyond the nation.[40]

For it is clear that, whatever else European Pan-nationalism may help to create, it will not be a European super-nation, a nation like all other nations but writ large. Neither will it resemble the United States of America, whose ethnic communities lack separate historic homelands; nor a Soviet Union whose national republics and communities may feel little cultural kinship beyond the common recent Soviet political experience. The new Europe will not even approximate to the British or Belgian models, if only in those cases one *ethnie* or nation dominates the others, though in these cases a greater cultural and historical affinity is apparent. If a European political community is created that will have an *popular* resonance, then we may be sure that it will be founded on the basis of a common European cultural heritage by a Pan-European nationalist movement that is able to forge common European myths, symbols, values and memories out of this common heritage, in such a way that they do not compete with still powerful and vigorous national cultures. Only in this way can Pan-nationalism create a new type of collective identity, which overarches but does not abolish individual nations.

CONCLUSION

It must be apparent by now that the chances of transcending the nation and superseding nationalism are at present slim. It is simply not enough to point to the powerfully trans-national impact of the new economic, political and cultural forces at work today, nor to the various global interdependencies that they undoubtedly create.

A growing cosmopolitanism does not in itself entail the decline of nationalism; the rise of regional culture areas does not diminish the hold of national identities. As I said at the outset, human beings have multiple collective identifications, whose scope and intensity will vary with time and place. There is nothing to prevent individuals from identifying with Flanders, Belgium and Europe simultaneously, and displaying each allegiance in the appropriate context; or from feeling they are Yoruba, Nigerian and African, in concentric circles of loyalty and belonging. It is, in fact, quite common, and very much what one would expect in a world of multiple ties and identities.

This does not mean that such ties and identities are entirely optional and situational, nor that some among them do not exercise a greater hold and exert a more powerful influence than others. It is the thesis of this book that what I have defined as national identity does in fact today exert a more potent and durable influence than other collective cultural identities; and that, for the reasons I have enumerated – the need for collective immortality and dignity, the power of ethno-history, the role of new class structures and the domination of inter-state systems in the modern world – this type of collective identity is likely to continue to command humanity's allegiances for a long time to come, even when other larger-scale but looser forms of collective identity emerge alongside national ones. In fact, as the European case suggests, a cultural Pan-nationalist movement to create large-scale continental identities may actually reinvigorate the specific nationalisms of *ethnies* and nations within the demarcated culture area; as if the individual members of a 'family of cultures' drew strength from their kinship bonds. Even the mingling of formerly more homogeneous cultures through immigration, guest-workers and waves of refugees can provoke strong ethnic reactions from indigenous peoples and cultures.

There is both danger and hope in the division of humanity into nations and the persisting power of national identity throughout the world. The dangers are clear enough: destabilization of a fragile global security system, proliferation and exacerbation of ethnic conflicts everywhere, the persecution of 'indigestible' minorities in the drive for greater national homogeneity, justification of terror, ethnocide and genocide on a scale inconceivable in earlier ages. Nationalism may not have been responsible by itself for the endemic instability, conflict and terror of the present century, but its presence among the prime causes, or in an accompanying role, is too frequent to be dismissed or excused.

At the same time a world of nations and national identities is not without hope. Nationalism may not be responsible for the many instances of reform and democratization of tyrannical regimes, but it is a frequent accompanying motive, a source of pride for downtrodden peoples and the recognized mode for joining or rejoining 'democracy' and 'civilization'. It also provides the sole vision and rationale of political solidarity today, one that commands popular assent and elicits popular enthusiasm. All other visions, all other rationales, appear wan and shadowy by comparison. They offer no sense of election, no unique history, no special destiny. These are the promises which nationalism for the most part fulfils, and the real reasons why so many people continue to identify with the nation. Until these needs are fulfilled through other kinds of identification, the nation with its nationalism, denied or recognized, oppressed or free, each cultivating its own distinctive history, its golden ages and sacred landscapes, will continue to provide humanity with its fundamental cultural and political identities well into the next century.

Notes

1 NATIONAL AND OTHER IDENTITIES

1. Sophocles (1947, 55).
2. Sophocles (1947, 71–124).
3. Sophocles (1947, 66, 74, 79, 117–121).
4. Usually those of class or nation, with feminist movements allying themselves with socialist and/or nationalist movements.
5. For the revolt in the Vendée, see Tilly (1963); on ethno-regional movements in the modern West, see Hechter and Levi (1979).
6. The divisions within the *Tiers État* are discussed in Cobban (1965); the infrequency of non-nationalist workers' socialist revolutions is examined in Kautsky (1962, Introduction); but cf. Breuilly (1982, ch. 15) for a different view.
7. For the revolutionary Mazdakite sectarian movement, see Frye (1966, 249–50). For Weber's analysis of the relationship between strata and classes and different kinds of religious experience, see Weber (1965, ch. 8).
8. See M. Spiro: 'Religion: Problems of definition and explanation', in Banton (1966).
9. For the Druse, see Hitti (1928, especially 12) and H. Z. (J. W.) Hirschberg: 'The Druses', in Arberry (1969).
10. For this argument, see the seminal study by Armstrong (1982, especially chs. 3, 7).
11. A striking case of religion reinforcing ethnicity is the role of Burmese Buddhism, on which see Sarkisyanz (1964); cf. also de Silva (1981) for the Sinhalese case. For the Anglo-Saxon fusion, see the interesting argument by P. Wormald: 'The emergence of Anglo-Saxon Kingdoms', in L. Smith (1984).
12. See the argument in Finley that covers Meinecke's points (1986, ch. 7); cf. Fondation Hardt (1962).
13. For early Western definitions of the nation, see Kemilainen (1964).

14. For the early Dutch case, see Schama (1987, ch. 1); for the various meanings of 'national territory', see A. D. Smith (1981b).
15. Schama (1987, ch. 2); and for persisting regionalism in late nineteenth-century France, see E. Weber (1979).
16. On these 'political cultures', see for example Almond and Pye (1965).
17. Nairn (1977, chs. 2, 9) emphasizes this 'inter-class', populist role. cf. also Gellner and Ionescu (1970).
18. For such linguistic revivals, see Fishman (1968); and for revivals in some Northern countries, including Ireland and Norway, see Mitchison (1980).
19. On French linguistic nationalism during the Revolution, see Lartichaux (1977); for rival myths of French descent, see Poliakov (1974, ch. 2).
20. For some of the many discussions of the problems of defining the nation and nationalism, see Deutsch (1966, ch. 1), Rustow (1967, ch. 1), A. D. Smith (1971, ch. 7) and Connor (1978).
21. See for example Tivey (1980).
22. Connor (1972) for this calculation; see also Wiberg (1983).
23. For economic aspects of nationalism, see Johnson (1968) and Mayall (1984).
24. An aspect stressed by Gellner (1983).
25. Klausner (1960) provides an interesting example of this consequence.
26. See the well-known critique of Kedourie (1960). A demonstration of the empirical multiplicity of national selves in modern Africa is provided by Neuberger (1986, ch. 3).
27. Kedourie (1960) and (1971, Introduction).

2 THE ETHNIC BASIS OF NATIONAL IDENTITY

1. The nationalist salvation drama is critically portrayed by Kedourie (1960) and Breuilly (1982).
2. For more extended discussions of these rival approaches, see the essay by Paul Brass in Taylor and Yapp (1979) and A. D. Smith (1986a, ch. 1).
3. For the Turks, see B. Lewis (1968, especially ch. 10); for the Slovaks, the essay by Paul in Brass (1985).

4. For fuller discussions, see Horowitz (1985, chs. 1–2) and A. D. Smith (1986a, ch. 2).

5. For this distinction, see Van den Berghe (1967).

6. See, for example, the discussions in Dobzhansky (1962), and Banton and Harwood (1975) and Rex (1986).

7. Horowitz (1985, ch. 2); cf. Schermerhorn (1970, ch. 1).

8. For the Roman case, see Tudor (1972, ch. 3); for the Swiss myths, see Steinberg (1976).

9. The significance of attachment to the land is discussed in Armstrong (1982, ch. 2).

10. On this, see Gellner (1973); for the symbolic use of these markers as 'boundary mechanisms' separating ethnic groups, see Barth (1969, Introduction).

11. To which we should add that ethnic traditions and their guardians, as well as the cultural modes in which they are expressed (languages, customs, styles, etc.), may exert a powerful and continuing, and shaping, influence for long periods; on all of which, see Armstrong (1982, passim).

12. Horowitz (1985, 64–74).

13. See Alty (1982); and Finley (1986, ch. 7).

14. The use of the concept of concentric circles of ethnicity had been pointed out in the African context long ago by Coleman (1958, Appendix); cf. Anderson, von der Mehden and Young (1967).

15. See on this Horowitz (1985, 51–4, 66–82); A. D. Smith (1984b).

16. For an attempt to synthesize the primordialist with the instrumentalist or mobilizationist approaches, see McKay (1982).

17. On which, see Cambridge History of Iran (1983, Vol. III, ch. 1).

18. See, on early Armenian history, Lang (1980); also Armstrong (1982, ch. 7).

19. Weber (1968, Vol. I, Part 2, ch. 5, 'Ethnic Groups').

20. For the western cases, see Tilly (1975, Introduction); for other pre-modern cases, see Mann (1986).

21. See Tilly (1975, especially the essays by Tilly and Finer); cf. A. D. Smith (1981c) and for the Great War, Marwick (1974).

22. For further details, see Armstrong (1982, chs. 3, 7) and A. D. Smith (1986a chs. 2–5).

23. For a brief account, see Woodhouse (1984, 36–8); cf. Ostrogorski (1956, 93–4, 192–4); for the Hellenic myth, see Campbell and Sherrard (1968, ch. 1).

24. On this revival, see Baynes and Moss (1969, Introduction) and Armstrong (1982, 174–81); and more generally, Sherrard (1959).

25. This is the argument presented by Carras (1983).

26. For the Nazi extermination of the Gypsies, see Kenrick and Puxon (1972); for the much-contested Turkish actions in 1915, see Nalbandian (1963).

27. On genocide generally, see Kuper (1981) and Horowitz (1982).

28. On which, see Moscati (1973, Part II, especially 168–9); other Punic cities were spared and so a Punic culture survived.

29. See Roux (1964, 301–4); and more generally on Elam and Elamite culture, see Cambridge Ancient History (1971, Vol. I, Part 2, ch. 23).

30. See Saggs (1984, 117–21); Roux (1964, 374).

31. As Assyrian art reveals, the object of Assyrian efforts and cult was increasingly the Assyrian state itself, rather than the culture or community; see the essay by Liverani in Larsen (1979). For the probable causes of Assyria's downfall and demise, see Roux (1964, 278, 290); and the discussion in A. D. Smith (1986a, 100–4).

32. On the Babylonian revolts, see J. M. Cook (1983, 55–6, 100); cf. Oates (1979).

33. See the essay by Werblowski in Ben-Sasson and Ettinger (1971); cf. Seltzer (1980) and Yerushalmi (1983).

34. Armstrong (1976) and (1982, ch. 7).

35. On the Samaritans in recent times, see Strizower (1962, ch. 5); for the Falasha of Ethiopia, see Kessler (1985).

36. On late Pharaonic religion, see Grimal (1968, 211–41).

37. On the Orthodox case, see Arnakis (1963).

38. For the Deuteronomic and Prophetic movements, see Seltzer (1980, 77–111); for the Mishnaic period, see Neusner (1981). For religious reform in the modern period, see Meyer (1967).

39. On which see Frazee (1969) and Kitromilides (1979).

40. See Tcherikover (1970) and Hengel (1980).

41. See Cambridge History of Iran (1983, Vol. III/1, ch. 3, and III/2, ch. 27) and Frye (1966, ch. 6).

42. See, for example, Saunders (1978); and in today's Iran, Keddie (1981).
43. Exodus 19: 5–6; Deuteronomy 7: 6–13.
44. A start has been made in O'Brien (1988); cf. Armstrong (1982).
45. For the role of priesthoods and religion in empires, see Coulborn and Strayer (1962) and Eisenstadt (1963); on their ethnic role, see Armstrong (1982, chs. 3, 7) and A. D. Smith (1986a, especially chs. 3, 5).
46. Armstrong (1982, ch. 7).
47. On these *regna*, see Reynolds (1984, ch. 8).
48. For a general outline of these processes, see Seton-Watson (1977, ch. 2); and the next chapter for fuller discussion.
49. For a general account of nationalism in Latin America, see Masur (1966); and the stimulating analysis in Anderson (1983, ch. 3).
50. The model here is less Yugoslav than Swiss or British, though without the required time-span that these two national states had at their disposal, but with the resources of a national*ist ideology* that the Swiss and British possessed only in the later stages of their national formation. This will be discussed more fully in Chapter 4 below. For the general sub-Saharan African picture, see Rotberg (1967) and Horowitz (1985).

3 THE RISE OF NATIONS

1. See Reiss (1955) for the German Romantic belief in the organic 'national soul' (*Volkseele*); for earlier scholars who upheld a 'perennialist' view of nations, see Walek-Czernecki (1929).
2. Good examples of the 'modernist' approach are Kedourie (1960) and Breuilly (1982); for a critique, see A. D. Smith (1988a).
3. See Gellner (1983, ch. 2).
4. For early intimations of democracy in Sumerian city-states, see Roux (1964, 105); for the early Swiss cantons, see Kohn (1957). The question: *When* was/is the nation? has only recently begun to receive attention; see Connor (1990).
5. See, for example, Frankfort (1954, ch. 4) and David (1982).
6. For these legal and educational differences between classes in ancient Egypt, see Beyer (1959); on the decline of ancient Egyptian religion, see Grimal (1968, 211–41).

7. See Moscati (1962, 110) for this inscription; cf. Pritchard (1958, 173–5). On early Egyptian sentiment, see Trigger *et al.* (1983, 188–202).

8. On the Dorian–Ionian dichotomy, see Alty (1982); and for its cultural ramifications, see Huxley (1966) and Burn (1960, especially 6–7, 48–50, 98–100, 210–14).

9. For Pan-Hellenic sentiments, see the essays by H. Schwabl and H. Ditter in Fondation Hardt (1962), and the essay by Andrewes in Lloyd-Jones (1965); for inter-city and social conflicts within the *polis*, see Forrest (1966) and Burn (1978, chs. 9–10).

10. For the hellenization crisis, see Tcherikover (1970); for the role of the prophetic and priestly movements in 7th century BC Judah, see Seltzer (1980, chs. 2–3); also Zeitlin (1984).

11. For these Zealot conceptions, see Brandon (1967, ch. 2) and Maccoby (1974); for an evaluation of the Brandon thesis, see Zeitlin (1988, ch. 10).

12. For such religious nationalisms, see the examples in D. E. Smith (1974).

13. For some Jewish conceptions of the Second temple and Mishnaic periods, see the essay by Werblowski in Ben-Sasson and Ettinger (1971) and Neusner (1981); for the political and economic history of late Roman and Talmudic Judea, see Avi-Yonah (1976) and especially Alon (1980, Vol. I, chs. 1, 4, 7–8).

14. Notably for Armenians, Ethiopians, Jews, Byzantine Greeks, Orthodox Russians, Catholic Poles, Irish, Welsh, English and French.

15. On these early medieval *regna*, see Reynolds (1983) and Wallace-Hadrill (1985).

16. On Poland and Russia generally, see Seton-Watson (1977, chs. 2–3); on Poland, see Davies (1982) and on Russia, Pipes (1977); cf. also Portal (1969).

17. We do find some earlier expressions in the sixteenth century, on which see Marcu (1976); but cf. the critique in Breuilly (1982, Introduction). For the debate on medieval nationalism, see Tipton (1972) and Reynolds (1984, ch. 8).

18. For the Declaration of Arbroath, see Duncan (1970); for the Swiss *Eidgenossenschaft* and Oath of the Rütli, see Thürer (1970).

19. On the Normans and their myth, see Davis (1976) and more generally Reynolds (1984, ch. 8).

20. A fuller discussion of the differences between lateral and vertical *ethnie* can be found in A. D. Smith (1986a, ch. 4); for the early Israelite confederacy, see Zeitlin (1984, chs. 3–5).

21. See Frye (1966, ch. 6); cf. Herrmann (1977). The Mazdakite movement of the fifth century AD was both social and religious, involving class protest and a Manichaean heresy in doctrinal matters; for Manichaean doctrines, see Runciman (1947).

22. The classic account is Lewis (1970); see also Saunders (1978).

23. For the feudal period in Armenia, see Lang (1980, chs. 7–8); for the later Armenian diaspora communities, see Nalbandian (1963).

24. For this transformation in Persia after the Arab conquest of the seventh century, see Frye (1966, ch. 7); for the Islamization (and Arabization) of Egypt from the seventh century AD on, see Atiyah (1968, Part I).

25. On which, see Levine (1965, ch. 2) and Ullendorff (1973, ch. 4).

26. For the political (state) aspects of this complex process, see Tilly (1975); cf. Seton-Watson (1977, ch. 2).

27. On which, see Geoffrey of Monmouth (1966) and Mason (1985).

28. For the growth of legal, economic and territorial unity, see Corrigan and Sayer (1985); cf. Brooke (1969) for the earlier period, and Keeney (1972) for the Anglo-French Wars.

29. For the 'Saxon' myth, see MacDougall (1982); for middle class religious and national sentiment in the sixteenth century, see Corrigan and Sayer (1985, chs. 2–3).

30. See Reynolds (1984, 276–89); cf. Bloch (1961, II, 431–7).

31. See Armstrong (1982, 152–9); cf. A. Lewis (1974, 57–70).

32. See on this E. Weber (1979); on French linguistic unification and standardization, see Rickard (1974) and, for the Revolution, Lartichaux (1977).

33. For a general account, see Atkinson (1960); cf. also Poliakov (1974, ch. 1).

34. For recent Basque and Catalan ethno-nationalisms, see Payne (1971), and Greenwood's essay in Esman (1977) and Llobera (1983).

35. See the thesis of Bendix (1964) that is also implicit in Tilly (1975, Introduction and Conclusion); cf. Poggi (1978).

36. This is true also in Germany, despite Prussia's vital role; we cannot overlook the parts played by memories of former ethnic ties — myths, symbols, customs, languages — or by the intelligentsia and bourgeoisie in the Customs Union; see Hamerow (1958) and Kohn (1965, especially ch. 8).

37. See Wallerstein (1974, ch. 3) and the essays by Tivey and Navarri in Tivey (1980).

38. For the position of the intellectuals, see Gouldner (1979) and Anderson (1983).

39. For fuller discussion of this process, see Strayer (1963) and A. D. Smith (1986a, chs. 6–7).

40. For examples of the problems of ethno-religious communities, see Arnakis (1963) on the Greeks under Ottoman rule, and A. D. Smith (1973b) on the nineteenth-century Arabs and Jews.

41. For these problems, as revealed in the writings of Arabists and others, see Haim (1962); for the institutional differences, see Rosenthal (1965).

42. See Sharabi (1970) for the Arab case, and Jankowski (1979) for Egyptian responses to these problems.

43. See Kedourie (1971, Introduction) and A. D. Smith (1971, ch. 10).

44. For discussions of these orientations among intellectuals, see the essay by Matossian in Kautsky (1962) and A. D. Smith (1979a, ch. 2). These debates dominated nationalist movements in Russia, India, Persia, Greece, Israel, Ireland and among Arabs and West Africans; see on the latter the fine study by July (1967); and Geiss (1974).

45. See on this Kedourie (1971, Introduction). The nineteenth-century Russian intelligentsia provided a classic example of this 'return to the people' and its ethno-history; see Thaden (1964).

46. For fuller discussion, see A. D. Smith (1984a); and Hobsbawm and Ranger (1983).

47. See Steinberg (1976) for the Swiss use of legends.

48. For the romantic interest in Stonehenge, see Chippindale (1983, chs. 6–7).

49. See A. D. Smith (1984b) and (1986a, ch. 8).

50. The visions of the Gaelic revival are analysed in the illuminating study of Hutchinson (1987); cf. also the subtle account in Lyons (1979).

51. See the Introduction by Branch to Kirby's translation of the *Kalevala* of 1907 (Branch 1985); for the wider political context, see Jutikkala (1962, ch. 8) and the essay by M. Klinge in Mitchison (1980).

52. See Honko (1985), who connects the historical interpretation of the *Kalevala* with periods of threat to national identity; for Sibelius and the *Kalevala*, see Layton (1985) and for Akseli Gallén-Kallela's art, see Arts Council (1986, esp. 104–15 and the essays by Sarajas-Korte and Klinge).

53. For some East European examples of these cultural crusades, see the essays in Sugar (1980) and, on the Slovaks, the essay by Paul in Brass (1985).

54. But not always. In Japan, tsarist Russia, Ethiopia and Persia, aristocrats and clergy held on for a long time. This is even true of some parts of sub-Saharan Africa, on which see Markovitz (1977, chs. 2–3).

55. It certainly made the division of the globe into 'nations' unnecessary, even where particular *ethnies* became the basis for kingdoms; the hold of often broad religious communities (Islam, Buddhism, Christendom), for all their ethnic sub-divisions, suggested a more universal basis for political loyalty, tied as it sometimes was to the concept of empire, as in Dante's vision (see Breuilly 1982, Introduction).

56. For the territorial aspects of the nation and nationalism, see Kohn (1967b) and A. D. Smith (1981b).

4 NATIONALISM AND CULTURAL IDENTITY

1. Gellner (1964, 168).
2. Kedourie (1960, 1).
3. For nationa*lism* in England, see Kohn (1940) and the essays by Christopher Hill and Linda Colley in Samuel (1989, vol. I). For West African nationalism, see July (1967) and Geiss (1974); for Arab nationalism, see Binder (1964).
4. On which, see Hutchinson (1987, 158–61, 285–90).

5. For fuller discussions of the problems of defining 'national*ism*', see Deutsch (1966, ch. 1), Rustow (1967, ch. 1), A. D. Smith (1971, ch. 7) and Connor (1978).

6. These propositions are adapted and modified from A. D. Smith (1973a, 2.1).

7. For the 'nation'/'state' distinction, see Connor (1972) and Tivey (1980, Introduction).

8. See Akzin (1964, ch. 3).

9. Shaftesbury (1712, 397–8); see also Macmillan (1986, ch. 3).

10. Rousseau (1915, II, 319, *Projet Corse*).

11. Cited in Berlin (1976, 182); cf. Barnard (1965).

12. For irredentist movements in the Third World, see Horowitz (1985, ch. 6); also Lewis (1983).

13. For discussion of David's *Horatii*, see Brookner (1980, ch. 5) and Crow (1978); for *fraternité* during the French Revolution, see Cobban (1957–63, Vol. I, Part 3) and Kohn (1967b).

14. For the case of the French Third Republic, see E. Weber (1979); for some early post-independence African regimes, see Apter (1963) and Rotberg (1967).

15. Josephus: *Jewish War*, II, 53 cited in Yadin, Y. (1966) *Masada*, London, Weidenfeld & Nicolson; Thucydides: *Peloponnesian War* II, 71, 2.

16. See Kedourie (1960, chs. 2–4) for Kant's influence; cf. A. D. Smith (1971, ch. 1).

17. The field of nationalist symbolism merits more intensive investigation; see Doob (1964) on Tyrolean symbolism, Dowd (1948) on the fêtes of the French Revolution, Mosse (1976) on the ceremonial of German nationalism, and Thompson (1985) on Afrikaner ceremonial.

18. For the self-referential quality of nationalism, see Breuilly (1982, ch. 16); on Durkheim and nationalism, see Mitchell (1931).

19. A point made by Debray (1977); see also Anderson (1983, ch. 1).

20. For the ethnic group as a 'super-family', see Horowitz (1985, chs. 1–2); for the masculine/feminine split in David's historical painting, see Herbert (1972).

21. An argument found in Kedourie (1960) and (1971), in Sathyamurthy (1983) and to some extent in Breuilly (1982).

22. For some earlier typologies, see Snyder (1954), Seton-Watson (1965), Symmons-Symonolewicz (1965) and (1970); cf. the recent typology in Gellner (1983).

23. Kohn (1955) and (1967a).

24. See the more detailed discussion in Hutchinson (1987, ch. 1).

25. See Pulzer (1964) and Mosse (1964) on support for Pan-Germanism; for Russian bourgeois support for Russian cultural nationalism, see Gray (1971).

26. See the essay by Plamenatz in Kamenka (1976).

27. This is a modified and simplified version of A. D. Smith (1973a, 3.4–7).

28. For Maurras' integral nationalism, see Nolte (1969); for Latin American populism, see Mouzelis (1986).

29. See Kohn (1960) and Davies (1982, Vol. II, ch. 1); on Jasna Gora, see Rozanow and Smulikowska (1979).

30. See Kedourie (1971, Introduction); cf. the essays by Crane and Adenwalla in Sakai (1961) for the nationalist use of the Hindu past.

31. For late medieval 'nationalisms', see Tipton (1972); for the Dutch example, see Schama (1987, I/2).

32. See especially the detailed work by Kemilainen (1964), to which the subsequent discussion is indebted; cf. also Barnard (1965, ch. 1).

33. Richardson (1725, 222–4).

34. Both cited in the essay by W. F. Church on 'France' in Ranum (1975).

35. La Font de Saint-Yenne (1752, 305–6); on which see Crow (1985, ch. 4).

36. Barry (1809, II, 248).

37. On this change in the meaning of the concept of nation in Europe, see Zernatto (1944); see also Bendix (1964).

38. See Poliakov (1974, esp. ch. 8); Nisbet (1969).

39. For the neo-classical style and movement, see Honour (1968).

40. Rousseau (1924–34, X, 337–8), cited in Cobban (1964); cf. Cohler (1970).

41. For Rousseau's Genevan attachments, see Kohn (1967a, 238–45) and Baron (1960, 24–8). On the Greco-Roman models in the French Revolution, see Rosenblum (1967, ch. 2) and Herbert (1972).

42. On the German Gothic revival, see Robson-Scott (1965).

43. See Macmillan (1986, ch. 3) on the 'poet of nature'; for British literary medievalism, see Newman (1987, ch. 5) and for some contrasts between French and British artistic trends, see A. D. Smith (1979b).

44. For this 'language', see Berlin (1976).

45. On national romanticisms, see Porter and Teich (1988); for its national uses in the later nineteenth century, see Hobsbawm's concluding essay in Hobsbawm and Ranger (1983).

46. For the artists' 'moral historicism' and 'archaeological drama', see Rosenblum (1967) and A. D. Smith (1987) and (1989); see also the catalogue of *La France* (1989).

47. For national feeling in music, see Einstein (1947, esp. 266–9, 274–82); for nationalist romanticism in art, see Vaughan (1978, ch. 3); for its imprint in Europe's cultural heritage, see Horne (1984). Many artists who were in no way nationalistic, could find their works of art appropriated for a particular nationalism, because of the 'evocative' aura of such works for those already permeated by nationalist feeling; such has been the fate of Constable and Delacroix, of Schumann and even Beethoven.

48. On the intellectuals, see Shils (1972) and Gella (1976).

49. See Baron (1960, ch. 2) and Anderson (1983, ch. 5).

50. See Kedourie (1960); and Breuilly (1982, Introduction and chs. 15–16).

51. See on the German Romantic contribution, Reiss (1955) and Kedourie (1960); for Kant, see also Gellner (1983).

52. See Cobban (1957–63, vol. I, Part 3) and Palmer (1940); on the *cahiers de doléances* and French nationalism in 1789, see Shafer (1938).

53. For the thesis that intellectuals are required for their modernizing skills, see Kautsky (1962, Introduction) and Worsley (1964). But Kautsky's 'intellectuals' are really the intelligentsia, the professionals. The same is true for some of the cases cited by Kedourie (1971, Introduction) including those of Gandhi and Kenyatta.

54. For Hess, see Hertzberg ·(1960, Introduction); for the European links between the intellectuals and nationalism, see A. D. Smith (1981a, ch. 5).

55. For the 'identity crisis' thesis, see Ayal (1966); and Kedourie (1960) and (1971, Introduction); for a critique, see Breuilly (1982, 28–35).
56. For this wider cultural crisis, see A. D. Smith (1971, ch. 10).

5 NATIONS BY DESIGN?

1. See Tilly (1975, Introduction and Conclusion); and Seton-Watson (1977, chs. 2–3).
2. See, *inter alia*, Corrigan and Sayer (1984, chs. 2–4); Newman (1987, chs. 5–6); and the essays by Hill and Colley in Samuel (1989, Vol. I).
3. See Pipes (1977, chs. 9–10); cf. Seton-Watson (1967).
4. See Dunlop (1985) and the essay by Pospielovsky in Ramet (1989).
5. See, for example, G. E. Smith (1989).
6. On Ottomanism, see Mardin (1965) and Berkes (1964); and the essay by Karpat in Brass (1985).
7. On which, see Lewis (1968, ch. 10); and Kushner (1976).
8. For modern Pan-Turkism, see Landau (1981).
9. On this history, see Ullendorff (1973); for the Dergue's problems, see Halliday and Molyneux (1981).
10. For some brief accounts, see J. Hall (1962) and A. Lewis (1974).
11. See Brown (1955).
12. For a detailed discussion of *nihonjinron* and its exponents, see Yoshino (1989).
13. See Alavi (1972); cf. Saul (1979).
14. See Horowitz (1985, ch. 2); cf. the essays by Asiwaju and Hargreaves in Asiwaju (1985).
15. For French policies in Africa, see W. H. Lewis (1965); and, more generally, Crowder (1968).
16. See Wallerstein (1965) and Lloyd (1966); cf. Geiss (1974) and Kedourie (1971, Introduction).
17. See W. H. Lewis (1965); Geiss (1974, ch. 15); and Legum (1964). For this selective colonial perception, see Enloe (1980).
18. See, *inter alia*, J. H. Kautsky (1962, Introduction), Kedourie (1971, Introduction) and Seton-Watson (1977).
19. See Kedourie (1971, Introduction); McCulley (1966).

20. There were also more general political and economic factors which continue to maintain the civic–territorial nation in Africa, Asia and Latin America, notably geo-political forces; see Neuberger (1986). On Négritude, see Geiss (1974).

21. For these influences, see Hodgkin (1964); for the Indian case, see Heimsath (1964).

22. See Sharabi (1970); and Vital (1975).

23. See Kedourie (1971, Introduction), Kushner (1976) and Hutchinson (1987).

24. See Vatikiotis (1969); and Jankowski (1979).

25. On Burmese Buddhism, see Sarkisyanz (1964).

26. See the essay by Rothchild on Kenya in Olorunsola (1972); on Zimbabwe's minorities and their environments, see Ucko (1983).

27. On the Nigerian ethnic background, see Hodgkin (1975, Introduction); see also Panter-Brick (1970) and Markovitz (1977).

28. See Gutteridge (1975).

29. On the early Ba'ath ideology, see Binder (1964); cf. Sharabi (1966).

30. For an account of the principal *ethnie* and their nationalisms in Pakistan, and of Islam's role there, see the essays by Harrison and Esposito in Banuazizi and Weiner (1986). For the Indian ethnic–linguistic mosaic, see Harrison (1960) and Brass (1974).

31. See McCulley (1966) and D. E. Smith (1963).

32. As the Pakistani case illustrates; see the essays by Binder and Harrison in Banuazizi and Weiner (1986). For African anxieties on this score, see Neuberger (1976).

33. On this OAU stand, see Legum (1964) and Neuberger (1986).

34. See the essay by Young in Brass (1985); and for the earlier mass-mobilizing African regimes, see Apter (1963).

35. For the Angolan resistance, see Davidson, Slovo and Wilkinson (1976); cf. also Lyon (1980) for Guinea-Bissau.

36. For a brief account of the Great Zimbabwe debate, see Chamberlin (1979, 27–35); and for the nationalist significance of the 'homeland', see A. D. Smith (1981b).

37. For the Ghanaian CPP, see Austin (1964).

38. See Gellner (1983) for the new importance accorded to public education; but it is as much a consequence as a cause of nationalist ideology and consciousness.

39. For linguistic education during the French Revolution, see Lartichaux (1977), and during the Third Republic, E. Weber (1979).
40. See Markovitz (1977, ch. 6).
41. Mannheim (1940); J. H. Kautsky (1962, Introduction); Gouldner (1979).
42. For the social composition of nationalist movements, see Seton-Watson (1960), the essay by Kiernan in A. D. Smith (1976) and Breuilly (1982, ch. 15); for a critique, see Zubaida (1978).
43. For the role of professionals, see Hunter (1962), Gella (1976) and Pinard and Hamilton (1984).
44. See, for example, Hodgkin (1956).

6 SEPARATISM AND MULTI-NATIONALISM

1. For this 'official' nationalism, see Anderson (1983, ch. 6); for some of the Eastern European classic ethnic nationalisms, see Sugar and Lederer (1969).
2. For the alien, metropolitan origins of the post-colonial state, see Alavi (1972); for some of these Third World ethnic movements, see R. Hall (1979).
3. For general surveys of the Western movements, see Esman (1977) and Allardt (1979).
4. See Deutsch (1966); and the classic critique in Connor (1972).
5. Connor (1984a).
6. For the Irish case, see Boyce (1982); for the Norwegian case, see Elviken (1931) and Mitchison (1980, 11–29); for Finland, see Jutikkala (1962); all flourished in the mid-nineteenth century.
7. A good example is the veneration accorded to the monastery of Yasna Gora in southern Poland with its Byzantine image of Our Lady, placed there in the late fourteenth century, a place of national pilgrimage ever since; see Rozanow and Smulikowska (1979). See also pp. 65–7 above.
8. For musical nationalism, see Einstein (1947, 266–9, 274–82) and Raynor (1976, ch. 8). See also pp. 92–3 above.
9. Weber (1968, Part I/2, ch. 5, p. 396).
10. For this process, see Kedourie (1971, Introduction).
11. For the 'culture of critical discourse', see Gouldner (1979). For

the role of the intelligentsia in classic European nationalisms, see Barnard (1965, ch. 1) and Anderson (1983, ch. 5).

12. See on this Nairn (1977, ch. 9); also Pech (1976).

13. For this Gaelic nationalism, see Lyons (1979); for 'Karelianism' in Finland, see Laitinen (1985) and Boulton Smith (1985).

14. See, for example, Kedourie (1960, chs. 5–6); Pearson (1983).

15. See, for example, Berkes (1964) for the impact of the French Revolution on Ottoman Turkey; for the Greek case, see Kitromilides (1980).

16. For the Kurdish struggles, see Edmonds (1971) and Chaliand (1980, 8–46).

17. For an overview of ethnic politics in Pakistan, including the Baluch, Sindhi and Pashtun movements, see the essay by Selig Harrison: 'Ethnicity and Political Stalemate in Pakistan', in Banuazizi and Weiner (1986, 267–98).

18. In the Eritrean case this has been particularly problematic: a common experience of Italian colonialism and Ethiopian repression undoubtedly helped to foster some sense of unity among the nine or more ethnic categories in the region. But divisions between predominantly Christian Tigrinnya-speaking peoples and the mainly Muslim 'Tigre' and other peoples led to periodic civil war which has only recently been contained by the Eritrean Peoples Liberation Front; see Cliffe (1989, 131–47). For the Palestinian experience, see Quandt et al. (1973).

19. For Biafra, see V. Olorunsola: 'Nigeria', in Olorunsola (1972) and Markovitz (1977, ch. 8). For an example of the use of a dominant *ethnie*, see D. Rothchild: 'Kenya', in Olorunsola (1972). For a careful analysis of the patterns of *ethnie*-state relations in Africa and Asia, see Brown (1989, 1–17).

20. Gellner, in fact, claims that nationalism is 'weak' precisely because there are many more 'objective' cultural differences than ethnic nationalisms. Only some differences become the sites for ethnic mobilization; the others 'fail' to provide bases for the development of nationalisms; see Gellner (1983, ch. 5). For African examples of 'tribes' that to date have 'failed' to produce correlative nationalisms, see King (1976).

21. Horowitz (1985, ch. 6) for the detailed exposition of his argument. My discussion is necessarily limited, since its main concern

is with the *consequences* for the construction of 'national identity'
of separatist ethnic nationalisms.

22. These factors are prominent in the essays on Pakistan and Iran
in the volume edited by Banuazizi and Weiner (1986).

23. For other discussions of the incidence and geo-politics of ethnic
secession and irredentist nationalisms in Africa and Asia, see
Bucheit (1981), Wiberg (1983) and Mayall (1985).

24. For ethnocide among such smaller groups, see Svensson (1978).
For the partial loss of indigenous traditions among the Indian
populations of Central and Latin America, see Whitaker and
Jordan (1966).

25. For the Kurds, see Chaliand (1980) and Entessar (1989, 83–100).
On pre-colonial ethnic categories in what is now Nigeria, see
Hodgkin (1975, Introduction).

26. For the community-creating nature of ethnic nationalist movements, see Hutchinson (1987) and Cliffe (1989, 131–47).

27. See the essays by Connor and Lijphart in Esman (1977); also
Allardt (1979).

28. For the renewal of nationalism in Lithuania, see Vardys (1989,
53–76).

29. For the Scots, see MacCormick (1970) and Webb (1977); for
the problem of 'dual loyalties' in Western democracies, see
A. D. Smith (1986c).

30. For the 'underdeveloped' ethno-regions of the West, see the
essays by Reece, and by Hechter and Levi, in Stone (1979); for
the lack of fit between ethno-nationalisms and particular economic backgrounds, see Connor (1984a).

31. For ethnic sentiment and mobilization in the Soviet Union, see
Szporluk (1973) and G. E. Smith (1985).

32. The popular aspect of ethnic nationalism is stressed by Nairn
(1977, chs. 2, 9), who speaks of recent 'neo-nationalisms'.

33. For a fuller discussion of the processes involved, see A. D. Smith
(1986a, chs. 7–8); see also Brock (1976) and Hutchinson (1987).

34. See in particular the role of intellectuals like Lonnröt and Runeberg in Finnish nationalism; see Branch (1985). For the Irish
case, see Lyons (1979); for the Breton revival, see Mayo (1974)
and the essay by Beer in Esman (1977).

35. On which see Schama (1987) and Hill (1968).

36. For details, see A. D. Smith (1981a, chs. 1, 9); for Catalonia, see Conversi (1990).
37. This is well illustrated in the detailed study by Hechter (1975) of the impact of the British state on ethnic regions.
38. This is the frequent charge of ethnic minorities against the centralized states of France, Britain and till recently Spain; see Coulon (1978).

7   BEYOND NATIONAL IDENTITY?

1. National movements have emerged in such apparently unlikely areas as Siberia, Papua–New Guinea and Melanesia; see, for example, Kolarz (1954) for Siberia and Central Asia, and May (1982) for Papua–New Guinea.
2. For a critique of the inflation of nationalism, see Breuilly (1982, 8–11). For the Chinese communist case, see Johnson (1969).
3. A point also made by Daniel Bell (1975) in respect of the conjunction of 'affinity' and 'interest' in ethnic mobilization.
4. For this evolutionary perspective in liberal sociology, see Parsons (1966) and Smelser (1968); and in Marxism and Marxist politics, see Cummins (1980) and Connor (1984b).
5. The strength of Italian regions and German *Länder* to this day, despite Italian irredentism and the desire for German reunification, is clear evidence of this. For the Swiss case, see Steinberg (1976).
6. For the history of Illyrianism and the Yugoslav struggle for independence, see Stavrianos (1961, esp. ch. 9) and Singleton (1985, ch. 5).
7. See Schöpflin (1980) and Djilas (1984).
8. See Fedoseyev *et al.* (1977); Bennigsen (1979).
9. See the analyses of these questions in Goldhagen (1968) and G. E. Smith (1985).
10. For Russian neo-nationalism, see Dunlop (1985) and, more generally, the essays in Ramet (1989).
11. See Kilson (1975) for 'neo-ethnicity' among the Whites; and Gans (1979) for its largely symbolic nature.
12. See Burrows (1982).
13. On the centrality of the providential Puritan myth in America, see Tuveson (1968) and O'Brien (1988).

14. As in the nineteenth-century German case; see Kahan (1968). For an earlier 'functional' analysis of the EC, see Haas (1964).

15. For this European debate, re-echoed today in Britain, see Camps (1965). De Gaulle might well have adduced the strong evidence of the continuing power of national sentiments and policies in the 1960s throughout Western Europe, presented by Benthen van den Berghe (1966). Even if a new generation is today more 'European' than its predecessors, is it any less nationalistic?

16. Notably by Galtung (1973) in his successful plea to the Norwegians not to join the enlarged Community. But the arguments for or against Europe becoming a 'super-state' should not be confused with those that portray it as a likely 'super-nation'. This is to confuse loss of sovereignty with loss of identity. The history of ethnic survival without sovereignty disproves any necessary connection; see A. D. Smith (1988b). As far as a purely *political* European nationalism is concerned, this is as yet confined to *segments* of the political, economic and cultural élites in each European nation; it has as yet no deep popular base.

17. For the immediate aftermath of the Second World War and the rise of giant power blocs, see Barraclough (1967) and Hinsley (1973).

18. See Bell (1973) and Kumar (1978) on this 'service society'.

19. For an analysis of these new movements − feminism, ecology, student and ethno-national movements, see Melucci (1989, chs. 3−4).

20. See Richmond (1984); and cf. Melucci (1989, 89−92).

21. See Warren (1980, ch. 7); cf. also Enloe (1986).

22. For a discussion of the media critics (Mattelaart, Morley, Hall) who demonstrate the role of ethnicity and class in structuring popular responses to modernist American media products, see Schlesinger (1987).

23. For the 'culture of critical discourse' of the humanistic intellectuals and their technical counterparts, see Gouldner (1979).

24. On these monuments and ceremonies, see Hobsbawm and Ranger (1983, especially the essay by Hobsbawm) and Horne (1984). For earlier imperial imagery, see Armstrong (1982, ch. 5).

25. For this idea of the nation as an imagined community whose

texts have to be deconstructed and read, see Anderson (1983); for an application to the British case, see Samuel (1989, esp. Vol. III).

26. See the parallel view in Anderson (1983, ch. 1); for these memorials, see Rosenblum (1967, ch. 2).

27. On Finnish national history, see Branch (1985) and Honko (1985).

28. For the rituals of nationalism, see Mosse (1976) and Horne (1984); on art and nationalism, see Rosenblum (1967).

29. For Slovak history, see Brock (1976); on the East European mosaic, see Pearson (1983).

30. For Iraqi and Turkish 'roots', see Zeine (1958); for royal tombs in ancient Macedon, see Yalouris (1980); on Transylvania, Giurescu (1967).

31. On these processes, see Wallerstein (1974, ch. 3) and Tilly (1975).

32. For Balkan nationalism, see Stavrianos (1957); for capitalism and nationalism in Africa, see Markovitz (1977) and A. D. Smith (1983, chs. 3, 5).

33. For this process, see A. D. Smith (1981a, ch. 6).

34. For this confusion, see Connor (1978); also Tivey (1980).

35. For state systems and non-interference, see Beitz (1979, Part II).

36. On which, see Kohn (1960).

37. For its recent history, see Landau (1981).

38. On which, see Geiss (1974).

39. For medieval sacred languages, see Armstrong (1982, ch. 8); on language and nationalism today, see Edwards (1985, ch. 2).

40. For this mythology, see, for example, de Rougemont (1965).

Bibliography

AKZIN, Benjamin (1964) *State and Nation*, London: Hutchinson

ALAVI, Hamza (1972) 'The State in Post-colonial Societies – Pakistan and Bangla Desh', *New Left Review* 74, 59–81

ALLARDT, Erik (1979) *Implications of the Ethnic Revival in Modern, Industrialised Society*, Commentationes Scientiarum Socialium 12, Helsinki, Societas Scientiarum Fennica

ALMOND, Gabriel and Lucian Pye (eds.) (1965) *Comparative Political Culture*, Princeton, Princeton University Press

ALON, Gedaliah (1980) *The Jews in their Land in the Talmudic Age (70–640 CE)*, 2 vols., Jerusalem, The Magnes Press, The Hebrew University

ALTY, J. H. M. (1982) 'Dorians and Ionians', *The Journal of Hellenic Studies* 102, 1–14

ANDERSON, Benedict (1983) *Imagined Communities: Reflections on the Origin and Spread of Nationalism*, London, Verso Editions and New Left Books

ANDERSON, Charles W., Fred von der Mehden and Crawford Young (eds.) (1967) *Issues of Political Development*, Englewood Cliffs, Prentice-Hall

APTER, David (1963) 'Political Religion in the New Nations', in C. Geertz (ed.), *Old Societies and New States*, New York, Free Press

ARBERRY, A. J. (ed.) (1969) *Religion in the Middle East: Three Religions in Concord and Conflict*, 2 vols., Cambridge, Cambridge University Press

ARMSTRONG, John (1976) 'Mobilised and Proletarian Diasporas', *American Political Science Review* 70, 393–408

— (1982) *Nations before Nationalism*, Chapel Hill, University of North Carolina Press

ARNAKIS, G. (1963) 'The Role of Religion in the Development of Balkan Nationalism', in Barbara Jelavich and Charles Jelavich (eds.), *The Balkans in Transition*, Berkeley, University of California Press

ARTS COUNCIL (1986) *Dreams of a Summer Night: Scandinavian Painting at the Turn of the Century*, London, Hayward Gallery, Arts Council of Great Britain

ASIWAJU, A. I. (ed.) (1985) *Partitioned Africans: Ethnic Relations across Africa's International Boundaries, 1884–1984*, London, C. Hurst & Company

ATIYA, A. S. (1968) *A History of Eastern Christianity*, London, Methuen

ATKINSON, W. C. (1960) *A History of Spain and Portugal*, Harmondsworth, Penguin

AUSTIN, Denis (1964) *Politics in Ghana, 1946–60*, London, Oxford University Press

AVI-YONAH, Michael (1976) *The Jews of Palestine: A Political History from the Bar-Kochba War to the Arab Conquest*, Oxford, Basil Blackwell

AYAL, E. B. (1966) 'Nationalist ideology and economic development', *Human Organisation* 25, 230–39

BANTON, Michael (ed.) (1966) *Anthropological Approaches to the Study of Religion*, London, Tavistock

— and Jonathan Harwood (1975) *The Race Concept*, Newton Abbott, London and Vancouver, David and Charles

BANUAZIZI, Ali and Myron Weiner (eds.) (1986) *The State, Religion and Ethnic Politics: Afghanistan, Iran and Pakistan*, Syracuse, New York, Syracuse University Press

BARNARD, Frederick M. (1965) *Herder's Social and Political Thought*, Oxford, Clarendon Press

BARON, Salo W. (1960) *Modern Nationalism and Religion*, New York, Meridian Books

BARRACLOUGH, Geoffrey (1967) *An Introduction to Contemporary History*, Harmondsworth, Penguin

BARRY, James (1809) *The Works of James Barry, Esq.*, London

BARTH, Fredrik (ed.) (1969) *Ethnic Groups and Boundaries*, Boston, Little, Brown and Co.

BAYNES, Norman and H. St L. B. Moss (eds.) (1969) *Byzantium: An Introduction to East Roman Civilisation*, Oxford, Oxford University Press

BEITZ, C. (1979) *Political Theory and International Relations*, Princeton, Princeton University Press

BELL, Daniel (1973) *The Coming of Post Industrial Society*, New York, Basic Books

— (1975) 'Ethnicity and Social Change', in Nathan Glazer and Daniel Moynihan (eds.), *Ethnicity: Theory and Experience*, Cambridge, Mass., Harvard University Press

BENDIX, Reinhard (1964) *Nation-building and Citizenship*, New York, John Wiley

BENNIGSEN, Alexandre (1979) 'Islam in the Soviet Union', *Soviet Jewish Affairs* 9, no. 2, 3–14

BEN-SASSON, H. and S. Ettinger (eds.) (1971) *Jewish Society through the Ages*, London, Valentine, Mitchell & Co.

BENTHEM VAN DEN BERGHE, G. van (1966) 'Contemporary Nationalism in the Western World', *Daedalus* 95, 828–61

BERKES, Niyazi (1964) *The Development of Secularism in Turkey*, Montreal, McGill University Press

BERLIN, Isaiah (1976) *Vico and Herder*, London, Hogarth Press

BEYER, W. C. (1959) 'The Civil Service in the Ancient World', *Public Administration Review* 19, 243–49

BINDER, Leonard (1964) *The Ideological Revolution in the Middle East*, New York, John Wiley

BLOCH, Marc (1961) *Feudal Society*, 2 vols., London, Routledge & Kegan Paul

BOULTON SMITH, J. (1985) 'The *Kalevala* in Finnish Art', *Books from Finland* 19, no. 1, 48–55

BOYCE, D. George (1982) *Nationalism in Ireland*, London, Croom Helm

BRANCH, Michael (ed.) (1985) *Kalevala: the Land of Heroes*, trans. W. F. Kirby, London, Athlone Press/New Hampshire, Dover.

BRANDON, S. G. F. (1967) *Jesus and the Zealots*, Manchester, Manchester University Press

BRASS, Paul (1974) *Religion, Language and Politics in North India*, Cambridge, Cambridge University Press

— (ed.) (1985) *Ethnic Groups and the State*, London, Croom Helm

BREUILLY, John (1982) *Nationalism and the State*, Manchester, Manchester University Press

BROCK, Peter (1976) *The Slovak National Awakening*, Toronto, University of Toronto Press

BROOKE, Christopher (1969) *From Alfred to Henry III, 871–1272*, London, Sphere Books Ltd

BROOKNER, Anita (1980) *Jacques-Louis David*, London, Chatto & Windus

BROWN, D. (1955) *Nationalism in Japan: An Introductory Historical Analysis*, Berkeley, University of California Press

BROWN, David (1989) 'Ethnic Revival: Perspectives on State and Society', *Third World Quarterly* 11, no. 4, 1–17

BUCHEIT, Lee C. (1981) *Secession, the Legitimacy of Self-determination*, New Haven, Yale University Press

BURN, Andrew R. (1960) *The Lyric Age of Greece*, London, Edward Arnold

— (1978) *The Pelican History of Greece*, Harmondsworth, Penguin

BURROWS, Edwin G. (1982) 'Bold Forefathers and the Cruel Stepmother: Ideologies of Descent in the American Revolution', Paper for Conference on *Legitimation by Descent*, Paris, Maison des Sciences de l'Homme

CAMBRIDGE ANCIENT HISTORY (1971) Vol. I, Part 2, *The Early History of the Middle East* (1971), third edn, Cambridge, Cambridge University Press

CAMBRIDGE HISTORY OF IRAN (1983) Vol. III, Parts 1 and 2, *The Seleucid, Parthian and Sassanian Periods* (ed. E. Yarshater), Cambridge, Cambridge University Press

CAMPBELL, John and Philip Sherrard (1968) *Modern Greece*, London, Benn

CAMPS, Miriam (1965) *What Kind of Europe? The Community since De Gaulle's Veto*, London, Oxford University Press

CARRAS, C. (1983) *3,000 Years of Greek Identity – myth or reality?*, Athens, Domus Books

CHALIAND, Gerard (ed.) (1980) *People without a Country: The Kurds and Kurdistan*, London, Zed Press

CHAMBERLIN, E. R. (1979) *Preserving the Past*, London, J. M. Dent & Sons

CHIPPINDALE, Christopher (1983) *Stonehenge Complete*, London, Thames & Hudson

CLIFFE, Lionel (1989) 'Forging a Nation: the Eritrean Experience', *Third World Quarterly* 11, no. 4, 131–47

COBBAN, Alfred (1957–63) *A History of Modern France*, 3 vols., Harmondsworth, Penguin

— (1964) *Rousseau and the Modern State*, second edn, London, Allen and Unwin

— (1965) *Social Interpretation of the French Revolution*, Cambridge, Cambridge University Press

COHLER, Anne(1970) *Rousseau and Nationalism*, New York, Basic Books

COLEMAN, James S. (1958) *Nigeria: Background to Nationalism*, Berkeley and Los Angeles, University of California Press

CONNOR, Walker (1972) 'Nation-building or Nation-destroying?', *World Politics* 24, 319–55.

— (1978) 'A nation is a nation, is a state, is an ethnic group, is a . . .', *Ethnic and Racial Studies* 1, no. 4, 378–400

— (1984a) 'Eco- or ethno-nationalism?', *Ethnic and Racial Studies* 7. no. 3, 342–59

— (1984b) *The National Question in Marxist-Leninist Theory and Strategy*, Princeton, Princeton University Press

— (1990) 'When is a Nation?', *Ethnic and Racial Studies* 13, no. 1, 92–103

CONVERSI, Daniele (1990) 'Language or race?: the choice of core values in the development of Catalan and Basque nationalisms', *Ethnic and Racial Studies* 13, no. 1, 50–70

COOK, J. M. (1983) *The Persian Empire*, London, J. M. Dent & Sons

CORRIGAN, Philip and Derek Sayer (1985) *The Great Arch: English State Formation as Cultural Revolution*, Oxford, Basil Blackwell

COULBORN, Rushton and Jack Strayer (1962) 'Religion and the State', *Comparative Studies in Society and History* I, no. 1, 38–57, 387–93

COULON, Christian (1978) 'French political science and regional diversity: a strategy of silence', *Ethnic and Racial Studies* 1, no. 1, 80–99

CROW, Tom (1978) 'The Oath of the Horatii in 1785: Painting and pre-Revolutionary Radicalism in France', *Art History* 1, 424–71

— (1985) *Painters and Public Life*, New Haven, Yale University Press

CROWDER, Michael (1968) *West Africa under Colonial Rule*, London, Hutchinson and Co.

CUMMINS, Ian (1980): *Marx, Engels and National Movements*, London, Croom Helm

DAVID, A. Rosalie (1982) *The Ancient Egyptians: Beliefs and Practices*, London & Boston, Routledge & Kegan Paul

DAVIDSON, B., J. Slovo and A. R. Wilkinson (1976) *Southern Africa: the New Politics of Revolution*, Harmondsworth, Penguin

DAVIES, Norman (1982) *God's Playground: A History of Poland*, 2 vols., Oxford, Clarendon Press

DAVIS, R. H. C. (1976) *The Normans and their Myth*, London, Thames & Hudson

DEBRAY, Regis (1977) 'Marxism and the National Question', *New Left Review* 105, 20–41

DE ROUGEMONT, Denis (1965) *The Meaning of Europe*, London, Sidgwick & Jackson

DEUTSCH, Karl W. (1966) *Nationalism and Social Communication*, second edn, New York, MIT Press

DJILAS, Aleksa (1984) 'Communists and Yugoslavia', *Survey* 28, no. 3, 25–38

DOBZHANSKY, Theodosius (1962) *Mankind Evolving*, Toronto and New York, Bantam Books

DOOB, Leonard (1964) *Patriotism and Nationalism: their Psychological Foundations*, New Haven, Yale University Press

DOWD, David (1948) *Pageant-Master of the Republic: Jacques-Louis David and the French Revolution*, Nebraska, University of Lincoln Press

DUNCAN, A. A. M. (1970): *The Nation of Scots and the Declaration of Arbroath (1320)*, London, The Historical Association

DUNLOP, John B. (1985) *The New Russian Nationalism*, New York, Praeger

EDMONDS, C. J. (1971) 'Kurdish Nationalism', *Journal of Contemporary History* 6, no. 1, 87–107

EDWARDS, John (1985) *Language, Society and Identity*, Oxford, Basil Blackwell

EINSTEIN, Alfred (1947) *Music in the Romantic Era*, London, J. M. Dent & Sons

EISENSTADT, Shmuel N. (1963) *The Political System of Empires*, New York, Free Press

ELVIKEN, A. (1931) 'The Genesis of Norwegian Nationalism', *Journal of Modern History* 3, 365–91

ENLOE, Cynthia (1980) *Ethnic Soldiers*, Harmondsworth, Penguin

— (1986) 'Ethnicity, the State and the New International Order', in John F. Stack, Jr, (ed.), *The Primordial Challenge: Ethnicity in the Contemporary World, op. cit.*

ENTESSAR, Nader (1989) 'The Kurdish Mosaic of Discord', *Third World Quarterly* 11, no. 4, 83–100.

ESMAN, Milton J. (ed.) (1977) *Ethnic Conflict in the Western World*, Ithaca, Cornell University Press

FEDOSEYEV, P. N. *et al.* (1977) *Leninism and the National Question*, Institute of Marxism–Leninism, CC CPSU, Moscow, Moscow Progress Publishers

FINLEY, Moses (1986) *The Use and Abuse of History*, London, Hogarth Press

FISHMAN, Joshua *et al.* (eds.) (1968) *Language Problems of Developing Countries*, New York, John Wiley

FONDATION HARDT, (1962) *Grecs et Barbares, Entretiens sur l'Antiquité Classique* VIII, Geneva

FORREST, William G. (1966) *The Emergence of Greek Democracy*, London, Weidenfeld & Nicolson

FRANKFORT, Henri (1954) *The Birth of Civilisation in the Near East*, New York, Anchor Books

FRAZEE, C. A. (1969) *The Orthodox Church and Independent Greece, 1821–52*, Cambridge, Cambridge University Press

FRYE, Richard N. (1966) *The Heritage of Persia*, New York, Mentor

GALTUNG, John (1973) *The European Community: A Superpower in the Making*, London, Allen & Unwin

GANS, Herbert (1979) 'Symbolic ethnicity', *Ethnic and Racial Studies* 2, no. 1, 1–20

GEISS, Immanuel (1974) *The PanAfrican Movement*, London, Methuen

GELLA, Aleksander (1976) *The Intelligentsia and the Intellectuals*, Beverley Hills, Sage Publications

GELLNER, Ernest (1964) *Thought and Change*, London, Weidenfeld & Nicolson

— (1973) 'Scale and Nation', *Philosophy of the Social Sciences* 3, 1–17

— (1983) *Nations and Nationalism*, Oxford, Blackwell

— and Gita Ionescu (eds.) (1970) *Populism, its Meanings and National Characteristics*, London, Weidenfeld & Nicolson

GEOFFREY OF MONMOUTH (1966) *The History of the Kings of Britain*, (trans. L. Thorpe), Harmondsworth, Penguin

GIURESCU, C. C. (1967) *Transylvania in the History of Romania*, London, Garnstone Press

GLAZER, Nathan and Daniel Moynihan (eds.) (1975) *Ethnicity: Theory and Experience*, Cambridge, Mass., Harvard University Press

GOLDHAGEN, Eric (ed.) (1968) *Ethnic Minorities in the Soviet Union*, New York, Praeger

GOULDNER, Alvin (1979) *The Rise of the Intellectuals and the Future of the New Class*, London, Macmillan

GRAY, Camilla (1971) *The Russian Experiment in Art, 1863–1922*, London, Thames & Hudson

GRIMAL, Pierre (1968) *Hellenism and the Rise of Rome*, London, Weidenfeld & Nicolson

GUTTERIDGE, William F. (1975) *Military Regimes in Africa*, London, Methuen & Co.

HAAS, E. B. (1964) *Beyond the Nation-State: Functionalism and International Organisation*, Stanford, Stanford University Press

HAIM, Sylvia (ed.) (1962) *Arab Nationalism, An Anthology*, Berkeley and Los Angeles, University of California Press

HALL, J. (1962) 'Feudalism in Japan', *Comparative Studies in Society and History* V, 15–51

HALL, John (1985) *Powers and Liberties: the causes and consequences of the rise of the West*, Oxford, Basil Blackwell

HALL, Raymond (ed.) (1979) *Ethnic Autonomy – Comparative Dynamics*, New York, Pergamon Press

HALLIDAY, Fred and Maxine Molyneux (1981) *The Ethiopian Revolution*, London, Verso and New Left Books

HAMEROW, T. (1958) *Restoration, Revolution, Reaction: Economics and Politics in Germany, 1815–71*, Princeton, Princeton University Press

HARRISON, Selig (1960) *India, the most dangerous Decades*, Princeton, Princeton University Press

HECHTER, Michael (1975) *Internal Colonialism: the Celtic Fringe in British National Development, 1536–1966*, London, Routledge & Kegan Paul

— and Margaret Levi (1979) 'The Comparative Analysis of Ethnoregional Movements', *Ethnic and Racial Studies* 2, no. 3, 260–74

HEIMSATH, C. (1964) *Indian Nationalism and Hindu Social Reform*, Princeton, Princeton University Press

HENGEL, Martin (1980) *Jews, Greeks and Barbarians*, London, SCM Press

HERBERT, R. (1972) *David, Voltaire, Brutus and the French Revolution*, London, Allen Lane

HERRMANN, Georgina (1977) *The Iranian Revival*, Oxford, Elsevier Phaidon

HERTZBERG, Arthur (ed.) (1960) *The Zionist Idea, A Reader*, New York, Meridian Books

HILL, Christopher (1968) *Puritanism and Revolution*, London, Panther Books

HINSLEY, F. H. (1973) *Nationalism and the International System*, London, Hodder and Stoughton

HITTI, P.K. (1928) *The Origins of the Druze People and Religion*, New York, Columbia University Press

HOBSBAWM, Eric and Terence Ranger (eds.) (1983) *The Invention of Tradition*, Cambridge, Cambridge University Press

HODGKIN, Thomas (1956) *Nationalism in Colonial Africa*, London, Muller

— (1964) 'The relevance of "Western" ideas in the derivation of African nationalism', in J. R. Pennock (ed.) *Self-government in Modernising Societies*, Englewood Cliffs, Prentice-Hall

— (1975) *Nigerian Perspectives, An Historical Anthology*, second edn., London, Oxford University Press

HONKO, Lauri (1985) 'The *Kalevala* Process', *Books from Finland* 19, no. 1, 16–23

HONOUR, Hugh (1968) *Neo-Classicism*, Harmondsworth, Penguin

HORNE, Donald (1984) *The Great Museum*, London and Sydney, Pluto Press

HOROWITZ, Donald (1985) *Ethnic Groups in Conflict*, Berkeley, Los Angeles & London, University of California Press

HOROWITZ, Irving Louis (1982) *Taking Lives: Genocide and State Power*, third edn., New Brunswick and London, Transaction Books

HUNTER, Guy (1962) *The New Societies of Tropical Africa*, London, Oxford University Press

HUTCHINSON, John (1987) *The Dynamics of Cultural Nationalism: The Gaelic Revival and the Creation of the Irish Nation State*, London, Allen & Unwin

HUXLEY, G. L. (1966) *The Early Ionians*, London, Faber & Faber

JANKOWSKI, J. P. (1979) 'Nationalism in Twentieth Century Egypt', *Middle East Review* 12, 37–48

JOHNSON, Chalmers (1969) 'Building a communist nation in China', in R. A. Scalapino (ed.) *The Communist Revolution in Asia*, Englewood Cliffs, Prentice-Hall

JOHNSON, Harry G. (ed.) (1968) *Economic Nationalism in Old and New States*, London, Allen & Unwin

JULY, R. (1967) *The Origins of Modern African Thought*, London, Faber & Faber

JUTIKKALA, Eino (1962) *A History of Finland*, London, Thames & Hudson

KAHAN, Arcadius (1968) 'Nineteenth-century European experience with policies of economic nationalism', in H. G. Johnson (ed.): *Economic Nationalism in Old and New States*, London, Allen & Unwin

KAMENKA, Eugene (ed.) (1976) *Nationalism: The nature and evolution of an Idea*, London, Edward Arnold

KAUTSKY, John H. (ed.) (1962): *Political Change in Underdeveloped Countries*, New York, John Wiley

KEDDIE, Nikki (1981) *Roots of Revolution: An Interpretive History of Modern Iran*, New Haven and London, Yale University Press

KEDOURIE, Elie (1960) *Nationalism*, London, Hutchinson

— (ed.) (1971) *Nationalism in Asia and Africa*, London Weidenfeld & Nicolson

KEENEY, Barnaby C. (1972) 'England', in Leon Tipton (ed.) *Nationalism in the Middle Ages*, New York, Holt, Rinehart & Winston, 87–97

KEMILAINEN, Aira (1964) *Nationalism, Problems concerning the Word, the Concept and Classification*, Yvaskyla, Kustantajat Publishers

KENRICK, Donald and Graham Puxon (1972) *The Destiny of Europe's Gypsies*, London, Chatto-Heinemann (for Sussex University Press)

KESSLER, David (1985) *The Falashas, the Forgotten Jews of Ethiopia*, New York, Schocken Books

KILSON, Martin (1975) 'Blacks and Neo-ethnicity in American Political Life', in Nathan Glazer & Daniel Moynihan (eds.); *Ethnicity, op. cit.*

KING, P. (1976) 'Tribe: conflicts in meaning and usage', *The West African Journal of Sociology and Political Science*, 1, no. 2, 186–94

KITROMILIDES, Paschalis (1979) 'The Dialectic of Intolerance: Ideological Dimensions of Ethnic Conflict', *Journal of the Hellenic Diaspora* VI, no. 4, 5–30

— (1980) 'Republican Aspirations in South-eastern Europe in the

Age of the French Revolution', *The Consortium on Revolutionary Europe, Proceedings* vol. I, 275–85, Athens, Georgia

KLAUSNER, S. (1960) 'Why they chose Israel', *Archives de Sociologie des Religions* 9, 129–44

KOHN, Hans (1940) 'The origins of English nationalism', *Journal of the History of Ideas* I, 69–94

— (1955) *Nationalism: Its Meaning and History*, Princeton, Van Nostrand

— (1957) *Nationalism and Liberty: The Swiss Example*, London, Macmillan

— (1960) *Pan-Slavism, Its History and Ideology*, second edn. revised, New York, Random House, Vintage Books

— (1965) *The Mind of Germany: The Education of a Nation*, New York, Scribners/London, Macmillan

— (1967a) *The Idea of Nationalism*, second edn, New York, Collier-Macmillan

— (1967b) *Prelude to Nation-States: The French and German Experience, 1789–1815*, Princeton, Van Nostrand

KOLARZ, W. (1954) *Peoples of the Soviet Far East*, London, Philip

KUMAR, Krishan (1978) *Prophecy and Progress*, Harmondsworth, Penguin

KUPER, Leo (1981) *Genocide*, Harmondsworth, Penguin

KUSHNER, David (1976) *The Rise of Turkish Nationalism*, London, Frank Cass

LA FONT DE SAINTE-YENNE (1752) *L'Ombre du Grand Colbert, Le Louvre et la ville de Paris, Dialogue*, Paris

LA FRANCE (1989) *Images of Woman and Ideas of Nation, 1789–1989*, London, South Bank Centre

LAITINEN, Kai (1985) 'The *Kalevala* and Finnish Literature', *Books from Finland* 19, no. 1, 61–64

LANDAU, Jacob (1981) *Pan-Turkism in Turkey*, London, C. Hurst & Co.

LANG, David M. (1980) *Armenia, Cradle of Civilisation*, London, Allen & Unwin

LARSEN, Mogens Trolle (ed.) (1979) *Power and Propaganda: A Symposium on Ancient Empires*, Copenhagen, Akademisk Forlag (*Mesopotamia*, Copenhagen Studies in Assyriology 7)

LARTICHAUX, J.-Y. (1977) 'Linguistic Politics during the French Revolution', *Diogenes* 97, 65–84

LAYTON, Robert (1985) 'The *Kalevala* and Music', *Books from Finland* 19, no. 1, 56–59

LEGUM, Colin (1964) *Pan-Africanism, A Political Guide*, second edn., London, Pall Mall Press

LEVINE, Donald N. (1965) *Wax and Gold: Tradition and Innovation in Ethiopian Culture*, Chicago and London, Chicago University Press

LEWIS, Archibald (1974) *Knights and Samurai: Feudalism in Northern France and Japan*, London, Temple Smith

LEWIS, Bernard (1968) *The Emergence of Modern Turkey*, London, Oxford University Press

— (1970) *The Arabs in History*, fifth edn., London, Hutchinson & Co.

LEWIS, Ioann (ed.) (1983) *Nationalism and Self-determination in the Horn of Africa*, London, Ithaca Press

LEWIS, W. H. (ed.) (1965) *French-speaking Africa: the Search for Identity*, New York, Walker

LLOBERA, Josep (1983) 'The Idea of *Volksgeist* in the Formation of Catalan Nationalist Ideology', *Ethnic and Racial Studies* 6, no. 3, 332–50

LLOYD, P. C. (ed.) (1966) *New Elites in Tropical Africa*, London, Oxford University Press

LLOYD-JONES, Hugh (ed.) (1965) *The Greek World*, Harmondsworth, Penguin

LYON, Judson (1980) 'Marxism and Ethno-nationalism in Guinea-Bissau', *Ethnic and Racial Studies* 3, no. 2, 156–68

LYONS, F. S. (1979) *Culture and Anarchy in Ireland, 1890–1930*, London, Oxford University Press

MACCOBY, Hyam (1974) *Judea in Revolution*, London, Ocean Books

MACCORMICK, Neil (ed.) (1970) *The Scottish Debate, Essays in Scottish Nationalism*, London, Oxford University Press

MACDOUGALL, Hugh A. (1982) *Racial Myth in English History: Trojans, Teutons and Anglo-Saxons*, Montreal, Harvest House/ Hanover, New Hampshire, University Press of New England

MACMILLAN, Duncan (1986) *Painting in Scotland: The Golden Age*, Oxford, Phaidon Press

MANN, Michael (1986) *The Sources of Social Power*, vol. I, Cambridge, Cambridge University Press

MANNHEIM, Karl (1940) *Man and Society in an Age of Reconstruction*, London, Routledge & Kegan Paul

MARCU, E. D. (1976) *Sixteenth-Century Nationalism*, New York, Abaris Books

MARDIN, Sherif (1965) *The Genesis of Young Ottoman Thought: A Study of the Modernisation of Turkish Political Ideas*, Princeton, Princeton University Press

MARKOVITZ, I. L. (1977) *Power and Class in Africa*, Englewood Cliffs, Prentice-Hall

MARWICK, Arthur (1974) *War and Social Change in the Twentieth Century*, London, Methuen

MASON, R. A. (1985) 'Scotching the Brut: the Early History of Britain', *History Today* 35 (January), 26–31

MASUR, G. (1966) *Nationalism in Latin America: Diversity and Unity*, New York, Macmillan

MAY, R. J. (ed.) (1982) *Micronationalist Movements in Papua New Guinea*, Political and Social Change Monograph No. 1, Canberra, Australian National University

MAYALL, James (1984) 'Reflections on the New Economic Nationalism', *Review of International Studies* 10, 313–21

— (1985) 'Nationalism and the International Order', *Millennium, Journal of International Studies* 14, no. 2, 143–58

— (1990) *Nationalism and International Society*, Cambridge, Cambridge University Press

MAYO, Patricia (1974) *The Roots of Identity: Three National Movements in Contemporary European Politics*, London, Allen Lane

MCCULLEY, B. T. (1966) *English Education and the Origins of Indian Nationalism*, Gloucester, Mass., Smith

MCKAY, James (1982) 'An Exploratory Synthesis of Primordial and Mobilisationist Approaches to Ethnic Phenomena', *Ethnic and Racial Studies* 5, no. 4, 395–420

MELUCCI, Alberto (1989) *Nomads of the Present: Social Movements and Individual Needs in Contemporary Society*, London, Hutchinson Radius

MEYER, Michael A. (1967) *The Origins of the Modern Jew: Jewish Identity and European Culture in Germany, 1749–1824*, Detroit, Wayne State University Press

MITCHELL, Marion M. (1931) 'Emile Durkheim and the Philosophy of Nationalism', *Political Science Quarterly* 46, 87–106

MITCHISON, Rosalind (ed.) (1980) *The Roots of Nationalism: Studies in Northern Europe*, Edinburgh, John Donald Publishers

MOSCATI, Sabatino (1962) *The Face of the Ancient Orient*, New York, Anchor Books

— (1973) *The World of the Phoenicians*, London, Cardinal, Sphere Books Ltd

MOSSE, George (1964) *The Crisis of German Ideology*, New York, Grosset and Dunlap

— (1976) 'Mass politics and the Political Liturgy of Nationalism', in Eugen Kamenka (ed.): *Nationalism, op. cit.*

MOUZELIS, Nicos (1986) *Politics in the Semi-periphery*, London, Macmillan

NAIRN, Tom (1977) *The Break-up of Britain*, London, New Left Books

NALBANDIAN, Louise (1963) *The Armenian Revolutionary Movement: the Development of Armenian political Parties through the Nineteenth century*, Berkeley, University of California Press

NEUBERGER, Benjamin (1976) 'The African Concept of Balkanisation', *Journal of Modern African Studies* XIII, 523–29

— (1986) *National Self-determination in Post-colonial Africa*, Boulder, Colorado, Lynne Rienner Publishers

NEUSNER, Jacob (1981) *Max Weber Revisited: Religion and Society in Ancient Judaism*, Eighth Sacks Lecture, Oxford, Oxford Centre for Postgraduate Hebrew Studies

NEWMAN, Gerald (1987) *The Rise of English Nationalism: A Cultural History, 1740–1830*, London, Weidenfeld & Nicolson

NISBET, Robert (1969) *Social Change and History*, Oxford, London and New York; Oxford University Press

NOLTE, Ernest (1969) *Three faces of Fascism*, trans. L. Vennewitz, New York and Toronto, Mentor Books

OATES, Joan (1979) *Babylon*, London, Thames and Hudson

O'BRIEN, Conor Cruise (1988) *God Land: Reflections on Religion and Nationalism*, Cambridge, Mass, Harvard University Press

OLORUNSOLA, Victor (ed.) (1972) *The Politics of Cultural Sub-Nationalism in Africa*, New York, Anchor Books

OSTROGORSKY, George (1956) *History of the Byzantine State*, Oxford, Basil Blackwell

PALMER, R. (1940) 'The National Idea in France before the Revolution', *Journal of the History of Ideas* I, 95–111

PANTER-BRICK, S. (ed.) (1970) *Nigerian Politics and Military Rule*, London, Athlone Press

PARSONS, Talcott (1966) *Societies: Evolutionary and Comparative Perspectives*, Englewood Cliffs, Prentice-Hall.

PAYNE, Stanley (1971) 'Catalan and Basque nationalism', *Journal of Contemporary History* 6, no. 1, 15–51

PEARSON, Raymond (1983) *National Minorities in Eastern Europe, 1848–1945*, London, Macmillan

PECH, Stanley (1976) 'The Nationalist Movements of the Austrian Slavs', *Social History* 9, 336–56

PINARD, M. and R. Hamilton (1984) 'The Class Bases of the Quebec Independence Movement: Conjectures and Evidence', *Ethnic and Racial Studies* 7, no. 1, 19–54

PIPES, Richard (1977) *Russia under the Old Regime*, London, Peregrine Books

POGGI, Gianfranco (1978) *The Development of the Modern State*, London, Hutchinson & Co.

POLIAKOV, Leon (1974) *The Aryan Myth*, New York, Basic Books

PORTAL, Roger (1969) *The Slavs: A Cultural Historical Survey of the Slavonic Peoples*, trans. Patrick Evans, London, Weidenfeld & Nicolson

PORTER, Roy and Mikulas Teich (eds.) (1988) *Romanticism in National Context*, Cambridge, Cambridge University Press

PRITCHARD, J. B. (ed.) (1958) *The Ancient Near East*, Princeton, Princeton University Press

PULZER, Peter (1964) *The Rise of Political Anti-Semitism in Germany and Austria*, New York, John Wiley

QUANDT, W. B., Fuad Jabber and Mosely A. Lesch (eds.) (1973) *The Politics of Palestinian Nationalism*, Berkeley & Los Angeles, University of California Press

RAMET, Pedro (ed.) (1989) *Religion and Nationalism in Soviet and East European Politics*, Durham and London, Duke University Press

RANUM, Orest (ed.) (1975) *National Consciousness, History and Political Culture*, Baltimore and London, Johns Hopkins University Press

RAYNOR, Henry (1976) *Music and Society Since 1815*, London, Barrie and Jenkins

REISS, H. S. (ed.) (1955) *The Political Thought of the German Romantics, 1793–1815*, Oxford, Blackwell

REX, John (1986) *Race and Ethnicity*, Milton Keynes, Open University Press

REYNOLDS, Susan (1983) 'Medieval *origines Gentium* and the Community of the Realm', *History*, 68, 375–90

— (1984) *Kingdoms and Communities in Western Europe, 900–1300*, Oxford, Clarendon

RICHARDSON, Jonathan (1725) *An Essay on the Theory of Painting*, second edn., London

RICHMOND, Anthony (1984) 'Ethnic Nationalism and Postindustrialism', *Ethnic and Racial Studies* 7, no. 4, 4–18

RICKARD, Peter (1974) *A History of the French Language*, London, Hutchinson University Library

ROBSON-SCOTT, William D. (1965) *The Literary Background of the Gothic Revival in Germany*, Oxford, Clarendon Press

ROSENBLUM, Robert (1967) *Transformations in late Eighteenth Century Art*, Princeton, Princeton University Press

ROSENTHAL, Erwin (1965) *Islam in the Modern National State*, Cambridge, Cambridge University Press

ROTBERG, Robert (1967) 'African Nationalism: Concept of Confusion?', *Journal of Modern African Studies* 4, 33–46

ROUSSEAU, Jean-Jacques (1915) *The Political Writings of Rousseau*, ed. C. E. Vaughan, 2 vols., Cambridge, Cambridge University Press

— (1924–34) *Correspondance Générale*, ed. T. Dufour, Paris, Vol. X

ROUX, Georges (1964) *Ancient Iraq*, Harmondsworth, Penguin

ROZANOW, Zofia and Ewa Smulikowska (1979) *The Cultural Heritage of Jasna Góra*, second revised edn., Warsaw, Interpress Publishers

RUNCIMAN, Steven (1947) *The Medieval Manichee; A Study of the Christian Dualist Heresy*, Cambridge, Cambridge University Press

RUSTOW, Dankwart (1967) *A World of Nations*, Washington DC, Brookings Institution

SAGGS, H. W. F. (1984) *The Might that was Assyria*, London, Sidgwick and Jackson

SAKAI, R. A. (ed.) (1961) *Studies on Asia*, Lincoln, University of Nebraska Press

SAMUEL, Raphael (1989) *Patriotism, The Making and Unmaking of British National Identity*, London, Routledge & Kegan Paul

SARKISYANZ, Emanuel (1964) *Buddhist Backgrounds of the Burmese Revolution*, The Hague, Nijhoff

SATHYAMURTHY, T. (1983) *Nationalism in the Contemporary World*, London, Frances Pinter

SAUL, John (1979) *State and Revolution in East Africa*, London, Heinemann

SAUNDERS, J. J. (1978) *A History of Medieval Islam*, London, Routledge & Kegan Paul

SCHAMA, Simon (1987) *The Embarrassment of Riches: An Interpretation of Dutch Culture in the Golden Age*, London, William Collins

SCHERMERHORN, Richard (1970) *Comparative Ethnic Relations*, New York, Random House

SCHLESINGER, Philip (1987) 'On National Identity: some Conceptions and Misconceptions Criticised', *Social Science Information* 26, no. 2, 219–64

SCHÖPFLIN, George (1980) 'Nationality in the Fabric of Yugoslav Politics', *Survey* 25, 1–19

SELTZER, Robert M. (1980) *Jewish People, Jewish Thought*, New York, Macmillan

SETON-WATSON, Hugh (1961) *Neither War nor Peace*, London, Methuen

— (1965) *Nationalism, Old and New*, Sydney, Sydney University Press

— (1967) *The Russian Empire, 1801–1917*, London, Oxford University Press

— (1977) *Nations and States*, London, Methuen

SHAFER, Boyd C. (1938) 'Bourgeois nationalism in the Pamphlets on the Eve of the French Revolution', *Journal of Modern History* 10, 31–50

SHAFTESBURY, Lord (1712) *A Letter concerning the Art or Science of Design*, written from Italy, on the occasion of the *Judgment of Hercules* to my Lord —, Naples

SHARABI, Hisham (1966) *Nationalism and Revolution in the Arab World*, Princeton, Van Nostrand

— (1970) *The Arab Intellectuals and the West: The Formative Years, 1875–1914*, Baltimore and London, Johns Hopkins University Press

SHERRARD, Philip (1959) *The Greek East and the Latin West*, London, Oxford University Press

SHILS, Edward (1972) *The Intellectuals and the Powers, and other Essays*, Chicago, Chicago University Press

SILVA, K. M. de (1981) *A History of Sri Lanka*, London, C. Hurst & Co./Berkeley & Los Angeles, University of California Press

SINGLETON, Fred (1985) *A Short History of the Yugoslav Peoples*, Cambridge, Cambridge University Press

SMELSER, Neil J. (1968) *Essays in Sociological Explanation*, Englewood Cliffs, Prentice–Hall

SMITH, Anthony D. (1971) *Theories of Nationalism*, (second edn. 1983), London, Duckworth/New York, Harper & Row

— (1973a) *Nationalism*, A Trend Report and Annotated Bibliography, *Current Sociology* 21, no. 3, The Hague, Mouton

— (1973b) 'Nationalism and Religion: the Role of Religious Reform in the Genesis of Arab and Jewish Nationalism', *Archives de Sociologie des Religions* 35, 23–43

— (ed.) (1976) *Nationalist Movements*, London, Macmillan/New York, St Martin Press

— (1979a) *Nationalism in the Twentieth Century*, Oxford, Martin Robertson

— (1979b) 'The "Historical Revival" in Late Eighteenth-century England and France', *Art History* 2, no. 2, 156–78

— (1981a) *The Ethnic Revival in the Modern World*, Cambridge, Cambridge University Press

— (1981b) 'States and Homelands: the Social and Geopolitical Implications of National Territory', *Millennium, Journal of International Studies* 10, no. 3, 187–202

— (1981c) 'War and Ethnicity: the Role of Warfare in the Formation, Self-images and Cohesion of Ethnic Communities', *Ethnic and Racial Studies* 4, no. 4, 375–97

— (1983) *State and Nation in the Third World*, Brighton, Harvester Press

— (1984a) 'Ethnic Myths and Ethnic Revivals', *European Journal of Sociology* 25, 283–305

— (1984b) 'National Identity and Myths of Ethnic Descent', *Research in Social Movements, Conflict and Change*, 7, 95–130

— (1986a) *The Ethnic Origins of Nations*, Oxford, Blackwell

— (1986b) 'State-making and Nation-building', in John Hall (ed.) *States in History*, Oxford, Blackwell, 228–63

— (1986c) 'History and Liberty: Dilemmas of Loyalty in Western Democracies', *Ethnic and Racial Studies* 9, no. 1, 43–65

— (1987) *Patriotism and Neo-Classicism: The 'Historical Revival' in French and English Painting and Sculpture, 1746–1800*, Ph.D. Dissertation, University of London

— (1988a) 'The Myth of the "Modern Nation" and the Myths of Nations', *Ethnic and Racial Studies* 11, no. 1, 1–26

— (1988b) 'Social and Cultural Conditions of Ethnic Survival', *Journal of Ethnic Studies, Treatises and Documents* 21, 15–26, Ljubljana

— (1989) 'The Suffering Hero: Belisarius and Oedipus in late Eighteenth Century French and British Art', *Journal of the Royal Society of Arts* CXXXVII, September 1989, 634–40

SMITH, Donald E. (1963) *India as a Secular State*, Princeton, Princeton University Press

— (ed.) (1974) *Religion and Political Modernisation*, New Haven, Yale University Press

SMITH, G. E. (1985) 'Ethnic Nationalism in the Soviet Union: Territory, Cleavage and Control', *Environment and Planning C: Government and Policy*, 3, 49–73

— (1989) 'Gorbachev's Greatest Challenge: *Perestroika* and the National Question', *Political Geography Quarterly* 8, no. 1, 7–20

SMITH, Leslie (ed.) (1984) *The Making of Britain: The Dark Ages*, London, Macmillan

SNYDER, Louis (1954) *The Meaning of Nationalism*, New Brunswick, Rutgers University Press

SOPHOCLES (1947) *The Theban Plays*, trans. E. Watling, Harmondsworth, Penguin

STACK, J. F. (1986), *The Primordial Challenge: Ethnicity in the Contemporary World*, New York, Greenwood Press

STAVRIANOS, L. S. (1957) 'Antecedents of the Balkan Revolutions of the Nineteenth Century', *Journal of Modern History* 29, 333–48

— (1961) *The Balkans Since 1453*, New York, Holt

STEINBERG, Jonathan (1976) *Why Switzerland?*, Cambridge, Cambridge University Press

STONE, John (ed.) (1979) 'Internal Colonialism', *Ethnic and Racial Studies*, 2. no. 3

STRAYER, J. (1963) 'The Historical Experience of Nation–building in

Europe', in K. W. Deutsch and J. Foltz (eds.) *Nation-Building*, New York, Atherton

STRIZOWER, S. (1962) *Exotic Jewish Communities*, New York and London, Thomas Yoseloff

SUGAR, Peter (ed.) (1980) *Ethnic Diversity and Conflict in Eastern Europe*, Santa Barbara, ABC–Clio

— and Ivo Lederer (eds.) (1969) *Nationalism in Eastern Europe*, Seattle and London, University of Washington Press

SVENSSON, F. (1978) 'The Final Crisis of Tribalism: Comparative Ethnic Policy on the American and Russian Frontiers', *Ethnic and Racial Studies* 1, no. 1, 100–23

SYMMONS-SYMONOLEWICZ, Konstantin (1965) 'Nationalist Movements: an Attempt at a Comparative Typology', *Comparative Studies in Society and History* 7, 221–30

— (1970) *Nationalist Movements: A Comparative View*, Meadville, Pa., Maplewood Press

SZPORLUK, Roman (1973) 'Nationalities and the Russian Problem in the USSR: an Historical Outline', *Journal of International Affairs* 27, 22–40

TAYLOR, David and Malcolm Yapp (eds.) (1979) *Political Identity in South Asia*, London and Dublin, Centre for South Asian Studies, SOAS, Curzon Press

TCHERIKOVER, Victor (1970) *Hellenistic Civilisation and the Jews*, New York, Athenaeum

THADEN, Edward C. (1964) *Conservative Nationalism in Nineteenth Century Russia*, Seattle, University of Washington Press

THOMPSON, Leonard (1985) *The Political Mythology of Apartheid*, New Haven and London, Yale University Press

THUCYDIDES (1963) *The Peloponnesian War*, New York, Washington Square Press

THÜRER, Georg (1970) *Free and Swiss*, London, Oswald Wolff

TILLY, Charles (1963) *The Vendée*, London, Arnold

— (1975) *The Formation of National States in Western Europe*, Princeton, Princeton University Press

TIPTON, Leon (ed.) (1972) *Nationalism in the Middle Ages*, New York, Holt, Rinehart and Winston

TIVEY, Leonard (ed.) (1980) *The Nation-State*, Oxford, Martin Robertson

TRIGGER, B. G., B. J. Kemp, D. O'Connor and A. B. Lloyd (1983) *Ancient Egypt; A Social History*, Cambridge, Cambridge University Press

TUDOR, Henry (1972) *Political Myth*, London, Pall Mall Press/Macmillan

TUVESON, E. L. (1968) *Redeemer Nation: The Idea of America's Millennial Role*, Chicago and London, University of Chicago Press

UCKO, Peter (1983) 'The politics of the Indigenous minority', *Journal of BioSocial Science, Supplement* 8, 25–40

ULLENDORFF, Edward (1973) *The Ethiopians, An Introduction to Country and People*, third edn., London, Oxford University Press

VAN DEN BERGHE, Pierre (1967) *Race and Racism*, New York, Wiley

VARDYS, V. Stanley (1989) 'Lithuanian National Politics', *Problems of Communism* XXXVIII (July–August), 53–76

VATIKIOTIS, P. J. (1969) *A Modern History of Egypt*, New York and Washington, Frederick A. Praeger

VAUGHAN, William (1978) *Romantic Art*, London, Thames & Hudson

VITAL, David (1975) *The Origins of Zionism*, Oxford, Clarendon Press

WALEK-CZERNECKI, M. T. (1929) 'Le rôle de la nationalité dans l'histoire de l'Antiquité', *Bulletin of the International Committee of Historical Sciences* II, 305–20

WALLACE-HADRILL, J. M. (1985) *The Barbarian West, 400–1000*, Oxford, Basil Blackwell

WALLERSTEIN, Immanuel (1965) 'Elites in French-speaking West Africa', *Journal of Modern African Studies* 3, 1–33

— (1974) *The Modern World System*, New York, Academic Press

WARREN, Bill (1980) *Imperialism, Pioneer of Capitalism*, New York and London, Monthly Review Press

WEBB, Keith (1977) *The Growth of Nationalism in Scotland*, Harmondsworth, Penguin

WEBER, Eugene (1979) *Peasants into Frenchmen: The Modernisation of Rural France, 1870–1914*, London, Chatto & Windus

WEBER, Max (1965) *The Sociology of Religion*, trans. E. Fischoff, London, Methuen

— (1968) *Economy and Society*, Vol. I, eds. G. Roth and C. Wittich, New York, Bedminster Press

WHITAKER, A. P. and D. C. Jordan (1966) *Nationalism in Contemporary Latin America*, New York, Free Press

WIBERG, Hakan (1983) 'Self-determination as international issue', in Ioann M. Lewis (ed.): *Nationalism and Self-determination, op. cit.*

WOODHOUSE, C. M. (1984) *Modern Greece: A Short History*, London and Boston, Faber & Faber

WORSLEY, Peter (1964) *The Third World*, London, Weidenfeld & Nicolson

YALOURIS, N. *et al.* (1980) *The Search for Alexander*, Boston, New York Graphics Society (Exhibition)

YERUSHALMI, Yosef H. (1983) *Jewish History and Jewish Memory*, Seattle and London, University of Washington Press

YOSHINO, Kosaku (1989) *Cultural Nationalism in Contemporary Japan*, Ph.D. Dissertation, University of London

ZEINE, Z. N. (1958) *Arab-Turkish Relations and the Emergence of Arab Nationalism*, Beirut, Khayats/London, Constable & Co. Ltd

ZEITLIN, Irving (1984) *Ancient Judaism*, Cambridge, Polity Press

— (1988) *Jesus and the Judaism of His Time*, Cambridge, Polity Press

ZERNATTO, G. (1944) 'Nation: The History of a Word', *Review of Politics*, 6, 351–66

ZUBAIDA, Sami (1978) 'Theories of Nationalism', in G. Littlejohn, B. Smart, J. Wakeford and N. Yuval-Davis (eds.) *Power and the State*, London, Croom Helm

Select Index

Italic page numbers indicate a main entry

READ MORE IN PENGUIN

In every corner of the world, on every subject under the sun, Penguin represents quality and variety – the very best in publishing today.

For complete information about books available from Penguin – including Puffins, Penguin Classics and Arkana – and how to order them, write to us at the appropriate address below. Please note that for copyright reasons the selection of books varies from country to country.

In the United Kingdom: Please write to *Dept. EP, Penguin Books Ltd, Bath Road, Harmondsworth, West Drayton, Middlesex UB7 0DA*

In the United States: Please write to *Consumer Sales, Penguin Putnam Inc., P.O. Box 12289 Dept. B, Newark, New Jersey 07101-5289.* VISA and MasterCard holders call 1-800-788-6262 to order Penguin titles

In Canada: Please write to *Penguin Books Canada Ltd, 10 Alcorn Avenue, Suite 300, Toronto, Ontario M4V 3B2*

In Australia: Please write to *Penguin Books Australia Ltd, P.O. Box 257, Ringwood, Victoria 3134*

In New Zealand: Please write to *Penguin Books (NZ) Ltd, Private Bag 102902, North Shore Mail Centre, Auckland 10*

In India: Please write to *Penguin Books India Pvt Ltd, 11 Community Centre, Panchsheel Park, New Delhi 110017*

In the Netherlands: Please write to *Penguin Books Netherlands bv, Postbus 3507, NL-1001 AH Amsterdam*

In Germany: Please write to *Penguin Books Deutschland GmbH, Metzlerstrasse 26, 60594 Frankfurt am Main*

In Spain: Please write to *Penguin Books S. A., Bravo Murillo 19, 1° B, 28015 Madrid*

In Italy: Please write to *Penguin Italia s.r.l., Via Benedetto Croce 2, 20094 Corsico, Milano*

In France: Please write to *Penguin France, Le Carré Wilson, 62 rue Benjamin Baillaud, 31500 Toulouse*

In Japan: Please write to *Penguin Books Japan Ltd, Kaneko Building, 2-3-25 Koraku, Bunkyo-Ku, Tokyo 112*

In South Africa: Please write to *Penguin Books South Africa (Pty) Ltd, Private Bag X14, Parkview, 2122 Johannesburg*

READ MORE IN PENGUIN

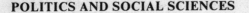

POLITICS AND SOCIAL SCIENCES

Anatomy of a Miracle Patti Waldmeir

The peaceful birth of black majority rule in South Africa has been seen by many as a miracle – or at least political magic. 'This book is a brilliant, vivid account of this extraordinary transformation' *Financial Times*

A Sin Against the Future Vivien Stern

Do prisons contribute to a better, safer world? Or are they a threat to democracy, as increasingly punitive measures are brought in to deal with rising crime? This timely account examines different styles of incarceration around the world and presents a powerful case for radical change.

The United States of Anger Gavin Esler

'First-rate . . . an even-handed and astute account of the United States today, sure in its judgements and sensitive in its approach' *Scotland on Sunday*. 'In sharply written, often amusing portraits of this disconnected America far from the capital, Esler probes this state of anger' *The Times*

Killing Rage: Ending Racism bell hooks

Addressing race and racism in American society from a black and a feminist standpoint, bell hooks covers a broad spectrum of issues. In the title essay she writes about the 'killing rage' – the intense anger caused by everyday instances of racism – finding in that rage a positive inner strength to create productive change.

'Just like a Girl' Sue Sharpe

Sue Sharpe's unprecedented research and analysis of the attitudes and hopes of teenage girls from four London schools has become a classic of its kind. This new edition focuses on girls in the nineties and represents their views on education, work, marriage, gender roles, feminism and women's rights.